The PTL Family Devotional

By Jim & Tammy Bakker

The PTL Family & Friends

PTL Television Network
Charlotte, NC 28279

Contributing Writers:	Lorraine Pakkala Emily Walker Ron Kopczick Jan White Hope Lippard
Coordinator:	Jean Scarborough
Copy Editor:	Sylvia McAllister
Proofreaders:	Rose Bradford Dorothy McAllister
Photography Staff:	Eddie Holder Lauri Braaten Ken Beebe
Photography Research:	Beverly Mahaley
Art Director:	Jerry Dunning
Cover Design:	Frank Clark
Typography:	Elsie Van Camp Ron Tucker
Production Artist:	Deborah Easley
Vice President of Marketing:	Rich Ball

The Devotionals published in THE PTL FAMILY DEVOTIONAL were written by PTL Staff writers based on information given by PTL guests on "Jim Bakker" a/k/a PTL Club and/or written or personal interviews with the individuals in this publication, or extracted from prior publications owned and copyrighted by PTL. Each devotional was edited for space, clarity, style and consistency.

©1981 by
Heritage Village Church & Missionary Fellowship, Inc.
PTL Television Network / Charlotte, NC 28279
All rights reserved
Printed in the United States
1st Printing: December 1981
All scriptures in King James Version unless otherwise noted.
LB-The Living Bible   RSV-Revised Standard Version
NAS-The New American Standard   NIV-New International Version
AB-Amplified Bible

I have never stopped thanking God for you. I pray for you constantly, asking God, the glorious Father of our Lord Jesus Christ, to give you wisdom to see clearly and really understand who Christ is and all that he has done for you. I pray that your hearts will be flooded with light so that you can see something of the future he has called you to share. I want you to realize that God has been made rich because we who are Christ's have been given to him! I pray that you will begin to understand how incredibly great his power is to help those who believe him. It is that same mighty power that raised Christ from the dead and seated him in the place of honor at God's right hand in heaven.

From Paul's letter to the Ephesians 1:16-20 (LB).

My Dear Friend,

You know, the most precious time we can spend with our family is the time we share together about the Lord.

Often in our home, it's around the dinner table, in the car, or piled up in "Mommy & Daddy's" bed on a Saturday morning.

But for those times of family devotional, when you gather the whole group together, we think you will find this book most helpful. Every day, the message is from a different PTL guest, from Jerry Clower to Bob Gass or Jeannie C. Riley to our own Jeanne Johnson.

We pray you enjoy this family devotional guide every day in your time of worship.

And, as you pray, remember our family, too, as we do you.

Love,

Jim + Tammy
Jim and Tammy

ACKNOWLEDGMENTS

Perhaps more than any other project, THE PTL FAMILY DEVOTIONAL is indeed a product of the entire PTL Family, both on the pages that follow, with some of your favorite PTL guests and to the behind-the-scenes work at PTL.

A special "thank you" is in order to the PTL guests and staff who shared with us their inspiring thoughts that have made up this book. Each and every devotional was a blessing to those who edited and put together this devotional guide, and we are so very thankful to those who shared with us in interview, in phone calls, in letters, and on the program to make this possible.

Also, there are some "unsung" anonymous heros of this publication. People like Elsie Van Camp, a retired typesetter who "happened" to be visiting Fort Heritage at the exact time we needed someone to do this book. Or Dorothy McAllister, a volunteer who proofread much of this devotional in her home. To these, and the others listed in the credits, we are so thankful for their good work.

So, from our "family" to yours, God bless you, and we pray you enjoy THE PTL FAMILY DEVOTIONAL.

                              Mary McLendon
                              Senior Editor

January 1

Unity In The Body

"Fulfill ye my joy, that ye be like-minded, having the same love, being of one accord, of one mind... Let this mind be in you, which was also in Christ Jesus." Philippians 2:2-5

We have declared 1982 to be a year of **prayer** and **unity** for the staff and Partners of PTL. With so much emphasis on prophecy and the signs that will usher in the end of the age and the return of Jesus Christ, there is one vital key that I believe must come to pass before our Lord's return.

And that key is unity within the Body of Christ (that we are "one" as Jesus and the Father are one). Throughout the Scriptures, we see the power of God manifested through unity, and especially in the early church where we find the people in one accord concerning the cause of the Gospel. The word "accord" is mentioned eleven times in the book of Acts alone.

Here at PTL, we have stood on the scripture Matthew 18:19, "...That if two of you shall agree on earth as touching any thing that they shall ask, it shall be done for them of my Father which is in heaven," and have seen God answer prayer in a marvelous way.

Let's you and I agree in prayer today concerning unity for the Body of Christ and within all our own relationships. For as our scripture today says, we should walk with love in one accord and with the mind of Christ.

I know that the power of the living God is being released for whatever is before you on this very day!

Bob Daniel
PTL General Manager

January 2

Small Beginnings

"Though thy beginning was small, yet thy latter end should greatly increase."

Job 8:7

When I was in Bible College, often when I had some time, I'd go down to the "skid row" area in Minneapolis and preach in the little missions and on street corners. Often my only "congregation" would be a half-asleep drunk lying on the sidewalk.

There was another young man at school that really made fun of me for that. He didn't understand why I would "waste" my time and energy for the pitiful few I could reach that way. "I'll never do that," he'd said, "I'm going to start at the top."

You know what, that man is not preaching or ministering at all, in fact, the last I heard, he is not even serving God. And I believe it is all because he wanted to start at the top.

If I've learned anything, it is that you never start at the top. You start at the bottom and take one step at a time. Maybe God has called you into a ministry, and you look around and see Oral Roberts and Billy Graham and you think, "What little I can do is nothing compared to those guys." But that is wrong. You have to start where you are. Your faith grows every time you step out. If you don't have the faith to believe God for a loaf of bread to feed your family, you certainly don't have faith to believe God for a City of Faith—not yet.

Do the task that God puts before you, and never despise small beginnings. You'll never know the end result until you step out and put God to the test.

Jim Bakker
PTL President

Don't Give Up!

"Commit thy way unto the Lord; trust also in him, and he shall bring it to pass."

Psalm 37:5

Have you ever gotten to the point of just giving up on God? Maybe you've prayed the same prayer for so long that you feel like maybe God isn't listening.

Well, don't give up! People, I know what I'm talking about. God promises in His Word that He will meet our needs, He will answer our prayers, and I've seen it time and again happening in my own life.

For two years, I had a special prayer need and every day I prayed the same prayer. And while I saw God answering all of my other prayers, it was like He ignored this one. I cried out on the inside, pleading with God to hear my prayer. My secretary knew what I was going through and was agreeing with me in prayer.

Finally, God did answer my prayer and in great way. The very time I expected it the least, He came down from heaven and met my need.

Some time after it happened, my secretary was praying and asked the Lord why I had to suffer so long and it was like the Lord said to her, "My timing is not your timing, tell Tammy to count it all joy, that I worked out many things that I could not have worked except in My perfect timing."

I praise God that He is in control and working in my life, and He is working in yours, too. Trust Him today and know that, in His timing, He will bring it to pass!

Tammy Faye Bakker
PTL Co-Host

January 4

Nothing Is Impossible With God

"...whosoever shall say unto this mountain, Be thou removed...and shall not doubt in his heart...he shall have whatsoever he saith."
Mark 11:23

When all seems lost, and man's wisdom or assistance fails, our eternal, magnificently powerful God performs the impossible. My husband and I witnessed an impossibility as it became a reality recently as our infant son, Tony, was restored to complete health after having drowned in our swimming pool. We experienced God's wonderful mercy and tender care even when we were not living for Him. This demonstration of His Grace touched all our lives. We have never been the same since.

While gardening one afternoon, I noticed that my son, who had been playing with our dog, grew very quiet. After looking all over the house for him, I checked the pool, and there he lay at the bottom. When I retrieved his lifeless, weighted body, he was already blue—he was dead! For twenty minutes he was dead. No heartbeat, no oxygen getting to the brain. I was gripped with guilt, fear, and concern. The doctors gave him one in a hundred chances to live, and then *if* he survived, he would have severe brain damage. Our prayers were, "Lord, take him home or give him to us whole." Weeks went by and he had begun breathing but was still unconscious. But God gave us a sign, he moved his

leg. Then we began to pray, "Lord, heal him completely!" because the Lord had shown us His will. I can truly testify to the fact that indeed we can ask anything of the Lord and He'll not deny His children. Our son is perfectly whole and normal now, because of the God of the impossible.

Sandi Trevisan
Mother

Nothing Separating

"For I am persuaded beyond doubt...that neither death, nor life, nor angels, nor principalities,...nor anything...will be able to separate us from the love of God..." Rom. 8:38-39 (AB)

During my teens and early twenties when I was going through a time of real soul-searching, my mind accepted the fact that God loved me because His Word said so, but my spirit had not received this truth. Accepting God's love for me has been one of the most difficult things I have ever encountered!

At a time when I was praying and searching for the answers to many, many questions and was particularly needing to have this settled once and for all, God made very real to me from His Word that I was secure in His love. In the Amplified Bible, it reads, "...nor things impending and threatening, nor things to come, nor powers. Nor height, nor depth, nor anything else in all creation will be able to separate us from the love of God which is in Christ Jesus our Lord."

There was an overwhelming joy in *knowing* that *nothing* could ever separate me from His love. That has been one of the most stabilizing influences of my entire life.

Every thought that entered my mind of something that might separate me from God's love fit into one of the categories of the list of things in Romans 8:38-39. It absolutely assures me that truly *nothing* will ever separate me from His love. Everything in my life was secondary to getting this settled once and for all.

Janelle Q. Young
*PTL's January
Employee of the Month*

January 6

Warning For The Last Days

"For I have determined not to know any thing among you, save Jesus Christ, and him crucified."   I Corinthians 2:2

Paul warned that just before Christ's return, there would be false teachers with false doctrine. "For the time will come when they will not endure sound doctrine; but after their own lusts shall they heap to themselves teachers, having itching ears; And they shall turn away their ears from the truth, and shall be turned unto fables" (II Timothy 4:3). Paul also warned Timothy that many would err from the faith because of their love of money, "For the love of money is the root of all evil: which while some coveted after, they have erred from the faith, and pierced themselves through with many sorrows" (I Timothy 6:10).

It is good to claim the promises of God but it is also important not to get caught up in what God can do for us. Are we guilty of going before God and letting the love of money overshadow our love of God? Could this be one of the false doctrines Paul warned Timothy about? To capitalize on a famous saying, has our generation of Christians become caught up in a "what can God do for me" religion instead of a "what can I do for God" religion? Is Christ really first and foremost in our lives or do we see Him as a means of getting what we want? Do we think of Him as a person to love and worship or just a name to tack on the end of our prayer demands?

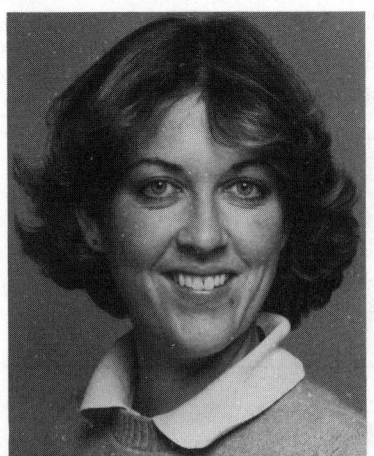

In these "last days" that Paul warned us about, we must with Paul "...determine not to know anything...save Jesus Christ, and him crucified."

Heidi Dove
Singer

January 7

"DO!"

"Those things, which ye have both learned, and received, and heard, and seen in me, do: and the God of peace shall be with you."
                                                                Philippians 4:9

To have the peace of God promised in verse nine, we must obey and *do* the commands from the preceding verse. We're told to, 'think on these things, things that are true, things that are honest, things just, things pure, things lovely, things of good report, things of virtue and things of praise.' Then God's peace shall be with you.

It's very difficult to turn the wheels of a parked automobile. The Lord is telling us here to get into motion, get into action. The great commission was, "...go into all the world...." You don't have to sit around and wait for directives from God, He's already told you—go—, just begin.

As I emphasized in my book *Yes Yes Living In A No No World,* the same goal can take twenty days or twenty years, it depends on when you do the work. There's an old poem by an unknown author that states, "Sitting still and wishing, Makes no person great, The good Lord sends the fishing, But you must dig the bait." Just name your goal and it will be clear that some digging is involved.

Begin to do it! A little today, a little tomorrow. Great monuments aren't built in a day, they are built one stone at a time. We're told, "Whatsoever thy hand findeth to do, *do it* with all thy might..." (Ecclesiastes 9:10). Aim as high as you can, work as hard as you can and the goal that others call "impossible" will be yours for the asking. DO IT!

Neil Eskelin
Director of Development
Evangel College

January 8

Look Up!

"Before I formed thee in the belly I knew thee; and before thou camest...I sanctified thee, and I ordained thee a prophet unto the nations."
Jeremiah 1:5

I see a growing alarm among the Israelites from events that are coming to pass. A rabbi described the kind of person their deliverer would be. Not God, but man with supernatural ability to perform miracles. I was amazed. "You've just described the false prophet," I told him. Matthew 24:24 prophesies, "There shall arise false Christs, and false prophets, and shall show great signs and wonders; insomuch that, if it were possible, they shall deceive the very elect."

I believe the stage is set, it's a most exciting time for the whole prophetic scenario. We're already locked into a countdown toward Armageddon, we're *the* generation! I'm not a doomsday prophet—it's joyous—we're falling into a plan prophesied long ago. The reason I'm full of hope is because we're living in the days the prophets and apostles would have loved to live in. Things are coming together rapidly. I'm not terrified, I'm thrilled! Jesus is coming soon. He promised, "Let not your heart be troubled...I go to prepare a place for you..." (John 14:1-3). That's our hope in the midst of all the trouble we see.

He gave us a definite promise when He promised our salvation in I Thessalonians 5:9-10.

His coming is very, very soon and we will live eternally together with Him. What a future!

Hal Lindsey
Author/Prophecy Teacher

January 9

Walking In The Light

"But if we walk in the light, as he is in the light, we have fellowship one with another, and the blood of Jesus Christ...cleanseth us from all sin." I John 1:7

All that I am or ever hope to be, I give the Lord Jesus Christ praise! How very generous He's been to me since I first began to walk in the light of His glorious love. Too often we think our destiny is in our own hands. What a distortion of facts. The fact is that Jesus Christ is a reality, a living, vital, part of our lives. Only He can give total fulfillment. I will be eternally grateful for how He directed my life from poverty, obscurity, and negative circumstances, and with a gift to sing, transformed me into a bold witness for Him. Praise the Lord! I walk in His strength, and His love, to do His Will.

My father was a noted concert violinist before suffering an accident that destroyed his promising musical career. Embittered, his uncontrollable temper ended other job possibilities, so we were trapped in severe poverty. Because of his frustrations, father tried to force the older children in our family to grasp his love and talent for music. But they refused. I, on the other hand, drank in every word of instruction. Joining the Glee Club at school, and the church choir, I was determined to broaden my musical talents.

I felt terribly inferior in my "poor box" clothes and hand-me-down shoes at church, but I clung to every word the preacher said. I had never heard that Jesus loved me. It was a beautiful message. I made Jesus my Lord and now it is my privilege to sing for Him. My highest ambition is to allow the light of His love to shine through me.

Norma Zimmer
Singer

January 10

A Worldwide Invitation

"Come unto me, all ye that labor and are heavy laden, and I will give you rest."
                              Matthew 11:28

Jesus speaks to *everyone* to "Come." His is a worldwide invitation to everyone in need. He is more than willing and wanting to help you carry your burdens and teach you to rest in His loving kindness.

From the time I was fifteen and the Holy Spirit came to abide in me, God's direction was clear—to come and follow Christ. Many times I didn't understand what God was doing and I often cried because I couldn't see the way ahead.

But God did not always answer my questions at the moment. Instead, He just let the circumstances unfold like a flower until finally I was able to see His purpose in the situation. Other times when the way seemed too hard and the burden too heavy, I thought God was being unfair. But as I developed a sense of faith in God and learned to obey and trust Him regardless of the circumstances, I learned that His Word is true and that He will never fail me.

It is important to realize, that if we choose to refuse to give Him our burdens and cares, we are promised nothing. But if we accept His freely extended invitation, we will find that in every situation He will meet our needs and direct our paths.

Come to Jesus if you are weary. Come with your sins. Come, no matter what your problem, and you will find rest unto your soul. For His yoke is indeed easy and His burden light.

Rev. Mrs. A.G. Garr
Minister/Pastor Emeritus

The Forever Principle

"We are troubled on every side, yet not distressed; we are perplexed, but not in despair."
II Corinthians 4:8

I am a happy person, not because I have no problems, but because I'm certain that God meets me there in my problems. We are given a glimpse of the reason for troubles in this life, the apostle Paul tells us in II Corinthians 4:10, "...that the life...of Jesus might be made manifest in our body."

There are two basic commitments we make where the world can see the power is from God and not from ourselves. The first commitment is foundational: to know Jesus and give our lives over to Him completely. Salvation is a commitment, a putting of our lives into His hands. The initial work of salvation is Christ's work, "For by grace are ye saved through faith; and that not of yourselves: it is the gift of God:" (Ephesians 2:8). However, the walk with Christ is a continuous walk, a developing discipleship. The moment Christ becomes your Saviour, He should become your Lord.

The second great commitment is to marriage (if you are married). Next to your relationship with God, your next most important relationship is to your spouse. The state of marriage is the most conducive to all that can be known of human happiness. Remember, conflicts in a marriage aren't bad, where there is growth, there will be conflicts; here's where too many rush to the divorce courts.

Within these two great commitments, to Christ and to your marriage, lies true freedom.

Maxine Hancock
Author

January 12

In The Power Of His Might

"Trust in the Lord with all thine heart; and lean not unto thine own understanding. In all thy ways acknowledge him, and he shall direct thy paths." Proverbs 3:5-6

I know what the power of God feels like. The Holy Spirit brings forth my music. I'm God's servant, the music flows from Him, to you—through me. He uses me as a vessel to pipe his music to the world, to tell the world that He reigns and that He's alive.

No human words can express being 'born again.' No one ever, ever told me *how* to be born again until I heard it on PTL. I was under such bondage, condemnation and guilt.

Then, one day my wife and daughters sat watching Jim Bakker. I heard him invite listeners to pray with him. Jim prayed, "Dear God, I'm a sinner, sorry for my sin. Today I give my life over to Jesus Christ. I accept Jesus Christ as my Saviour, Christ, the Son of God who died on the cross and rose again. Come into my heart. I give you my past, future and life." I prayed that prayer with Jim and something wonderful happened. I became a new creature, born anew. The guilt, condemnation, and bondage slipped away.

Then, I realized the Lord has led in the different phases of my life in a beautiful way. If we will really trust, really not live by our own understanding but acknowledge Him, He will direct every aspect of our lives. When we honestly say, "Lord, I will trust You," then we can know the power of His might, then we stand in His power.

Jimmy Clanton
Singer/Musician

_____ January 13

Decreasing For Glory

"He must increase, but I must decrease."
                              John 3:30

John 3:30 cuts out all the nitpicking and the pride. It gets right down to the heart of serving the Lord. Being a simple fellow, I can understand that He should increase and I should decrease. By having that attitude, God will let me reap all the benefits of His wonderful blessings.

The verse became my favorite because any time I would hear an individual, whom I thought was a maximum Christian, express themselves about God or about their work, they always, without exception, said, "To God be the glory." You ask a great man of God a question and start bragging on him and say how wonderful he is, he will interrupt you and go to pointing toward heaven.

Another of my favorite scriptures is John 14:1-3. "Let not your heart be troubled: ye believe in God, believe also in me. In my Father's house are many mansions: if it were not so, I would have told you. I go to prepare a place for you. And if I go and prepare a place for you, I will come again, and receive you unto myself; that where I am, there ye may be also."

I was saved on the fourth Thursday in July, 1939. My mother and my brother Sonny went to an old country church to a revival meeting, and it was that evening that I heard the Gospel preached. At the end of the service I walked down the aisle and had that experience of grace that only comes from the saving power of God.

Jerry Clower
Entertainer

January 14

Believing Comes First

"...whosoever shall say unto this mountain, Be thou removed, and be thou cast into the sea; and shall not doubt in his heart....he shall have whatsoever he saith." Mark 11:23,24

A combination of these two verses brought me off the bed of sickness into a life of health many years ago. I was bedfast, almost totally paralyzed and medical science gave me no hope. I was reading these verses and believing as much as I knew how to believe, but I didn't know enough. I didn't have light on this scripture. We need knowledge of the Word. When this light of knowledge from the Word comes, faith is automatically there.

In that moment, I saw exactly what that verse meant. I saw that I was looking at my body and testing my heartbeat to see if I had been healed. But suddenly I saw it. The verse says that you have to believe *when* you pray. The having comes after the believing. I had been reversing it. I was trying to have first and then believe second. And that is what most folks do.

"I see it. I see it," I shouted. "I see what I've got to do, Lord. I've got to believe that my heart is well while I'm still lying on this bed, and while my heart is not beating right. I've got to believe that my paralysis is gone while I'm still lying here flat on my back and helpless." I prayed and then I began to say out loud in my room, "I believe that I receive my healing for my body. I believe that I receive my healing for the heart condition." (I specified each thing.) I declared what I believed and I then received healing. I was totally healed.

Kenneth E. Hagin, Sr.
President
Kenneth Hagin Ministries

_____ January 15

Christ Living—Faith

"...He that believeth on me, the works that I do shall he do also; and greater works than these shall he do...."   John 14:12

When faith is exercised, it becomes an unlimited power. Faith reproduces itself, making full proof of Christ's supremacy over all. The proof of Christ's resurrection and the reality of the Gospel stirs me up to good works.

Christianity is distinctive from other religions because of the healings, miracles and joy of the new converts, confirming God's Word.

When I became a believer in Jesus Christ, I became a new creature. "Therefore if any man be in Christ, he is a new creature: old things are passed away; behold, all things are become new" (II Corinthians 5:17). When Jesus rose from the dead, He left behind an eternally defeated Satan. As a 'new creature in Christ,' I become what Christ is—Jesus and I now have equal dominion and authority. I found that the strength of increase depends absolutely on how much I believe and exercise my faith in God and His words.

In John 15:16, Jesus said, "I have chosen you and ordained you...that ye should go and bring forth fruit...that whatsoever ye shall ask of the Father in my name, he may give it you." God has always stood by me and honored His Word that goes out of my mouth; it has always accomplished the purpose it has been sent out for.

Rev. Dr. Benson Idahosa
Evangelist

January 16

Developing Spiritual Muscles

"It is a good thing to give thanks unto the Lord, and to sing praises unto thy name, O Most High; to show forth thy loving-kindness in the morning...." Psalm 92:1-2

I accepted Jesus as a small boy, more than fifty years ago. There have been times when God was so close I felt I could touch Him. He has seemed very far away at other times. The silence of God is the greatest test of our faith. His silence is not a silence of indifference, it is the silence of higher thoughts.

Just as a muscle which has nothing to resist becomes soft and weak so it is with our 'spiritual muscles.' What are the times and experiences which help us grow the most? The days of green pastures? No, they have their value; but the days which advance us most are the days of stress and cloud. As long as we whine in the circumstances, we shall continue in them until we have learned our lesson. God must come first in our lives. The hope we have in Him is like a star that twinkles on a dark night.

In the "Chanticleer," Rostand has a beautiful thought on praise. Every morning, the noble bird, Chanticleer, would crow and the sun would rise. He thought his crowing brought up the sun. Then, one morning he overslept, and the sun came up anyway. To this conclusion he speaks profoundly and echoes the conviction of the believing soul of man: "It may be that it is not my poor voice which brings on the day, but this at least I can do, and nothing can deprive me of the joy of it: if I cannot cause the sun to rise, I will lift up my voice to celebrate its rising." He knew the satisfaction of praise.

Elwood Coggin
PTL Pastoral Staff

The Person Of The Holy Spirit

"He that spared not his own Son, but delivered him up for us all, how shall he not with him also freely give us all things?"
Romans 8:32

I got saved in Israel in 1968, but the person of the Holy Spirit didn't become real to me until 1973 at a Katherine Kuhlman meeting. I had heard of the Holy Spirit, had received the baptism, spoken in tongues, but every time I heard Him mentioned, it was in relation to the gifts. I had never heard the Holy Spirit, Himself, mentioned as a real person.

While we waited that night to hear Miss Kuhlman, I could feel the presence of the Lord. I literally shook at His closeness, and it became more intense. When Katherine came out on the platform, I felt a rush of wind. There were no open windows or doors, it was the Holy Spirit sweeping over the auditorium.

She began by asking, "Do you know Him?" I knew she meant the Holy Spirit, and I knew I didn't know Him. Tears started streaming down my cheeks as I asked the Lord to take my life and use it. That day I was introduced to the Holy Spirit, the Third Person in the Holy Trinity. I felt like I was charged with electricity. This experience caused me to remember a similar experience I had as a child. I had seen a vision of Christ and felt this same sensation, one of power, excitement, and expectation. I spent hours in prayer and communion with my new found friend. Even the speech impediment I was born with disappeared, causing my parents to become believers. Discover for yourself this mighty, comforting person, the Holy Spirit.

Benny Hinn
*International Evangelist
Healing Ministry*

January 18

A Future And A Hope

"For I know the plans that I have for you...plans for wealth and not calamity...come and pray...seek me...And I will be found by you."
Jeremiah 29:11-14 (NASB)

A few years ago, when I was traveling on the road with a singing group, about halfway through the tour I started asking the Lord what He was doing with my life. At sixteen I already knew I wanted to be a singer, but I started to get anxious about it, anxious about how the Lord was going to do it. When would it happen? Would I get the big break? Should I initiate any interest in my talent? It all seemed so slow. I was ready to see my dreams realized. Then during a church service as I was waiting for our cue to go on and sing, I began reading my Bible and these verses blazed up at me. I'm sure now that the Lord gave them to me at that time to assure me He did have specific plans for my life. It wasn't just a random chance, here or there, but a definite plan.

Since then, God has opened up the doors. I haven't formally auditioned for anything. God spoke to me to move on from that group. A wise friend told me, "Sometimes you have to get in motion before the Holy Spirit can start working." So after I resigned from the group, that very day I was asked to join the PTL Singers.

When we take the time to get on our knees and call on the Lord, He will honor His promises; "and call upon me in the day of trouble: I will deliver thee, and thou shall glorify me" (Psalms 50:15).

God truly has a design and specific plan for all of us. Trust, obedience, and a yielded will secures God's best for us.

Shari Larson
PTL Singers

January 19

Remember All His Benefits

"Christ hath redeemed us from the curse of the law, being made a curse for us; for it is written, Cursed is every one that hangeth on a tree:"
Galatians 3:13

Concerning our redemption, often we restrict our thinking just to salvation and we tend to forget the other benefits we can enjoy because of the redemptive power we received due to Calvary.

In Psalm 103:2 David said, "Bless the Lord, O my soul, and forget not all his benefits:" As we meditate on redemption, we must also remember that at Calvary, Jesus not only defeated sin but sickness, poverty, death, hell, and the grave.

The thing we should impress upon our minds is that we must not limit the abilities of the power of God in our individual lives. If we place that limitation on ourselves, we limit our ability to do and be all that God wants us to do and be.

Colossians 2:15 tells us, "And having spoiled principalities and powers, he made a show of them openly, triumphing over them in it." God made an open display to the whole world through Christ's triumph at the cross. After defeating Satan, God publicized it before the whole world. He was letting us know that Satan is not the ruling force over us but a defeated foe and under our feet.

We are no longer under the curse, no longer under anything. Christ has redeemed us from the curse. Step out and enjoy all the benefits that are yours through this wonderful redemption.

Rev. Ken McNatt
Evangelist

January 20

Spiritual Farmers

"For God so loved the world, that he gave his only begotten Son, that whosoever believeth in him should not perish, but have everlasting life."   John 3:16

God loved, and He gave. If we love, we must give. The Bible teaches Christ is coming soon, we should have an urgency to win souls for Him because He commanded us to.

My grandmother had faith because an evangelist cared enough to come to Russia preaching under the great anointing of the Holy Spirit. He shared Jesus and showed us our need for a Saviour. His message was, "Believe on the Lord Jesus Christ, and thou shalt be saved, and thy house" (Acts 16:31). My grandmother accepted the love gift and because of that, I'm saved.

The Lord tells us, "My people are destroyed for lack of knowledge:..." (Hosea 4:6). People are actually perishing spiritually if we fail to bring them the knowledge of Christ. We're also promised great reward if we give forth His Word. Mark 10:29-30 sets forth the promise, "There is no man that hath left house, or brethren...for my sake, and the gospel's, But he shall receive an hundredfold now in this time, houses, and brethren... with persecutions; and in the world to come eternal life." That's God's law of blessing.

God is responsible for His Word. When we give out His Word, He is bound to bless His Word. I'm a good spiritual farmer—I want to plant the seed of God's Word and I want to reap a harvest. Let's all join the Lord of the Harvest and be spiritual farmers.

Bill Basansky
Evangelist

January 21

Wash Me With Your Words

"Husbands, love your wives, even as Christ also loved the church, and gave himself for it;"
Ephesians 5:25

After fifteen years of marriage, without Jesus as Head of our home, Bill and I found we had wounded each other in many, many areas. Each of these areas had to be healed. When Jesus became the Lord of our lives and the Head of our home, we began applying the principles set forth in His Word and found we must be 'doers' of the Word. As doers of the Word we would reap a positive healing and restoration to our relationship.

We are told how husbands should love their wives in the next verse, Ephesians 5:26, "...sanctify and cleanse it with the washing of water by the word." Christ being the bridegroom (husband) of the church, He washes her with His words. Now we as wives and husbands are to wash each other with our words that we may be able to present our husbands (or wives) to ourselves—faultless, hurts healed and with faith and trust built up in each other. When a husband or wife speaks words of life to each other, it washes them and encourages them, gives confidence to them, gives life to them and builds trust.

We must learn to be transmitters of love, joy, peace, patience, kindness, gentleness, faithfulness and goodness. According to the law of sowing and reaping, if we transmit love, we will receive a lover. Don't give up on your marriage relationship if it seems to be on the rocks. His Word works if we humble ourselves to do it!

Bea Basansky
Author

January 22

O Taste And See

"O taste and see that the Lord is good: blessed is the man that trusteth in him." Psalm 34:8

The Lord has, through many promises, provided bountifully for those who walk in fellowship with Him. We can enjoy His unlimited love, unfailing mercy, divine protection as we partake (taste) of His holiness. When we are filled with the Holy Spirit, we can really see His goodness.

In times of distress, we can take refuge in the Lord and learn how to dwell in "the secret place of the Most High," as recorded in Psalms 91. These promises are rich and real but cannot be obtained without submission to His discipline and Lordship. Many today want God's provision without submitting to His requirements. But, His standards are already set.

Early one morning as I prepared for my regular devotions, I received a blessed assurance of God's goodness. Mark 11:24 seemed to leap out at me as I read it, "What things soever ye desire, when ye pray, believe that ye receive them, and ye shall have them." I felt confident that I could ask Him anything. How can we dare not trust in His wonderful love? Continuing to read, the next two verses seemed to point out the prerequisite of forgiveness to the receiving mentioned in verse 24. "when ye stand praying, forgive," verse 25 and "if you do not forgive, neither will your Father which is in heaven forgive your trespasses." I'm convinced that forgiveness is the real key to opening up God's promises in our lives.

Jim Noblitt
Evangelist

_____ January 23

He Selected Me To Set Free

"Ye have not chosen me, but I have chosen you...that ye should go and bring forth fruit... that whatsoever ye shall ask of the Father in my name, he may give it..."   John 15:16

After reading this verse many times, it suddenly struck me how much is involved. To realize that He chose me means so much to me. Since being born again, I have loved Jesus with all my heart, but knowing that He chose me made me love Him even more and want to be like Him all the more. It gave me further confirmation of the creation when all things in the beginning were a part of the Master's plan throughout eternity. The Lord's promise that, "your fruit should remain..." means that the souls who come to Christ because of me will remain in Him. The Father promises whatsoever I ask "in His name, He will give it." All good things come to my mind when I consider this phrase, love, kindness, and giving.

Contemplating this verse, I realize I was not so magnanimous in choosing Him...He selected me as one of all the people on the earth to be set free...like picking up one grain of sand from all the deserts and beaches. It is so humbling.

I had attended church casually for many years and been a sporadic church-goer. Then one day in 1978, I went to Church on the Way. That experience left me with a totally different feeling. I felt the power of the Holy Spirit in that meeting. I knew that people could be moved under the power of the Holy Spirit, knew that something was missing from my own life. Then, I prayed and asked the Lord to fill in what was missing and He did. Now I have let Jesus be Lord of my life.

Jay Stewart
Television Announcer

January 24

Fulfilling The Great Commission

"Go ye into all the world, and preach the gospel to every creature."   Mark 16:15

My parents were both preachers, fulfilling the "Great Commission" was our whole life. However, that verse took on new meaning for me at age thirteen when I came to the realization that I had to make a personal commitment to Christ. I realized the truth of John 14:6, "...I am the way, the truth and the life: no man cometh unto the Father, but by me."

After that I noticed we weren't going "into all the world" very fast. Only about eighty people attended church in that big old building in Hot Springs, Arkansas. The Great Commission then became my personal commission. I knew I had to do something about attendance at our church services. I took my guitar, went to the local radio station and asked for the manager. When I asked to sing, he asked, "What for?" I replied, "I want to sing Gospel songs and tell your listeners about my dad's church." He took me into a studio and said, "Sing!" I did and the response from listeners was so great, he asked me to sing regularly. Within a year, attendance at Dad's church grew from eighty to more than a thousand. I've been in broadcast ministry ever since.

In 1952, I became aware of the potential of television for

fulfilling the Great Commission, "And this gospel of the kingdom shall be preached in all the world for a witness unto all nations; and then shall the end come" (Matthew 24:14). I have been ministering over television since then and, in 1982, I will have been in radio and television ministry for thirty years. Praise be to God.

Rex Humbard
TV Evangelist

The Divine Helper And Keeper

"I will lift up mine eyes unto the hills, from whence cometh my help. My help cometh from the Lord, which made heaven and earth....The Lord is thy keeper:..." Psalm 121

The 121st Psalm became very real to me a few years ago when I had to have surgery. I was very depressed although I am God's child and I knew He would take care of me. But the night before the surgery it seemed I couldn't touch the hem of His garment like I wanted to for that peace of mind I needed.

A little nurse came in that night and picked up my Bible and read the 121st Psalm. It was just what my soul needed. Peace flooded my heart.

The next morning I went up to surgery and the minor surgery turned out to be major. Five hours later they brought me out and the doctor said, "Rev. Humbard, we did all we could do to save your wife, and we might have lost her except a higher power stepped in." That day in the operating room, the Lord reached down His hand and said my work was not through on this earth.

Since that time, the songs that I've sung have become more real. I believe with all of my heart that is why I'm here today, because of that portion of Scripture, "I will lift up mine eyes unto the hills, from whence cometh my help."

God does not slumber, nor doth He fall asleep. If He takes note of the little sparrow that falls, how much more does He take note of His children.

Maude Aimee Humbard
Evangelist's Wife

January 26

Fervent Love

"...obeying the truth through the Spirit unto unfeigned love of the brethren, see that ye love one another with a pure heart fervently:"
I Peter 1:22

After accepting the Lord, I thought of putting on a circus in the winter at churches because winter is the slack season for us. Several years later when things were slow in my career and the Lord was dealing in my life, I recommitted my life completely to Him. I prayed, "Lord, I just want You to use me."

Shortly after that, Pastor Nevil Gritt asked if I would entertain for his church. We prayed mightily and many people were touched in that performance. That's when I realized circus could be more than entertainment but could be used to reach people for the Lord. Earlier, my attitude had been wrong, I'd wanted to fill a slack season. God wanted my all—not just the leftovers. I pray before every show, not just for church performances but every show, for both the performers and the audience.

God wants our very best not just in our circus performance but in our family relationships. Love is the glue that holds relationships together. Love overwhelms our problems. We must 'love fervently' to coexist. It makes no difference if it's a circus performance, relating to your family, washing the dishes, or walking the high wire; the Lord wants our very best for Him.

We're told, "And whatsoever ye do, do it heartily, as to the Lord, and not unto men" (Colossians 3:23).

Tino Zoppe
Circus Manager

_____ January 27

Power In Joy

"He healeth the broken in heart, and bindeth up their wounds."   Psalm 147:3

The highway to heaven is lighted all the way with glorious revelations from God's Word, plus illumination from the Holy Spirit. When I begin a sermon, the material from the Holy Spirit creates such a spontaneous combustion when it comes, there's no holding back.

So many Christians have internal hurts. If we could see into hearts, we would see much scar tissue caused by strife, anger, and resentment. Christ cares for His bride—He's promised to heal the brokenhearted—to bind up and care for our wounds.

God is solid and non-changing, "Jesus Christ, the same yesterday, and today, and for ever" (Hebrews 13:8). His job in the changed life is to mend the brokenhearted. There's never been a time of such deceitfulness, betrayal, and hurt; but praise God, when we get to heaven, there won't be any hurts or wounds. The only wounds there, will be on Christ's body for our sakes. Our wounded hearts will be full of love and joy because of Christ's wounds. But, we already *have* God's healing, here and now, through Christ's wounds.

The Holy Spirit, in these days, is getting the bride ready for resurrection. The oil and wine are for healing. The Holy Spirit wants to transform our brokenness into a changed life for Him.

The Lord stated a deep truth when He said, "...the joy of the Lord is your strength" (Nehemiah 8:10). His joy will transform you. His joy will allow you to say, "Devil, move over!"

Jerry B. Walker
Evangelist

January 28

Saved To Overcome

"To him that overcometh will I grant to sit with me in my throne..." Revelation 3:21

You don't get experience in the controlled environment of the classroom, you get it in the real world of tribulation and trial. One man looked and thought he saw a light at the end of the tunnel, but it was only a freight train that ran him down. That's how it seems to us sometimes, but that's how the Lord helps us become overcomers of problems that could run us down, even unexpectedly.

Think of the crushing problems of the Old Testament saints, the Lord says of their troubles in I Corinthians 10:11, "These things happened to them for examples: and they are written for our admonition." God's way is not out, but through. We plead, "Lord get me out of this problem...," but God promises to be with us through the problem. "When thou passest through the waters, I will be with thee...through the fire, thou shalt not be burned...For I am the Lord thy God..." (Isaiah 43:2,3). God doesn't promise to deliver us from but develop us through.

We are being prepared for the millennium. God said, "To him that overcometh will I grant to sit with me in my throne..." (Revelation 3:21). He referred to overcoming again in Revelation 3:5, "He that overcometh...I will confess his name before my Father..."

The new birth is only five percent of the Christian life. The other 95 percent is growing. We must be grounded in His Word and strengthened by overcoming.

Bob Gass
Evangelist

January 29

Our Peaceful Inheritance

"...he was wounded for our transgressions, he was bruised for our iniquities: the chastisement of our peace was upon him; and with his stripes we are healed." Isaiah 53:5

Many Christians are in good physical and spiritual condition, but are emotionally crippled. Jesus left us with a gift, "Peace I leave with you, my peace I give unto you" (John 14:27). Inner healing is a healing of the mind, the emotions, and memories. Romans 12:2 says, "...be not conformed to this world: but be ye transformed by the renewing of your mind..." One day as I read the story of when the spies were sent into Canaan and they reported that the land was flowing with milk and honey, to receive their rightful inheritance they had first to defeat the giants, I realized that all of us have giants that we need to defeat, if we are to receive our rightful inheritance which is righteousness, peace, and joy.

We need to defeat the hindering giants of depression, anxiety, worry, fear, rejection, pride, inferiority, lust, inadequacy, etc. God took me through a very painful, but precious, day several years ago, when the Holy Spirit revealed to me where Satan had hidden hurts and painful memories. Inner healing, I discovered, is firstly confronting the giants in our lives, then conquering them. I was quick to discover that unforgiveness is another giant, responsible for resentments, bitterness and self-pity. Indeed, we can receive and experience peace of mind (a renewing of the mind) and the joy of the Lord can be ours and obvious in our lives.

Have you reclaimed your inheritance?

Heather Gass
Wife of Evangelist Bob Gass

January 30

Suicide To Joy Unspeakable

"Whom...ye love; in whom...though now ye see him not, yet believing, ye rejoice with joy unspeakable and full of glory."   I Peter 1:8

My high school years were turbulent after being raised in England and moving to the United States when I was thirteen. When I reached the age of seventeen, I knew something was missing, but there were no Christians to help me. During high school, I got wrapped up in my job with television. I immersed myself in my work and a week before Christmas of my senior year, I had a complete physical breakdown. When I got out of the hospital, I went right back to the compulsive work habit.

After high school, when my TV job came to an end, I felt like a limb had been severed. A big part of me was gone. I was unable to get a job and I was caught up in a vicious circle. No job, so I had no experience; with no experience I couldn't get a job, so the vicious circle went on. I was terribly pressured.

Finally, I volunteered at a TV studio for eight months. One day we heard a group called PTL was coming. I'd never heard of PTL, but a fellow worker was a Partner and explained it to me. By now I'd worked myself into a frenzy and decided to commit suicide. I'd figured out the time, place, and method. However, the minute I saw the PTL group, I knew they were different. The associate producer said, "You have a problem; we have the answer." I was at the point where I'd do anything to be happy. I accepted Christ and when they prayed with me, a great burden lifted and joy unspeakable poured in.

Paul King
*Assistant Manager,
PTL Broadcast Division*

January 31

No Room For Compromise

"Therefore with joy shall ye draw water out of the wells of salvation."   Isaiah 12:3

I remember how easy it was to praise the Lord when I first met Him. How that wellspring of new found joy made my heart just want to burst. The more I praised the Lord, the more He filled me back up with joy.

As time went on, I began to compromise on some things in my walk with the Lord. Little by little, my joy began to fade. It was so gradual, I didn't realize it at first. Not until it dawned on me I was thirsty for that "living water" that used to fill my soul did I realize my inner wellspring had dried up. That strong surge of hope and joy in my salvation was gone. I found I couldn't praise the Lord like I used to...I was lonely for Jesus.

God's Word says, "with joy shall ye draw water out of the wells of salvation." The cup of praise I raised to the Lord was the same cup He filled up with His joy and poured back inside me. By compromising, I had chipped holes and cracks in my cup. It wouldn't hold my praise so it couldn't hold joy; so I couldn't draw water from the wells of salvation.

When I got the compromises out of my life, my cup became whole again. Now I don't want to stop praising the Lord because His joy is more real to me than ever before.

If joy is missing in your life, ask the Lord to show you where you may be compromising with the world. Get back to really walking with Jesus. Start praising the Lord and He'll keep your cup filled up to overflowing.

Andrae Crouch
Songwriter/Singer

_____ February 1

Great Is Thy Faithfulness

"This I recall...therefore I have hope...because his compassions fail not. They are new every morning: great is thy faithfulness..."
Lamentations 3:21-26

God is so faithful to us, His children. I love to dwell on His goodness and am always strengthened and encouraged when I think about this portion of Scripture.

From Genesis to Revelation, the entire Word of God is proof of His love and steadfastness to us.

Learning to be faithfull will bring a meaningful life of joy and contentment.

Faithfulness to ourselves—holding fast, in His strength, to our faith in God and Jesus' sacrifice and *decide* to go to heaven.

Faithfulness to our loved ones and friends—showing through our actions the love of Christ Jesus.

Faithfulness to our commitments—determining to honor and continue in the covenants we have made.

Faithfulness to God—as foremost in our lives. To love and honor His Son—who never tires of us, never leaves us and never becomes bored with us, but instead He seeks us out and longs to be with us, to love us, and to give us His perfect peace.

To attain these things would please God, and yet, I know in my own self, this would be impossible. Only through Jesus can we begin to reach this high standard.

Above all else, I want to be found faithful. Don't you?

Sylvia McAllister
*PTL's February
Employee of the Month*

February 2

Grafted In

"But some of these branches from Abraham's tree, some of the Jews, have been broken off...So now you, too, receive the blessing..." Romans 11:17 (Living Bible)

For years I heard people say, "All the promises God made to Israel are available to us as adopted Jews." Recently, I searched it out for myself, and you know, it's true!

Throughout history, God has used the Jewish people to keep His name alive in this earth, and to write and preserve the Holy Scriptures. The Lord also used them to prove to us that we need Christ. He used the example of Moses who wrote, "That if a person could be perfectly good and hold out against temptation all his life and never sin once, only then could he be pardoned and saved" (Romans 10:5 Living Bible). What great love He has for them—Abraham's descendants.

The Apostle Paul also had a deep love for the Jews. He loved them so much he would even give up his place in heaven if it would save them.

What a blessed privilege we have to receive such inheritance and rich nourishments, just as His own original chosen people, the Jews. However, God warns us not to brag. Spiritual pride is something He frowns on. He warns us, "But you must be careful not to brag about being put in to replace the branches that were broken off. Remember that you are important only because you are now a part of God's tree; you are just a branch, not a root" (Romans 11:18 LB). We're partakers of the blessing, not because of who we are, or of what we are, but because of *whose* we are.

Henry Harrison
PTL Co-Host

February 3

Love As I've Loved

"This is my commandment, That ye love one another, as I have loved you." John 15:12

When I think on this commandment, and consider the great love in the heart of God for me, I am overwhelmed. One day God gave me a glimpse of the depths of this love.

I am a nurse but I have never witnessed such suffering as endured by my own son years ago. Day and night his wife and I stood by, helpless to relieve that horrible pain. As I stood by the bedside of my dying son, I was made to see a truth I would otherwise never have known.

I'd often slip away to the prayer chapel to cry to God, "Please don't take him, he's my only son." Always the soft answer from the Father came back, "Susan, I know, Jesus was my only son." Then it was that I turned and really looked upon the cross as Jesus was hanging there in a million times more agony, shame, and suffering than my son. I could see the agony of His son, knowing God had a choice as I didn't in my son's suffering. I cried, "Oh, God! How could you love me that much?"

Then He charged me, "Susan, I command you to go and love as I've loved!" I cried out, "God I cannot! It's too much to ask. I am incapable of so great a love." In a beautiful and sweet voice, He answered, "Susan, just let Me do it through you. That's all I ask, let Me do it."

That is all He asks, not that we strive or stretch or do, but allow Him to live and love through our lives.

Susan Harrison
PTL Hostess

February 4

Spirit Building Strength

"I can do all things through Christ which strengtheneth me." Philippians 4:13

As a professional body builder, my life has been built around strength. I have goals of building up my strength.

This verse tells us Christ gives us strength. I draw my physical strength as well as my spiritual strength from Jesus. There is nothing too big or too hard for my God and me to conquer together. I need the kind of strength only Jesus can give to live victoriously. Satan tries constantly to make people think that they can't do this or that, but they can do anything through Jesus! Exodus 15:2 reminds us, "The Lord is my strength..."

I grew up thinking I was saved, but I hadn't really made a commitment to give my life totally to God. One day the doctors told me I had cancer and that they could do nothing to help me. I turned to the Lord then, eleven years ago, and God healed me. He cleaned me up inside and out, physically and spiritually. The Lord has made promises to us all through His Word; to take care of our every need. In Luke 17:19 He said rise and go, your faith has made you well. I use my body to give glory to God who gave me back my body.

Physical strength is important and often emphasized, but spiritual strength is equally important. So praise the One who tells us, "I can do all things..."

Bill Ashpaugh
Mr. World Contest Winner

February 5

A New Life In Christ

"Jesus answered and said unto him, Verily, verily, I say unto thee, Except a man be born again, he cannot see the kingdom of God."
John 3:3

At one point in my musical career, a friend named Irvin and I had gotten hooked smoking pot, just trying to be hip. After Irvin had disappeared for six months, he came back and said he had found Jesus and told me, "Jesus will change your life." I had been singing and playing Gospel music for years, but I didn't really believe Jesus had anything to offer me that would change or make a difference in my life.

Irvin encouraged me to go to church with him, but I agreed to go only on Wednesday night. That evening the speaker shared on Romans. He called it the Roman Road as it explained what it means to be born again. I couldn't believe it as I listened, this guy was saying, "When you're born again, you get a new spirit, a new life." I asked Irvin, "Is this what you've been talking about?" He told me, "Yes." I told Irvin I didn't believe it and walked out of the church.

The next morning I was driving my car to the repair shop, when a man on the radio began preaching the same thing that I had heard before. I knew that Irvin was trying to get me to become a Christian, so I figured he had rigged the radio. But it wasn't Irvin, it was the Lord. When I heard this minister say the same thing, and give those scriptures, I asked the Lord to come into my heart, right there driving on a street. Perhaps you can encourage someone to attend church with you or to accept Christ as their personal Saviour. It could change their life into something new.

Jessy Dixon
Gospel Music Artist

February 6

God Of Our Total Supply

"Now unto to him that is able to do exceeding abundantly above all that we ask or think, according to the power that worketh in us," Ephesians 3:20

God, if we allow Him, will supply us with all that we need for prosperous, victorious, fruitful, and effective living. He, alone, is our provider and keeper.

A song God laid on my heart sums up my appreciation for God's provision and eternal love. It is entitled, "The More." I share it with you:

"The deeper the valley, the higher the mountaintop,
The heavier the burden, the greater His grace;
The more bitter the conflict, you just keep on fighting,
The sweeter the victory, at the end of the race.
The more you've been wounded, the more soothing the healing,
When someone wrongs you, the more you forgive,
And the more that you're tempted, when you just keep on trusting,
The more you'll be strengthened every day that you live.
The more that you hunger and thirst after Jesus, He promised to fill you more with His love, And the less you're concerned about worldly riches, that's the more He'll supply you with wealth from above."

You can rely on God's faithfulness. Trust Him with your all. He delights in blessing and using "Ordinary People," just like you and me.

Danniebelle Hall
Gospel Singer

February 7

A Product Of Love

"And I will give them one heart, and one way, that they may fear me for ever, for the good of them, and of their children..."
Jeremiah 32:39

I am a product of much love and careful training. That is quite a bold statement to make, to be sure, but I say it with much appreciation to godly parents who lived a life of dedication to God and to us. I am a preacher's kid, and glad of it. "PK's," as we are sometimes called, are somehow stereotyped as "do-gooders" and "goody two-shoes," who have no individuality, or personal aspirations.

That is not my upbringing. My parents taught me that self worth is not dependent on social acceptance but is based on one's ability to surrender all to the Lord and walk in His ways. Harmony with God brings peace, joy, success, for He has made us His children by a divine act of love, so are we to continue.

Priorities were set very early in my home. Our family always came first, even though my father is dedicated to the ministry. We were told every day that we were loved. We were never made to feel like our problems were not important. My parents never set themselves up as judges, they were not always right, neither were we. We always felt involved, because special effort was made to make us feel secure and a very important part of our parents' lives and ministry. Honesty was the order of the day, every day. Sounds rigid? Too structured? It was a way of life. Love administered consistently, gently, carefully and with every intention of teaching us God's order. All that I am, I owe to this labor of love.

Mark Gorman
Singer

February 8

Illness Brings Empathy

"For we know that all things work together for good to them that love God, to them who are the called according to his purpose."
Romans 8:28

A few years ago I suffered from anorexia nervosa. It's a disease where people are frightened of being fat and go to the other extreme. You get to a place where you can't eat or can't keep food on your stomach. It's accompanied by depression and sometimes anxiety.

I consider my good health today as a direct answer to prayer. Only one third of the victims of anorexia nervosa ever recover—the rest die of starvation.

Only by the grace of God was I able to recover. My mother, Shirley Boone, prayed for me constantly. She went to every friend and acquaintance, called up every relative, prevailed upon everyone she knew and asked them to pray for me. She had people all across the country praying for me. I am proof of the scripture, "...The effectual fervent prayer of a righteous man (woman) availeth much" (James 5:16.) Prayer literally drew me back to health. Gradually, over a long period of time, I have recovered.

However, I firmly believe in the truth of Romans 8:28, that all things work together for good. I gained an understanding and sympathy for those going through illness that I could have gained in no other way. Because of my own illness, I have an empathy and prayer burden for those going through any illness that I never had before.

Cherri Boone O'Neil
Co-Author

February 9

God Didn't Just Say "Some"

"....whosoever shall say unto this mountain, Be thou removed...and shall not doubt in his heart, but shall believe...he shall have whatsoever he saith." Mark 11:23

I could have given up my childhood dream of becoming Miss America after the car accident that left my face scarred and one leg two inches shorter than the other. But through the strong support and love of my family and the knowledge that God really loved me, I held onto that dream.

Even though my family prayed and read the Bible together, I had never asked God to do a miracle right in front of my eyes. Not until some precious Spirit-filled friends, who had the love of God in their hearts, shared with me the promise of Mark 11:23-24.

I began to read that verse over and over and ask God to help me understand it. At a certain point, I noticed it said, "Whosoever." It didn't say "some" people, but "whosoever" and that included me.

It told me I had the authority to say, "Hey, God, if I come to You and confess I'm going to have a longer leg, You can do this, and not only *can* You do it, but You love me enough that You *want* to do it." From that point I began to confess positive thoughts, not only concerning my healing but in everything about my life. As I got into God's Word and got God's Word into me, I prepared my spirit, mind and body to receive a miracle. That miracle happened and six years later I was crowned Miss America 1980.

God is so good and His Word is so true! Claim His promises in your life and believe for your miracle.

Cheryl Prewitt Blackwood
Miss America 1980
Singer/Author

February 10

Religion Or Christianity?

"See to it that no one makes a prey of you by philosophy and empty deceit, according to human tradition...the universe, and not according to Christ." Colossians 2:8 (RSV)

The Word tells us the Holy Spirit is the teacher and will lead us into all truth. It's important to walk in the Spirit so we won't be encumbered with the philosophies of the world.

Not long ago I heard a motivation speech by a very dynamic gentleman and much of what he said was good—believe your potential, emphasize the positive—that sort of thing. But the more he expounded, the more apparent it became that everything he pointed to revolved around the individual's ability and confidence in himself.

I realized how contrary this teaching is to the Word of God, as the Lord shows us we're to be totally dependent on Him. "In whom are hid all the treasures of wisdom and knowledge" (Colossians 2:3).

I picked up a book recently, written by an Eastern Religionist teacher. It said if "we did enough, went through the proper requirements and qualified ourselves," God would eventually be pleased and listen to us. This reminded me that all religions portray man trying to qualify and reach God, but Christianity alone shows God reaching down in love, mercy, and forgiveness to unqualified man. This dramatically points out how vain the philosophies and deceits of man are. No human reasoning can ever bring us the all encompassing forgiveness we received through Christ's death on the cross. In Christ dwells all knowledge, wisdom, and understanding.

Eric AuCoin
Heritage Village Church
Music Coordinator

February 11

Acknowledge Him

"Trust in the Lord with all thine heart; and lean not unto thine own understanding. In all thy ways acknowledge him, and he shall direct thy paths."   Proverbs 3:5-6

Trust is a word easily said but not easily committed to action. Demonstrating complete trust in the Lord is a lesson He's been teaching me lately. In this same process of growth, I'm discovering how much the Lord really loves, too. We all realize how very much we love our own children, how difficult it is to see them suffer in any way. God's love for us is much greater. So great, He's willing for us to suffer if we can accomplish more for His glory or if we can be more conformed to the image of His dear Son. His ways are higher than our ways, we can never fully comprehend the depths of His love.

In Colossians 3:17, we're instructed, "And whatsoever ye do in word or deed, do all in the name of the Lord Jesus, giving thanks to God and the Father by him." Sometimes we are tempted not to give thanks in the stressful, trying situations that confront us. How many more blessings we would enjoy if we could believe that it is the time when the situation looks the bleakest, that our thanks are most precious to Him. When we acknowledge Him in all situations, we can give thanks because we know He is working everything out to His glory and every thing out to His glory and perfect will.

Acknowledge the presence of God in every situation, praise Him in the midst of trials, trust completely in His love for you, and experience joy and peace in abundance.

Rosalinde AuCoin
Singer

February 12

Whatever It Takes

"Beloved, think it not strange concerning the fiery trial which is to try you...But rejoice, inasmuch as ye are partakers of Christ's sufferings; that...ye may be glad..." I Peter 4:12-13

I came from a strong Christian background. My father was the editor of the small paper called, "The Sunday School Times," and my parents were missionaries, so it was not unusual that I became a missionary, too. I have learned through many years of dedication to Gospel evangelism that God can take on all of our questions and suspicions about circumstances that confront us. All He truly wants and expects from us is conformity to the image of Jesus Christ. Only God knows, too, what it will take to bring you and me into that conformity. We may not like what happens to us, but if we sincerely want His perfect will in our lives, we say "Yes Lord, whatever it takes!"

I was on the mission field working in a tribe in Ecuador when my first husband, Jim Elliot, was killed by another tribe in 1956. When I first heard he was missing, the Lord whispered Isaiah 43:2 to my heart. How graciously God fulfills all His promises, for comfort, strength, and continued direction. After his death, I continued at my station, and with my ten month old daughter, fulfilled my responsibilities as well as taking over Jim's role. We had a church, school, store, clinic, and I had been building an airstrip. But God supplied the strength and the will to continue.

I refused to allow fear, worry, or despair to sink in, because I had known God's love too long. I was never disappointed in God, because He continually reassured me of His love, He still does today.

Elizabeth Elliot
Author/Speaker

February 13

You Can Do It!

"I can do all things through Christ which strengtheneth me."   Philippians 4:13

Obstacles are a reality we all face daily. They provide opportunities for God to be God in our lives and give us the privilege to be faithful and obedient to His Word. What tremendous strength we receive when we overcome through God's presence and power in us.

I was raised in a home where God was not welcomed. My mother physically abused me, and my father sexually abused me, and because of these stresses I went out into the world. I became a prostitute. For thirteen years, I was involved in that sordid, empty lifestyle, until one day I opened a Gideon Bible I had stolen out of a motel. I met a real man, Jesus! He gave His life for me just because He loved me. Then He rose from the dead to prove He is the Son of God. It broke my heart and I gave Him my life that day.

When I was a new babe in Christ, I was asked to share in front of hundreds of people and I was petrified. A brother in Christ said, "Judy, you can't, but Jesus can," and he quoted Philippians 4:13. That was the beginning for me to share across the world the miracle that Jesus had transformed my life. And because He is no respecter of persons, He will do the same for anyone.

As I go into the highways and byways to minister love to the unlovable, the enemy will try to tell me it is no use. But I live by faith not by sight, and the Word is my weapon!

Judy Mamou
Evangelist

February 14

Harper Valley To Mountain Top

"Greater love hath no man than this, that a man lay down his life for his friends."
John 15:13

I recently wrote a book on my life with the help of Jamie Buckingham. When we started, I was worried what I should share and what I should hold back. I wanted to write the Lord's message. While I was in this dilemma of what to include, I was praying and my Bible fell open to Acts 5, where Ananias and his wife Sapphira kept back a part of the price of the land they sold. Peter said to Ananias, "..Satan filled thine heart to lie to the Holy Ghost..." (Acts 5:3).

The Lord spoke to me and said, "That was their money they could have kept—the sin was they lied to the Holy Ghost. This is your story so don't hold back or you'll be lying to the Holy Spirit." It frightened me that the Lord required me to be so totally, painfully honest. The Lord made me willing to be honest. I went through such a range of emotions, I said, "Lord, I don't think I can take it." He answered, "I'll give you what you need when you need it." The Scripture promises us, "My grace is sufficient for you" (II Corinthians 12:9).

I shared all my scars in my book, there are no secrets, no unturned stones. Before, I feared when people saw my imperfections they'd reject me, but that hasn't been true, they've showered me with love.

I've learned love is something you do...a commitment. He'd have died for even one person, but He did die for *all*. "Greater love hath no man than this, that a man lay down his life for his friends."

Jeannie C. Riley
Singer

February 15

Waiting On The King

"...they that wait upon the Lord shall renew their strength; they shall mount up with wings as eagles; they shall run, and not be weary...shall walk, and not faint." Isaiah 40:31

As a young man without God, I wearied from pursuit of ideals crushed by corruption; dreams evaporated in shallow, worldly success and pleasure—all temporal and fleeting. Then, Christ came and made all things new. He poured His loving strength in me. What a difference!

He lifted my thoughts above the emptiness and ugliness of self. He gave me new, pure vision to love even as He loved me. I found great adventure with purpose in His service. There is lasting pleasure and eternal victory in leading the lost to Christ and seeing the effectual working of His power in them also. There is rest and assurance knowing that in all things His limitless power is at work and He is carrying the greatest share of the burden.

Learning to wait on the Lord and find His direction and purpose has given me a confidence, a winning attitude toward life that is unbelievable in the amount of strength and perseverance that it has given me.

I have known Jesus as my Saviour for nearly thirteen years. Before salvation, my insatiable lust drove me in a way that I didn't expect to live to my thirtieth birthday. Jesus bought my debt to sin, brought me out of darkness and prison and set me free. He is my King and I will wait on Him forever!

Jeff Park
PTL Director
Ministries Services

February 16

Wholeness In God

> *"And the very God of peace satisfy you wholly; and I pray God your whole spirit, and soul and body be preserved blameless...."*
> I Thessalonians 5:23

As a single woman, I found myself coping with loneliness and groping for my identity by putting categories on life. At my job as a marketing director, I acted out a businesswoman personality. When I was on a date, I lived my social personality. While at church, I put on my religious personality.

My parents lived a long distance from me and through my letters I portrayed another image of myself. The real me was standing in the background directing these phony fronts. Living a fragmented life resembled looking at myself in a broken mirror.

My emotions reacted differently to similar situations under various circumstances. People who knew me in two areas of my life, like at church and at work for example, saw marked changes in my lifestyles.

I needed that "whole" spirit, soul, and body that Paul mentions in I Thessalonians. One day I asked God to make me the person He wanted me to be. By combining the best qualities of my categories, He is transforming me into a whole person.

You may feel fragmented today. The weight of problems and pressures might threaten to shatter you to pieces. But I can tell you from experience that the God of peace will come into your life and begin to make you whole.

Andrea Wells Miller
Author/Consultant

February 17

A Man Called Job

"There was a man in the land of Uz, whose name was Job; and that man was perfect and upright, and one that feared God, and eschewed evil."
Job 1:1

Who was Job? He was not called to be a king, prophet, or priest but was only a layman to whom God chose to reveal some of His deepest secrets. God allowed Satan to bring about some great tragedies in Job's life. First, the deaths of Job's seven children and second, the loss of his health, not to mention lesser tragedies involving the loss of his servants and livestock.

Job 2:10 says, "...In all this did not Job sin with his lips." When the Lord knows that we are able to cope with a particular degree of trouble, showing our total submission and dependence on Him alone, He then is able to reveal more of Himself and His ways to us.

Job 38 through 42 records a great depth of communion between God and man. God speaks directly to Job and shares with him the mysteries of His vast universe, presenting Job with His own job description as God of the universe. Yes, even God Himself wanted to share something of His work, His accomplishments, and His greatness. And it was Job, the layman, who: (1) avoided all evil; (2) blessed the name of the Lord during tribulation; and (3) trusted in God in all circumstances; with whom God chose to share so intimately.

God's desire for us is that the attitude of our hearts and lives be such that we, like Job, can say, "I have heard of thee by the hearing of the ear; but now mine eye seeth thee" (Job 42:5). Our Heavenly Father longs for us to come to know Him more intimately.

Bruce Mumm
*Executive Producer,
Thailand PTL*

February 18

A Special Security

"...for I know whom I have believed, and am persuaded that he is able to keep that which I have committed unto him against that day."
II Timothy 1:12

I was brought up in an old-fashioned Pentecostal church and that's great, except that in the revivals we used to have, we'd always know we were going to have a great revival because we'd always pray the same people through in every revival. This always worried me, until I got out and began to work in a lot of different kinds of churches. A lot of Pentecostal people would always say they wanted to go and convert all the Baptists. Well, the Baptists really helped me in this one area.

Personally, I believe that when we're born again, we become the children of Jesus Christ and we commit ourselves to Him. Then He is able to keep us. We're not able to keep ourselves, but everything that we have committed to the Lord Jesus Christ, He is able to keep. If I can keep myself committed to Him, then I find this to be true in every aspect of my life. If I can keep my health committed to Him, then Jesus is able to keep me in perfect health. If I can keep my finances committed to Him, He is able to keep me with plenty of finances. He is able to supply all of my needs according to His riches in glory. Everything that I can commit to the Lord, He will keep, and to me, this is the reason why this scripture is great.

For He is able to keep that which I have committed into His trust. If I can learn to commit my all to the Lord, He is able to keep that.

Buck Rambo
Gospel Music Artist

February 19

The Providing Shepherd

"The Lord is my shepherd; I shall not want. He maketh me to lie down in green pastures: he leadeth me beside the still waters. He restoreth my soul:..." Psalm 23:1-3

Psalm 23 seems old because so many people use it as a favorite passage, but it is special to me because it says the Lord is my shepherd, I shall not want.

I knew a gentleman that became like a second father to me. He was a minister, a missionary to Baghdad. He came back to New Orleans and started one of the first Charismatic churches in that city, down near Bourbon Street. He won a lot of people to the Lord, especially young people and those that were confused and involved in things like alcohol and prostitution. He was an artist, such as a painter, and also a songwriter, just a very creative person. My father was not a Christian, and so this man became like my father. His name was John Thomas.

Getting to know him real well, I found out he had worked with the Assyrians quite a bit. He had an Assyrian Bible and as he read to me and asked me if I knew what Psalms 23:1 said in the Assyrian Bible, I said, "No, I don't." And he said, "The Lord is my provider, I shall not want for anything." That covers a lot of territory. I shall not want for anything, for He is my provider.

Psalm 23 has been an incredible scripture for me as it's great to have the Lord as a father, mother, a brother, a doctor, and a lawyer. Someone to help us stand our trials and help us through our problems. That is why this passage is one of my favorites.

Dottie Rambo
Gospel Music Artist

February 20

Cry Out To God

"In my distress, I cried unto the Lord and he heard me."

Psalm 120:1

How faithful God is in keeping all of His promises! Five years ago, at the lowest ebb in my life, Jesus was waiting to hear my cry of help and bring me back to Him.

My marriage of 25 years was a total wreck. Every fact of our relationship had been battered, physically, mentally, financially...it all seemed hopeless. Finally, we separated after several ugly scenes. We were far from the Lord, and each day our lives became a greater hell.

I got to the point I just wanted to die. Everything I cared about was messed up. In my anguish, I cried out to God, "Lord, help me. Please help me..."

Thank God, in His love and mercy, He saved me. He picked me up out of my despair and made a complete new creature out of me. It wasn't long before my husband also found the Lord, and our marriage was totally and completely healed. Then our three children found the Lord!

No matter what situation you may be facing today, God wants to help you. Cry unto Him, and let Him hear you and help you.

Mikki Howie
Reservations Clerk

Just Obey

"And Samuel said, Hath the Lord as great delight in burnt offering...as in obeying the voice of the Lord? Behold, to obey is better than sacrifice..." I Samuel 15:22

Shortly after I accepted the Lord, I began seeking some way to express to Him my gratitude for His love and mercy. I thought of preaching, that seemed the logical thing to do, but there wasn't a door open for me to do that.

Frustrated, I further searched myself for some great way to show the Lord how much I loved Him. I thought that if the time ever came that I be placed in a position of renouncing Christ or be put to death, I would gladly go to my grave for Him. That seemed the ultimate way to show Jesus how much I love Him.

About this time, I was invited to go to a full Gospel prayer meeting, and a young man started sharing about obedience. The message of his sermon and this verse startled me!

God began showing me that, more than anything else, He wanted His children to obey Him. Pure and simple...just obey.

Certainly, not all of us are called to preach, and not every Christian will be asked to die for Christ, but all of us are charged with obeying God. That is the greatest way we can show the Lord our love.

In every situation, seek the Lord's will and obey His gentle voice. It's the only way to really serve Him.

Kenneth "Buck" Howie
*Campground Manager
Fort Heritage*

February 22

But For His Grace

"For the eyes of the Lord run to and fro throughout the whole earth, to show himself strong in the behalf of them whose heart is perfect toward him." II Chronicles 16:9a

At seven years of age, I was involved in an accident while riding my bike. A man who was intoxicated hit me, mangling my body. The top of my head was cracked, my brains exposed, and my ear nearly severed. I was so badly hurt that funeral arrangements were discussed. My parents who had just begun the Spirit-controlled walk with Jesus walked into the hospital emergency room, knelt, prayed, asking God for a miracle. The doctors told them to pray for my death, because if I recovered, I would be a vegetable. They continued to pray for my healing, but with this stipulation, that if I were not going to live for Jesus, to take me home, now. God is so gracious, for in five days, I regained consciousness, with no pain. I could reason and speak normally and I had no paralysis. Bless the Lord!

That was the first of many near-death experiences I have encountered in my lifetime. The time came that, because I had recovered from such impossible accidents, I thought myself invincible and became a daredevil. I challenged God constantly. But through it all, God's faithfulness and demonstration confirms, beyond a shadow of a doubt, that we serve a mighty God, who is well able to do the impossible, even save a wretch like me. I will be eternally grateful to God and praying parents who persisted in prayer until I recognized my need for Him. I should have been destroyed many times over, but for His grace, I live to praise His wonderful name.

Jim Riley
Evangelist/Singer

February 23

The Fruit of the Righteous

"The fruit of the righteous is a tree of life; and he that winneth souls is wise."   Proverbs 11:30

The only thing important enough to bring our Saviour all the way from the ivory palaces of heaven to our planet, earth, was to seek and to save the lost, to win and to woo them into the loving arms of our Heavenly Father!

As one who has been reached by Him and for Him, my burning desire now is to reach out in His name and win others to Him. As God's children, I believe we are saved to serve, won to win, and told to tell! I am saved because someone told me about Jesus.

I was reared in the rugged outlaw country of the mountains of southeastern Oklahoma in a family of eleven children. For years, there wasn't a church of any denomination for miles! The area was called "The Land that God forgot!" I was sixteen before I darkened the doors of a church building, not because I didn't want to go to church, but because there were none to go to for miles. We had no car and our only means of transportation was walking or by horse.

I prayed, "Dear God, send us a preacher so I can be saved and live for you." God answered my prayer and sent missionaries who came and told us about Jesus Christ. They had to risk their lives among moonshiners, cattle rustlers, and fugitives from justice who had made the mountains their hideout from the law. After being saved, God called me to preach His message. Since salvation, God has used me to lead nearly my entire family and more than 100,000 others to Christ.

Cecil Todd
Revival Fires Ministry

February 24

I've Got Confidence

"And the peace of God, which passeth all understanding, shall keep your hearts and minds through Christ Jesus." Philippians 4:7

My confidence is in Christ Jesus, my Lord. I'm loved and I like it. We need love and we need to give love. Love isn't love until you give it away.

God is my staying power. My success as a singer is only through the grace of God. I had no plan, no formal education, but God had a plan. My friend Jesus Christ takes care of me, He's consistent and He's constant.

I wouldn't be here if it were not for God. I suffered an aneurysm in the brain while on the Johnny Carson show and was pronounced dead.

Lying on the floor, I prayed over and over, "Lord, help me, hold me and keep me." The doctors thought I wouldn't make it, but I had confidence in God and I made it. I told those doctors, "I was healed when I came here, God just needed you to get that thing out of my head."

God kept me from dying, but He also helps me to live. Day by day, God and I have a good time together. We look through a hole in the fence, but God sees the panoramic view. He's ever present. Believe, and you will receive.

The peace of this world can be broken and destroyed, but His is the peace that passes all understanding.

Della Reese
Singer

February 25

An Eternal Promise Of Perfection

"Being confident of this very thing, that he which hath begun a good work in you will perform it until the day of Jesus Christ."
Philippians 1:6

Basically, I like this scripture because in life we all have valleys and peaks. And to me, Philippians 1:6 assures us that for every valley, there will be another peak. Also when we look around us and see friends, colleagues, and business associates who have faults, just like we do, we're then assured that God has promised us that He will finish His work in us and make us perfect before Him on the Day of Judgment.

I went through a phase in my Christian walk where I expected perfection from myself and perfection in others. One of the greatest steps in my growth was when I realized man's inhumanity to man, the frailty of man, and that perfection was not an overnight thing. I also learned that the gifts of the Spirit did not mean overnight perfection. It was this scripture through which I taught myself not to be overly concerned with my own imperfections. From that point on, Philippians 1:6 has been the guiding light for me, so that eventually, one day, I will be the type of Christian, or the type of individual, that I believe God wants me to be.

Because we're all flesh, I don't really believe that too many of us exist in the form of perfection. In fact, no one ever was or no one will ever be perfect in this world, except Jesus Christ. But with His promises, we will be perfect on the Day of Judgment because of Him. And that's what really counts—in the final analysis.

Walter Richardson
*PTL Vice-President
Affiliates Division*

February 26

Marrying For Life

"Whoso findeth a wife findeth a good thing, and obtaineth favor of the Lord."
Proverbs 18:22

The institution of marriage is in a state of disaster in this country. Unless the trend changes, by the end of this decade there will be more children raised by single parents than those raised by two parents.

There is a correlation between juvenile delinquency and divorce. If we're going to solve the juvenile delinquency problem, we must first solve the marriage and divorce problem. A child's first exposure to loyalty is wife to husband, husband to wife as they make commitment to each other and to their home and children.

There is a definite correlation, too, with mortality and survival in a marriage relationship. The mortality rate in a given age group is 58 percent higher in the single adult. There is a 76 percent higher rate seeking psychiatric help in divorced and single. The suicide rate is double in singles. God has a good reason for marriage. This scripture is true.

For a marriage to work, we must employ basic skills: 1. The skill of loving—the mutual concern for each other. 2. Basic honesty, don't be a martyr. If you don't like salt on your egg, say so, don't suffer in silence. Be a communicator. 3. Compassion, look at the situation from the other person's point of view. Christ tells us, "...Thou shalt love thy neighbour..." (Matthew 5:43). Be sure that love includes your mate. If your mate does something you don't like, take the advice of Matthew 18:15, "...tell him his fault between thee and him alone...."

Dr. Ray Vath
Psychiatrist/Author

Don't Give Up

"My brethren, count it all joy when you fall into divers temptations."   James 1:2

At the Orange Bowl game in 1981, they came up to me and said, "J. C., for the second consecutive year, you are our most valuable offensive player."

I threw my hands up in the air and I said, "Thank you, Jesus!" I wasn't thanking Him for just that one football game—I was thanking Him for the presence of His person in every part of my life. I was thanking Him for the encouragement after I'd had a series of defeats and sat down one day and decided to give up. That's when the Lord reminded me of David. David went out against a giant—at great odds. David kept his eye on the giant, not the complications, not the past defeats but on the reward, the goal.

Then I thought about my team mates. I thought of all my prayer partners. Often when we have a challenge we want to quit. But the Lord says, "Don't be disillusioned." HE reminded me, "My brethren, count it all joy when you fall into divers temptations." It was like I could hear the Lord saying, "I'm with you; I believe in you, J.C. Get back in the game, don't give up."

Those next seven games had a story book finish. When I threw my hands up in the air and shouted, "Thank you, Jesus," it wasn't just for that one time—it was for all the power He's pumped into my playing and into my life!

J.C. Watts
Football Star

February 28

Surrender Your Problems

"Let your conversation (life) be without covetousness; and be content with such things...he hath said, I will never leave thee, nor forsake thee." Hebrews 13:5

After reaching success in the music world, my life began to decline. God sent me messages and warnings, but I ignored them until the Lord got my attention in a drastic manner.

The situation the Lord used was concerning my dearly loved son, born out of wedlock. I'd raised him for five years, and we were very close. His mother wanted him back and I refused to release custody. The mother went to the police and told them I was a drug user, armed and dangerous. Soon my house was surrounded by cops with bullhorns and sirens, it was altogether a terrifying situation.

I had to go into court for permanent custody. I knew I'd have to connive, trick, and lie, and was planning to do just that when the Lord started speaking to me. He said, "Look at the universe, look at the world. I can handle all this smoothly and if you'll let ME, I can handle your situation." I surrendered it to Him and, in one month, everything changed. With no conniving, tricking, or lying, it was all settled. I prayed, "Lord, if You can do that with that situation, what could You do with my whole life?" I left the record company I was with so I could just serve the Lord.

For the next nine months, the Lord miraculously undertook in my finances and in every other way in my life. HE was true to His promise, "I'll never leave thee nor forsake thee...." Praise His name, it's true!

Frank Wilson
Record Producer
Composer

March 1

Motivated For Christ

"Casting all your care upon him; for he careth for you." I Peter 5:7

Christians have the faith for the incredible but no faith for the everyday problems of life. "You can walk on the water, Lord, but You don't know my finance company—You can make the world, but You don't know my wife." Practice faith in the affairs of your life.

Many say, "If I become a Christian, I'll have to give up so much. It's true. I've given up late nights, worrying, and emptiness. I used to worry concerning what I'd speak about at the seminars, now I pray the Lord will let His Spirit flow through me. I didn't give up anything I couldn't live without.

If you're a Christian, smile and show it. A lot of people expect Christians to look like we're the cruise director for the Titanic. We don't have to carry our own cares. Christ said, "...cast all your cares on me...."

Positive thinking is good, but positive believing is based on a reason for believing that you can move any mountain. The Lord put us together and He knows how we function best. We're told to feed our minds on good things. "...whatsoever things are true, whatsoever things are honest, whatsoever things are just, whatsoever things are pure, whatsoever things are lovely, whatsoever things are of good report; if there be any virtue, and if there be any praise, think on these things" (Philippians 4:8).That's good, practical advice for a motivated life. Our salvation is reflected to the unsaved that we have God with us.

Zig Ziglar
Speaker/Author

March 2

Complete Love And Forgiveness

"For God so loved the world, that he gave his only begotten Son, that whosoever believeth in him should not perish, but have everlasting life." John 3:16

Because I needed to know, and still need to be reminded of the mercy, grace and love of Jesus Christ, John 3:16 shows me complete love and forgiveness in Jesus Christ.

Several years ago I walked out of a night club knowing I was going to commit suicide. I crossed the street and began walking to the railroad tracks a few blocks away, where I was going to throw myself on the rails and wait for a train to crush me. As I walked, I cried and prayed. I passed by an old church as I staggered down the street and fell on the steps leaning back against the stone pillars. I literally beat my head against that church crying.

"God let me live for you—give me the strength—somehow."

I'm not sure exactly what happened at this point. All I remember is that a feeling came over me—an awareness of God's love for all men, even those such as me who cursed His name. And in a moment there was a feeling of peace and security. I realized that I could live, but it would have to be for God, not myself. The meaning in my life would have to be translated in terms of what God wanted—not what I wanted.

I sat there for a few minutes as the Spirit of Christ began filling my heart. This was the conversion my father and mother had always prayed for. This was the moment of truth when the power of righteousness overcame the power of evil. It was as if I had been born again, given new hope and a new way.

Dave Boyer
Gospel Singer

March 3

He Restores All

"And I will restore to you the years that the locust hath eaten, the cankerworm, and the caterpillar....And ye shall eat in plenty...."
Joel 2:25-26

"Tough." That had been my middle name for years. I made sure that everyone understood perfectly who was in charge. If only everyone had known that I was not really in charge. Sometimes things happen to us that we have no control over, especially if we have not committed our lives to the Lord Jesus Christ. My life of drugs, crime, and degradation began with grief, a deep sense of loss and abandonment when my grandmother died. It was just a few weeks after I had married. She had raised me and was my life. I can remember praying to God to spare her life, and when she died, I blamed God and began drinking and doing drugs, even heroin.

A life of turmoil with no peace, direction, or stability resulted. So it was inevitable that I ended up in a women's institution, sentenced to the California Rehabilitation Center for one year for treatment, with prison terms in the not too distant future. While there, I had an accident that eventually led to the amputation of my arm. But I was still mean and bitter. There seemed to be so many changes to go through there. I constantly questioned, how, why this had happened to me?

I stayed in prison for five years, most of it in solitary. When I was released, I vowed never to return. I met Jesus face to face just after coming home. The Lord changed my life completely, He sent me to Bible school, made me an evangelist for Him and sent me back to prison, this time as His witness.

Darlene Deharo
Evangelist

March 4

Put His Word In Action

"So shall my word be that goeth forth out of my mouth: it shall not return unto me void, but it shall accomplish that which I please, and it shall prosper in the thing whereto I sent it."

Isaiah 55:11

This verse in Isaiah and the two that follow are very meaningful to me. God promises in this passage that His Word shall not ever return void—what a powerful thought! His Word always works!

If you digest this verse, and continue on in the Word, you'll see what will happen when you put the Word in action, "For ye shall go out with joy, and be led forth with peace: the mountains and the hills shall break forth before you in singing, and all the trees of the field shall clap their hands" (v. 12). What a glorious tribute to God! Aren't joy and peace what all of us seek? And here He promises it to us IF we are putting His Word in action.

And the Lord continues the promise in verse 13: "Instead of the thorn shall come up the fir tree, and instead of the brier shall come up the myrtle tree: and it shall be to the Lord for a name, for an everlasting sign that shall not be cut off."

In the forest, the animals always hide under fir trees, and here God promises that, instead of the thorn. Why? To glorify Him and to show the world how great our God is and how He takes care of His children.

I challenge you today to study the Word, and put it into action in your own life. God promises so much for our simple act of faith in Him. Try it today!

Sam McLendon
PTL Vice President
Fort Heritage

March 5

Come Back To Jesus

"If we confess our sins, he is faithful and just to forgive us our sins, and to cleanse us from all unrighteousness." I John 1:9

When I was a little girl, we lived right around the corner from a little Methodist church. Sunday morning, Sunday night, Wednesday prayer meeting, choir practice...whatever the occasion, when the doors opened, we were there.

Our pastor taught often about the forgiving nature of Jesus, and that was very easy for me to accept because I was a "good girl." My little sins weren't so bad.

But, when I went off to college, I slowly drifted away. My little sins became big sins (in my eyes), and further and further from God I strayed. To escape the guilt I felt, I began drinking heavily.

I knew I had failed God, but I could not understand that He would take me back, that He wanted me to come back to Him. The verse above became my lifeline back to Jesus. I asked Jesus to forgive me, to take me back and use me for His Glory.

That was almost six years ago, and in that short time, God has blessed me with a Christian husband and has allowed me to write for Him at PTL and for magazines like the *Saturday Evening Post*. What God has given to me is greater than I could have ever dreamed!

If you have strayed from God, as I did, come back to Jesus today. He loves you so much, and is waiting with open arms!

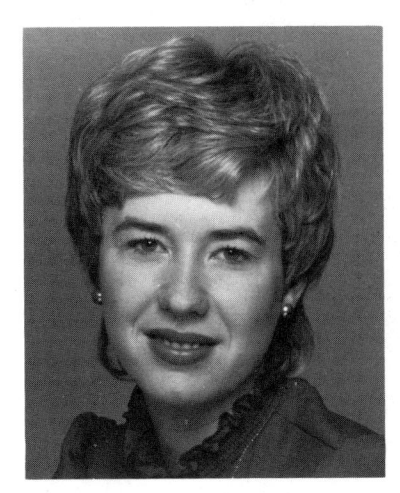

Mary McLendon
Editor/Writer

March 6

Remain Steadfast

"Therefore, my beloved brethren, be ye steadfast, unmovable, always abounding in the work of the Lord,...as ye know...your labor is not in vain in the Lord." I Corinthians 15:58

Any person who has genuinely committed his life to Jesus Christ and accepted Him as Lord is going to find repeated barriers to everything God is telling him to do. This will be true financially, spiritually, emotionally, morally, in every way. And the great temptation again and again is going to be to quit. But men who changed history and made an overwhelming impact in this world for the Kingdom of God were men who understood the need to be firm and unmovable. They realized that, regardless of the situation, their success would not fail to come, even if it were not according to their timetable. I firmly believe, and have often stated, "God made you to win!" So, be firm, steadfast, unmovable, also, abide in the work of the Lord, for inasmuch as He lives, your labor is not in vain.

During the early years of my ministry, we went into high school assemblies to evangelize with a group called *Dove*. We returned for an evening service where multitudes came to accept Christ as Lord and Saviour. Our greatest struggle was financial. We were reaching young people by the thousands, but young people do not give money in offerings. We were doing wonderfully well in reaching people but going dead broke financially. Many times I actually considered leaving the ministry. Now, our old evangelism team is still together and God is blessing us beyond our wildest dreams. It's true, "...Eye hath not seen, nor ear heard... the things which God hath prepared for them that love him" (I Cor. 2:9.)

Richard L. Hogue
Pastor, Television Host

March 7

I Want To Minister, Not Perform

"Love is very patient and kind, never jealous or envious, never boastful or proud...Love does not demand its own way..."
I Corinthians 13:4-5 (LB)

This chapter contains the best of all definitions of love and is a detailed portrait of God Himself, both as He is and as He can be in my life. It exposes legalism and other pseudo-spirituality, showing us a true satisfaction for the deepest longings of our soul. As a child, I memorized this chapter, but its real meaning has come to me in bits and pieces over the years in the school of life.

I write songs because I have a need to express deep feelings and my point of view, lyrically and musically, concerning God, His Word and my Christian experience. I think of my singing as an extension of my writing. I want the listener to identify, to say, "Hey, I've gone through that too," or "I've never quite looked at it that way before," that blesses me.

I feel Gospel music represents the Kingdom of God, and God selects and equips people to represent Him. I want the Spirit of the Master to speak to the heart and soul of a person who will listen and receive the message that God gives me through song.

This verse reminds me not to be boastful when I have success, not to be jealous when others have success. It reminds me to never demand my own way but to practice patience and kindness in every situation. What a fantastic blueprint for the Christian life!

Gordon Jenson
Songwriter/Singer

March 8

Loving Discipline

"He that hath my commandments, and keepeth them, he it is that loveth me; and he that loveth me shall be loved of my Father, and I will love him and manifest myself to him." John 14:21

Effective parenting is the goal of millions of families today. Several thousand years ago, the Bible was written describing in detail appropriate parenting practices. Its basic concept is that love and discipline go hand in hand.

Parents should endeavor to bring wholeness to their children. The Word of God is essential, especially in helping us realize that a child is a special gift from God. This gift can be treasured by holding them accountable for their actions; by giving them guidelines to live by; and by administering discipline in a loving manner. Ephesians 6:4 in the Living Bible says, "And now a word to you parents. Don't keep scolding and nagging your children, making them angry and resentful. Rather, bring them up with loving discipline the Lord Himself approves, with suggestions and godly advice."

In my book, *Parenthood Without Hassle,* we outline these basic points as also essential to effective parenting. First, respect your child's efforts, not overburdening him or her with unfair expectations. Second, remember that actions speak louder than words. Demonstrate or illustrate fully limits and privileges. Third, be consistent, carry out discipline with love and firmness. Fourth, go easy on criticism, respect each child's individuality. And fifth, never act in anger. Loving discipline is never destructive.

Remember, too, that Jesus, our example, always blended tenderness and strength. We should do no less.

Kevin Leman
Author

March 9

Understanding Of God's Salvation

"I am crucified with Christ: nevertheless I live; yet not I, but Christ liveth in me:...I live by the faith of the Son of God, who loved me, and gave himself for me." Galatians 2:20

This scripture gives a detailed illustration of what true salvation is all about. The old things in my life are passed away and all things are made new. Each of us must first experience Galatians 2:20 before we can ever be a blessing to anyone else. Jesus told His disciples, "...ye shall receive power after that the Holy Ghost is come upon you." This Holy Ghost power begins in this verse in Galatians, and it enables us to be witnesses to all the world.

In Acts 1:8, the word "power" in the Greek is "dunamis" and from this we get the word "dynamite." God has made each born-again believer a literal stick of dynamite and the next best thing for each of us to do, after being made dynamite, is to go somewhere and detonate. When we do explode, we shall reap constructive damage on the kingdom of the adversary.

After my salvation, I began to study the Bible to try and find out if there were words to explain my Christian experience. I was still in the U.S. Navy and one night while standing guard duty, I was reading the Bible and came across Galatians 2:20. I was so eager to understand in simple words what salvation was all about that these words jumped off the page and into my heart.

This was the first scripture that came alive to me spiritually. Since that experience, I have had many scriptures come alive, building a spiritual house within my heart. But the foundation of all I have and will learn shall rest on Galatians 2:20.

Larry Allen
Evangelist

March 10

A Real Love And Guidance

"And though I have the gift of prophecy, and understand all mysteries, and all knowledge; and though I have all faith, ...and have not charity, I am nothing."   I Corinthians 13:2

Salvation is the first step in the Christian life. I was saved in August of 1968 when I was witnessed to on a softball field by several different people. Swallowing my pride, I knelt there and asked Jesus to be my Saviour and Lord.

Secondly, the baptism in the Holy Spirit is absolutely essential for the Christian. Attempting to live a victorious Christian life by leaning to one's own understanding is a dangerous and unfruitful undertaking.

The Holy Spirit must be your daily guide and companion. He is to become the single, most important guiding influence in your life. Through the Holy Spirit's power, your faith will surge, decisions will be made correctly, and you will be able to love the unlovely.

There are times in my life when I find myself limited and not having enough strength or love, but the Holy Spirit is unlimited and can live and love through us if we will allow Him. The baptized believer lives in a new realm as opposed to the Christian who has not asked the Holy Spirit to have control.

Through God's grace, I was allowed to see myself, as in a mirror, without His Holy Spirit. For through a neighbor, the Lord showed me, as an unfilled believer, I was only willing to help someone if people would notice or if it didn't require a serious commitment on my part. But that all changed with my baptism in the Holy Spirit.

Mike Adkins
Evangelist/Songwriter

March 11

A Changing Image

"But we all, with open face beholding as in a glass the glory of the Lord, are changed into the same image from glory to glory, even as by the Spirit of the Lord." II Corinthians 3:18

Have you ever wished you could change? Have you been told that you are trapped by your heredity, your background, your circumstances into being who you are (and you don't really like that person very much)?

Well, we here at PTL's Heritage School of Evangelism have discovered a liberating truth in God's Word. We are standing on the promise that we can be changed daily, little by little, into the very image of Jesus Christ.

Every morning I look in the mirror and make the kind of cosmetic improvements that help me present the best face possible to the world. But there's something better than Oil of Olay, folks! It's an eternal radiance that comes to the person who looks into the mirror of God's own countenance and begins to reflect that likeness.

If, each morning, as religiously as I turn to that mirror to scrub my face, I turn to the Word of God and to prayer, I am giving my soul a cleansing and refreshing it sorely needs. And to benefit fully from this, look into God's mirror. I mustn't lean to the right or left but look straight to the Lord for every decision, every insight, every direction. With a commitment to total openness with God, the changes will come from plateau to plateau, from "glory to glory" until we see Him face to face in heaven. I Corinthians 13:12 holds quite a promise for us also. Claim it!

Sue Crider
Teacher
Heritage School Faculty

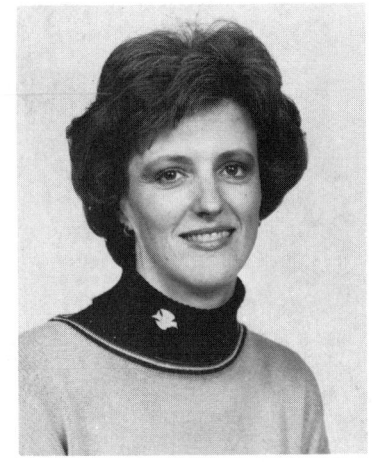

March 12

Truly Seeking

"But seek ye first the kingdom of God, and His righteousness; and all these things shall be added unto you."   Matthew 6:33

Many perplexing questions about the future and God's perfect will concern some Christians today. They wrestle with attitudes of uncertainty: What will the Lord do with my life? What is His perfect will concerning this or that? However, now, more than ever, I'm convinced we should set one definite goal in this life: to seek the Lord with all our energies and place our relationship with Him as priority number one. If we do, He has promised to supply all our needs in return.

Making time to cultivate intimacy with, dependency on, and faith in God is not an option for the sincere Christian. Our lives are a continual learning, growing experience. As we experience God's provision, love and mercy, it motivates us to learn more about Him and become even more involved in His transforming power.

Often we are reminded that the Lord is never slow to fulfill His promises. We get disturbed sometimes when things don't go as we think they should and impatience creeps in. We want an immediate response to our need, rather than waiting for His best. In those times when we must "wait on the Lord," we should never forget that His timing is always perfect and wrapped up in the "all these things" are the desires of our hearts.

Impatience breeds faithlessness. Faithlessness is sin and breeds anxiety. You can trust in His promises. He will perform His Word.

Margaret Douroux
Composer

March 13

Life Triumphant!

"...in all these things we are more than conquerors through him that loved us."
Romans 8:37

Christians should be, according to Scripture, "more than conquerors," victorious, triumphant and overcoming. The secret of this overcoming, conquering life is to saturate yourself in God's Word. When you read the Word—believe it! Act on it! Act in obedience to what the Word instructs. When we try to move around the Word, disobey what we clearly know is God's will, then we get in trouble.

I'm asked, "How do I really know it's the voice of the Lord speaking?" Become familiar with the Lord's presence. Know His voice as definitely as the voice of your mate or child. As you walk with the Lord, you come to know His voice and His commands to you. There is a Spirit witness, "The Spirit itself beareth witness with our spirit..." (Romans 8:16). When you need to make a major decision, don't go to your best friend for advice. They are liable to advise you to do what they know you desire to do. Go to someone you respect as being well grounded in God's Word.

Remember, whatever God speaks will *always* be in conformity with His Word. Just as lights in the harbor must line up for you to be on the right course, so must any decision line up with Scripture. Christ said, "My sheep know my voice..." (John 10:3). Know the voice of the Lord—and act on it!

Allan Hamilton
Pastor/Teacher

March 14

The Author Of Our Faith

"...seeing we also are compassed about with so great a cloud of witnesses, let us lay aside every weight, and...let us run with patience the race...before us."   Hebrews 12:1-2

All my life I have been actively involved with sports and athletics. To participate or be a spectator can often be an exhilarating experience. Regardless of the contest, there always exists a set of fair and just rules to aim one toward the ultimate goal. During the process of reaching this goal, one often encounters fatigue. At moments like these, the alternative of giving in and quitting presents itself. This is the very instant one needs to try the hardest. What a contrast! Quit or try hardest. Quit or finish the race. With God's resources, we, like Jesus, must look beyond the shame of any cross we have to bear, and keep the faith, finish the race. I have relied many times on this admonition, "to run the race with patience."

My grandmother was a major influence in my life. She was special, always singing songs about Jesus as she went about her work. At the age of ten, I gave a childlike commitment to serve Christ. I didn't have godly parents to share with and to give me guidance. I went through years of being good and trying to do the "right thing." Then in 1974, I realized God wanted total commitment from me. He wanted to be Lord and I needed Him to be.

I put aside my trying and striving and let Him be Lord of my life. I laid hold on eternal life as it is set forth in I Timothy 6:12, "Fight the good fight of faith, lay hold on eternal life, whereunto thou art also called, and hast professed a good profession before many witnesses."

Perry J. Bradshaw
*PTL's March
Employee of the Month*

_____ March 15

The Power Within You

"But ye shall receive power, after that the Holy Ghost is come upon you."   Acts 1:8

The Holy Ghost is God's creative power at work in our lives. We are not alone! When speaking about His departure plans, Jesus spoke these words in John 14, "I will not leave you comfortless:" (v. 18), "And I will pray the Father, and he shall give you another Comforter," (v. 16). Then He went on to promise, "...he shall teach you all things, and bring all things to your remembrance, whatsoever I have said unto you" (John 14:26).

Jesus spoke of Him as a distinct person! He shall guide you! He shall remind you! He shall be in you! Jesus, Himself had been the power source for His disciples, but He was going away, and they were in need of comfort, power, guidance, help in certain areas of life. Jesus was *not* going to leave them alone.

The Holy Ghost is our teacher. And a teacher imparts knowledge. Also, the Holy Ghost thinks, feels, moves and is easily grieved. He knows God's mind. He is forming the Body of Christ and bringing it into perfection.

Having a good Holy Ghost prayer meeting can change your mind about your future plans, revive you in your labor for the kingdom of God. Letting the Holy Ghost control your life can inspire you, equip you for the job ahead and establish new confidence in yourself and in your Father God.

The Holy Ghost knows God's will for your life and you will come to know it when you seek God in the Spirit. "...though our outward man perish, yet the inward man is renewed day by day" (II Corinthians 4:16).

Nancy Harmon
Evangelist/Singer

March 16

Like The Beasts That Perish

"Man that is in honor, and understandeth not, is like the beasts that perish." Psalm 49:20

My wife and I were always in church; I guess you could call us "churchians." We went to church because it was the social thing, the nice thing to do. But, we didn't know Christ.

Our life was good, but after the moon flight I experienced great frustration. I'd had all this intense training of Apollo and no place to channel it at work. At home, our marriage was falling apart. I was the most important person in the world to my wife and I wasn't doing a good job of being a husband.

She continued going to church and I started a beer business. After two years, I got frustrated with the beer business and gave it up. The very next month, I had an experience similar to Paul's when Ananias laid hands on him and said, "...be filled with the Holy Ghost. And immediately there fell from his eyes as it had been scales..." (Acts 9:18). Scales fell from my eyes and Jesus asked, "Who do you say that I am?" I realized then I'd have to make a decision that would determine where I'd spend eternity. Jesus said, "Whosoever therefore shall confess me before men, him will I confess also before my Father which is in heaven" (Matthew 10:32).

Shooting for the moon is the highest goal a person can have. I did it. I learned that personal success, landing on the moon or making a million dollars doesn't make for joy, peace or happiness; a close personal relationship with Jesus Christ does! Man without God is like a beast.

Charles Duke
Astronaut

March 17

Forgive!

"...condemn not, and ye shall not be condemned; forgive, and ye shall be forgiven."
Luke 6:37

The Lord tells us we are not to have any other idol but to worship Him alone. I worshiped my husband, Charles. Nothing should be more important than God to a person—not your husband, your children or your job. Husband first is not the divine order! When I got my priorities straightened out, my marriage was healed.

I was in deep depression and suicidal when I came to the Lord. I learned that "things" don't bring happiness. I had a famous husband, lots of money, two beautiful children, the moon on a string, and I was desperately unhappy.

I went to a series of weekend meetings at my church and the Holy Spirit ministered to me through the testimonies and lives of the people there. They all had such love, joy and peace. I had such a longing to know Him too. I prayed, "Lord, I've made mistakes. I'm turning my life over ot you." The Holy Spirit made me understand it wasn't just for one day but a total, lifetime commitment.

He said, "I forgive you. If you want your marriage to work, forgive Charles." I had a lot to forgive because I remembered every bad thing he'd ever done. I wanted a divorce and the Lord said again, "Forgive him." I didn't want to, but in obedience to God, I made a decision to forgive Charles. The Lord did a cleansing, healing work in my life so that I not only forgave but forgot my grievances. Once I had forgiven, I no longer hurt from the past.

Dottie Duke
Wife of Astronaut

March 18

Reasons To Praise

"Let everything that hath breath praise the Lord. Praise ye the Lord."   Psalm 150:6

Time and time again in the Bible, God tells His children to praise Him. The Book of Psalms, in particular, gives us reasons to praise Him. Chapter after chapter proclaims His mercy, faithfulness, deliverance, mighty works, salvation, goodness and many other praiseworthy virtues of God.

As a musician in full-time ministry for God, I sing His praises everywhere I go whether at churches, concerts, or on Christian television programs. For over ten years, I've lifted up the name of Jesus through music using my God-given talent for His glory. I praise the Lord for the opportunity to sing at Billy Graham Crusades and on record albums.

One of the most memorable experiences in my musical career occurred when I was chosen to sing the theme for the movie, "Born Again," the story of Charles Colson's conversion.

I have shared with you reasons from the Bible for giving thanks to God and specific instances in my life for which He deserves the praise. An album I recorded two years ago featured a song entitled "Everybody Praise The Lord." That song emphasizes Psalm 150:6. Each day during your free moments, think about the blessings God has given you and you will always have a reason to praise the Lord.

Larnelle Harris
Singer

_March 19

Be Constant In Prayer

"If my people, which are called by my name, shall humble themselves, and pray, and seek my face...then I will hear from heaven..."
II Chronicles 7:14

The Scriptures indicate we have a duty and responsibility to uphold our country in prayer. We should be especially vigilant in these United States because of the fact that this country has such a wide outreach in spreading the Gospel all over the world.

By being steadfast in prayer, we can help usher in Christ's Kingdom, "And the gospel must first (before His coming) be published among all nations" (Mark 13:10). The United States sends out 85 percent of all missionary monies for evangelization of the world, and our country sends out 82 percent of missionary personnel in the world. Satan would love to repress this outreach and this aiding of the ushering in of His Kingdom. As a great nation and a strong nation, we must continue to spread the Gospel to *all* nations.

To keep our nation strong, we're admonished to pray for our leaders, and we should do it daily. "I exhort therefore, that first of all, supplications, prayers, intercessions, and giving of thanks, be made for all men; For kings, and for all that are in authority; that we may lead a quiet and peaceable life in all godliness and honesty. For this is good and acceptable in the sight of God our Saviour" (I Timothy 2:1-3).

Be prayerful, people, we could be the generation to usher in the Kingdom.

Dr. David Lewis
Prophecy Teacher

March 20

Be An Example And Be Used

"Let no man despise thy youth...be...an example to the believers, in word, in coversation, in charity (love), in spirit, in faith, in purity."
                                    I Timothy 4:12

Two years ago while I was on tour with the Heritage School Chorale, traveling through the Greath Northwest and Canada, I realized that God could use me even though I was just a young man of 19. Before we left on tour, Jim Bakker told each of the students that if we would step out in faith, and be bold in the Spirit, God would use everyone of us in a very special and mighty way. We took what Jim said and acted upon it-and it worked. We saw hundreds of people saved, healed, filled with the Spirit, and delivered.

The highlight of the tour for me happened at a church in Toronto, Canada. We were singing our last song of the night, and people were coming to the altar to be prayed for. In the very back of the room, I saw a lady get up to make her way toward the altar. God spoke to my heart and said, "Les, I want you to go pray for that lady." She told me that she had been blind in her left eye for over forty years. You can imagine the initial shock, as I'd never prayed even for a runny nose befsore, and now I had to pray for a lady who was blind. Then I remembered the words that Jim had spoken. I laid my hands on her and prayed like I had never prayed before. The Spirit of God began to speak through me. Praise God, when she opened her eyes, she could see in her left eye after 42 years. God showed me that night that my age didn't matter, nor did my inexperience. The only thing that did matter was my willingness and desire to be used of Him.

Les Marple
*Record Promotion
Coordinator/Singer*

March 21

A Good Steward

"Behold, I will bring it health and cure, and I will cure them, and will reveal unto them the abundance of peace and truth." Jeremiah 33:6

"You are what you eat." How many times have you heard this saying? Yet, there are many instances of abuses and sicknesses directly linked to neglect of good health habits. Of all the things that concern Americans today, diet is number one. Everyone wants to look and feel better, but we must realize, that if we don't take care of our diet, we can't possibly be healthy. If we are not careful with our diet, our brains won't work any better than a body would if it were crippled and somehow handicapped. Good health practices, a balanced diet, proper rest and exercise will keep our bodies strong to do and be witnesses for our Lord.

For years, I have advocated the benefits of using honey, the most perfect, well-balanced food on this earth. Sugar is dangerous to our bodies, I equate its effects with the most treacherous effects of deadly poison. If, indeed, we are to be good stewards of all that God has entrusted into our care, can we do any less than to guard over our health?

We have been given these bodies to house our soul and spirit, and to accommodate normal daily activity. It, too, was designed and equipped by the Lord Jesus with other special gifts and capabilities to witness effectively. Without good health, we cannot get maximum performance from this very unique machine. When we jeopardize our health, we deny ourselves the richness of direction, strength, and power intended for us.

Joe Parkhill
P.R. Dir., Passion Play
Eureka Spgs., Arkansas

March 22

Glory Be To God

"Glory to God in the highest, and on earth peace, good will toward men." Luke 2:14

By the time we had applied to become foreign missionaries to Mexico in 1965, the health of our oldest daughter Betty Ann had seriously deteriorated. The doctors told us that we would have to be brave. "This child is going to die in just a matter of days, perhaps hours, even minutes," they told us. She was then placed in an oxygen tent.

For seven days, we stood vigil at her bedside hoping for a miracle and trying to prepare for that moment. The seventh night Betty called me to her side and asked me, "Daddy, am I going to die? Tell me the truth. I must know the truth."

Although it was hard for me to tell her that she was going to die, God gave me the right words. I said, "Betty, when you were born, the doctor told us that you were not going to live more than six years, but you are almost 16. God has given you ten extra years, and with the same power He can give you more. But if He wants to call you home, you must be ready because it is true that you could be called."

She took my hand and said, "Daddy, I'm not afraid. I'm ready to go at any time. I know when we die we go to heaven. Since Jesus in in heaven, why should I be afraid?" Then she smiled. Eight minutes later she said five times, "Gloria a Dios, Gloria a Dios," in Spanish which means, "Glory be to God." And she closed her eyes and went to heaven.

All the glory belongs to God. "Glory to God in the highest."

Juan Romero
Host-Club PTL

March 23

Strengthen The Hand Of The Poor

> "....this was the iniquity of thy sister Sodom, pride, fullness of bread, and abundance of iddleness...neither did she strengthen the hand of the poor...." Ezekiel 16:49

I see this description in Ezekiel as the condition our country is in now. People are so full of pride in their jobs, pride in their appearances, their homes, cars and the little things they are doing for Jesus. They are full of bread, overweight, idle, not caring for the poor and wandering to and fro. This was exactly the condition of Sodom before the vile, lewd, perverted sex sins took over and brought that country under the wrath of God. When sin became overpowering, God had to destroy Sodom.

If we will get up and get busy, humble ourselves and start helping the poor as we are commanded in the Word, God promises to restore peace to our nation, to heal it. Jesus said, in Matthew 25:35-36,"For I was ahungered, and ye gave me meat: I was thirsty, and ye gave me drink: I was a stranger, and ye took me in: Naked, and ye clothed me: I was sick, and ye visited me: I was in prison, and ye came unto me." If the people in our country would practice what the Lord asked us to do in these verses, He might spare our country. He stated He would have spared Sodom if He had found only ten righteous men.

The Lord gave us a test verse to prove our love to Him, "But whoso hath this world's goods, and seeth his brother have need, and shutteth up his bowels of compassion from him, how dwelleth the love of God in him?" (I John 3:17). Let us show compassion for His sake!

Julia (Mom) Taylor
Pass It On Ministry
President

March 24

Value Of The Person

"Greater love hath no man than this, that a man lay down his life for his friends."
John 15:13

There is a term businessmen use, "Quality Circle," which means the value of a person is predominant, above output, above profits, above net gains. As a mediator, the acting peacemaker between labor and management, I've seen what can happen when Jesus is brought into the work place and the "Value of the Person" then becomes predominant over the value of the machine.

I've seen businesses near ruin, rebuilt through divine intervention. Even more personally, if my faith in Jesus Christ were not paramount, I could never walk the thin line between pro-management and pro-labor factions.

The value of a person, through the pro-worker philosophy, is recognized in the work place but is even more highly regarded in God's eyes. This fact was brought to my attention quite dramatically when I was eighteen years old. Then serving in World War II, my friend, Red Preston and I were suddenly face to face with a German soldier. The enemy dropped a live grenade at my feet and in reflex action I killed him. Just then, the grenade exploded in my face, and as the blood spurted, I could see my friend hadn't run to safety. He had thrown his arms around me in protection. He protected me as he died...he gave his life for me. "Greater love hath no man than this... ."

It was through this experience that I realized the depth of Christ's willingness to give His life for me.

Wayne Alderson
*Labor Management
Peacemaker*

March 25

Spirit And Flesh

There is therefore now no condemnation to them which are in Christ Jesus, who walk not after the flesh, but after the Spirit." Romans 8:1

My girlfriend's brother, a Christian, started talking to me about God. He was faithful, he lost sleep to sit up late when I brought his sister home, so he could talk to me. I learned a lot about the salt from him— "Ye are the salt of the earth..." (Matthew 5:13). The purpose of salt is to make us thirsty. If we don't go out and touch people, then we can't make them thirsty for that only living water.

Finally, he convinced me to go to a Bible study with him. It was on Romans 7:18 where it says, "For I know that in me (that is, in my flesh,) dwelleth no good thing: for to will is present with me; but how to perform that which is good I find not." That stated the dilemma and then I read Romans 8:1 which states the answer.

Driving back home that night her brother said, "How would you like to be saved?"

I shook my head, "I'd mess up the whole kingdom." But I prayed with him and confessed my sins and asked Christ to save my soul. Light filled my whole body, I felt so alive! I just floated for the next few days.

But it's lasted, it's real! You can know success in the world and be a failure in your own heart without Jesus Christ.

Leon Patillo
Recording Artist

March 26

The Restoring Shepherd

"Because the Lord is my Shepherd, I have everything I need! He lets me rest in the meadow grass and leads me beside the quiet streams."
Psalm 23:1-2 (LB)

This scripture is ingrained in my spirit because at a time when I desperately needed peace, the Holy Spirit of God came to me in a dream, in the symbol of water as if beside a quiet steam.

On Friday, May 21, 1971, I received my final divorce papers from my lawyer. On Saturday, May 22, 1971, my five-year-old son was struck and killed in front of my home.

Needless to say, it was more than I could bear. But, the Lord Jesus Christ came to me in a beautiful way and gave me comfort.

In the following few months, every time I laid down to sleep, I would dream of swimming in a quiet stream. It was so refreshing that I would awake supernaturally peaceful.

Since attending a Bible school, I have learned that water is a symbol of the Holy Spirit. It was the Holy Spirit that was coming to me in my subconscious and leading me beside the still waters and restoring my soul.

Now, ten years since this supernatural experience, the Holy Spirit continues to lead me beside still waters and restore my soul. As long as the soul remains in our earthly bodies, we will need this restoring daily. Only Jesus Christ can restore us.

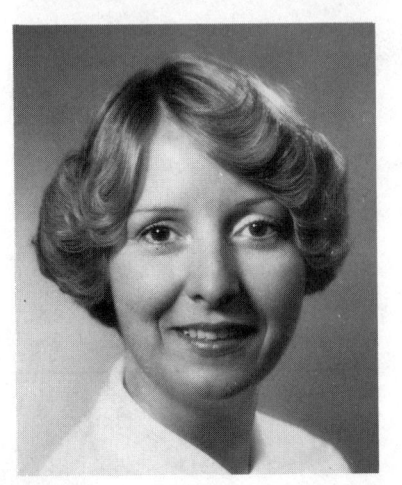

Jesus wants to to be your Shepherd. He wants to restore your soul.

Will you let Him?

Jean Scarborough
PTL Creative Services
Secretary

March 27

A New Creation

"Therefore if any man be in Christ, he is a new creature: old things are passed away; behold, all things are become new."
II Corinthians 5:17

Eleven years ago I was an atheist turned off to anything dealing with the Lord. As I listened to Dave Boyer singing on the radio, "He Touched Me," I began to take stock of my relationship with life and the Lord. I called a choir director who had talked to me about Christ, I told him what had happened to me that morning and asked if I might sing some time in his church.

He consented and on a warm May evening in 1970, my wife, JoAnn, and I drove to that little country church. Somehow I felt as though something great was about to happen!

As we listened to the minister preach on II Corinthians 5:17, I knew God was speaking to me. My life really could be changed! My sinful past could be forgiven! Life could have meaning! All I needed to do was receive Christ. Salvation is a free gift.

After the sermon, I walked to the front of the church and sang "The Lord's Prayer." As I sang, "Thy kingdom come, Thy will be done on earth as it is in heaven," I sensed the overwhelming power of the Holy Spirit and began weeping, "Oh, God!" Something welled up within me. "Oh, God! My, God!"

In that blessed moment of truth, I found what I had been searching for all along. At last, life had meaning. As I walked back to my seat with tear-filled eyes and a peaceful heart, I knew He had found me and touched me. I was indeed a new creature in Christ.

Tony Valenti
Singer

March 28

Restored By His Word

"O Lord, open thou my lips; and my mouth shall show forth thy praise."   Psalm 51:15

This nation's need for stability will be satisfied, in part, by getting back to the grassroots and basics; respect for human dignity, life, and equal opportunity for all to experience the "American Dream." Right after his victory, I talked briefly with then President-Elect Reagan. His openness and honesty touched me as we shared about this nation's need. His acknowledgement of God during his campaign demonstrates to me his consciousness of God as supreme. It is truly comforting to know that this kind of administration is at the helm of our nation's government.

Mr. Reagan continued by saying he believes it is God's time for this nation to get off its knees, straighten its back, and do a job for the Gospel of Jesus Christ, for the world, and to be an honor to God. He designed us to be His instruments for evangelism. When our nation repents and is restored by His Word, revived by His Spirit, then we will see the glory of the Lord returned to this great nation.

All over the world, today we are seeing this same kind of revival and a hunger for God. God is making the difference between success and failure, intellect and ability—as humble servants, of little preparation but with a hunger for God, are falling on their faces before Him for His direction and power. Even in our churches, we see a mighty spiritual hunger being satisfied as powerful, bold messages are coming forth. Your life, too, is a mighty message. Be restored to serve.

Thurnace York
Pastor/Spiritual Motivator

March 29

To Know Him

"And this is life eternal, that they might know thee the only true God, and Jesus Christ, whom thou hast sent."   John 17:3

I love this verse because it states that the heart of the Christian experience is in knowing God personally, and this happens through Jesus Christ. Christianity is a religion that centers around our personal experience of God and our relationship with Jesus Christ. Unless we are experiencing Him personally, we are not really "walking in the Spirit." I know, because I did not always walk in the Spirit.

Although I was saved when I was only eleven years old, I wasn't baptized in the Holy Spirit until 1959 when I was rector of St. Mark's Episcopal Church in Van Nuys, California. The *Encyclopedia Britannica* in the year book for 1973 credits me with being the first "Charismatic." My church was the first of the historic churches where a group of people began to acknowledge the baptism in the Holy Spirit and to speak about it openly. For the last twenty-one years, I have been speaking worldwide about this Pentecostal experience as recorded in Acts 2:4, "And they were all filled with the Holy Ghost, and began to speak with other tongues, as the Spirit gave them utterance."

I have found if there is a deep hunger in the heart, the Lord will give His Holy Spirit baptism as He promised in Matthew 5:6, "Blessed are they which do hunger and thirst after righteousness: for they shall be filled." When a heart hungers for the fullness of God, it will surely be filled. With this filling comes a closer knowing.

Dennis J. Bennett
Rector

March 30

Struggle Stimulates!

"These that have turned the world upside down...." Acts 17:6

I have spoken God's Word in great coliseums and amphitheaters, in tiny country churches and in storefronts. Over my lifetime, the Lord has moved me from the storefronts to the forefront with congregations in the thousands.

When I was growing up, Pentecostalism was not popular; I struggled under adversity. We wore black eyes with dignity. God delivered us from the namby-pamby. Jesus was no namby-pamby figure. HE was accused of everything but was never accused of being dull. Jesus was a threat to the undertakers after He caused the widow's son to rise; a threat to cemeteries after Lazarus rose from the grave; a threat to bakeries after He fed the five thousand with five loaves and two fishes and a threat to fishermen after He walked on the water. But, Jesus was never dull!

It's the struggle system that puts pizzaz in life. St. Paul was a small, bowlegged, myoptic threat; they said of him, "...these that have turned the world upside down..." (Acts 17:6). At one time, Jesus turned to the twelve, ordinary men like us and said, "Ye are the salt of the earth..." (Matthew 5:13). Ordinary men, but they got in the struggle and revolutionized history.

Get in the struggle! Stand up and be counted for Christ! You'll never hit the ball unless you get the bat off your shoulder.

Dr. C.M. Ward
Minister/Author

March 31

That You Might Believe

"But these are written, that ye might believe that Jesus is the Christ, the Son of God; and that believing ye might have life through his name."
John 20:31

Everybody calls it an "overnight success story" a young actor landing a major role in the hottest movie of the day. But in reality, it was a good break, well deserved after many years of hard work and bit parts on Broadway. Or so I thought then. I was to later realize the plan of God to bring me into a relationship with Himself through this film and other precious Christians whose love and concern taught me what real love is all about.

I have become more convinced than ever that God has a plan for each of our lives and fulfills His will in us at His own time, His own way. Little did I suspect in 1953 when I got off the Greyhound bus in Hollywood that the part of Caesar in the movie, "The Robe," was to be mine. In fact, all the casting had been done, except for this part, and I had no agent and was not established. So I went to the Yellow Pages, picked out an agent, went to the studio for a screen test and landed the part. Incredible! But the success of the film and my performance in it, was too much, too soon, my ego soared. The essence of the message of the film didn't sink in until I had nearly ruined my life with drugs parties, and bankruptcy. While I was serving a prison sentence, the film was shown on Easter Sunday. The impact of who Christ really is, and the price He paid for me, hit me broadside, and then when I was released and was making the film "Born Again" with Chuck Colson, I became a Believer. It took all of this that I might believe.

Jay Robinson
Actor

_____ April 1

Two-Par-Bar-Four AnniVERSEry

"At Par-bar westward, four at the causeway, and two at Par-bar."   I Chronicles 26:18

This has been one of my favorite verses for a long time. First, we have to go back to the original language. There we notice a series of numbers. Let's take the last number first—which seems appropriate on this day. First of all, we need to realize the number "2," comes directly after the number "1." And, speaking of the number "2," two people that should be in our prayers today are Jim and Tammy, this is their anniversary.

The next number that literally jumps out of this verse is the number "4"—which of course, reminds me there are four in Jim and Tammy's family. We should not only pray for Jim and Tammy on their anniversary, but we should pray for Tammy Sue and Jamie Charles also.

The other thing this verse brings to mind is the worldwide outreach of the PTL Television Network. If we send missionaries into some countries in the world today, we would be carrying them out on stretchers three days later. However, being able to produce television programs in their own language is a vital and exciting way to communicate the Gospel to millions who would otherwise not hear the claims of Christ.

On this April Fools' Day, as always, this verse, "At Par-bar westward, four at the causeway, and two at Par-bar" is tremendously significant. Realizing something like this would make it into God's Word means there is always hope for me.

Roger L. Flessing
*PTL Executive
Vice President*

April 2

God Is The Absolute Authority

"For God hath not given us the spirit of fear; but of power, and of love, and of a sound mind."
II Timothy 1:7

I dedicated my heart and life to Christ when I was eight years old. I was nineteen when my brother, R.W. Blackwood, was killed in an airplane crash. The brilliance of his work has never faded from my memory. I was asked to replace him in the Blackwood Brothers. I didn't think I'd be able to fill his shoes—and I still feel that way. "...God hath not given the spirit of fear..." has been a real encouragement to me and the Blackwood Brothers because of the work we do. Day in and day out, we are gone from home, preaching and singing. Satan tries to depress us and fill our minds with doubt and fear, but God says, "...the spirit...of power, and of love, and of a sound mind." The deceiver tries to tell us that this ministry can't stand, that it may fall apart; but God's Word is the *absolute authority*. Satan has to flee when we claim His Word. God is the power and authority over Satan and all our fears, "...greater is he that is in you, than he that is in the world" (I John 4:4).

Every day, I thank God for helping me. I praise God that my life and my work are to magnify Jesus through Gospel singing. With the humblest heart, I thank God for each minute, each hour, each day and each year that He allows me the great joy of serving Him. This verse echoes my heart's feeling, "Behold, God is my salvation; I will trust, and not be afraid: for the Lord Jehovah is my strength and my song; he also is become my salvation" (Isaiah 12:2).

Cecil S. Blackwood
Manager/Singer
Blackwood Brothers

God's Added Blessings

"But seek ye first the kingdom of God and his righteousness; and all these things shall be added unto you." Matthew 6:33

Over 25 years ago, my wife and I were visiting in the home of my wife's girlfriend and her husband. Being Christians, they invited us to take part in their nightly devotions, and during the devotion, my wife began to pray out loud—something I had never heard her do before. When she concluded, my heart was gripped; an inner voice seemed to say to me, "Al Duren, this is your time!" I cried out to God with all the anguish of my lost and desperate soul. I don't know what I said or how long I prayed, but I do know I felt Christ's actual presence and completely threw myself on His mercy. Somehow I knew without doubt that He loved me regardless of my problems. He forgave me—this was the crucial difference.

For a long time, I was conscious only of His supernatural presence. When I finally rose to my feet, the sins and sorrows of 45 years had fallen away. A desire for whiskey, my favorite drink, was not there, unlike the times I had fought this desire and lost. It was like being a child again. True to His Word, the Lord Jesus Christ had brought the joy of salvation and deliverance to this hopeless, hell-bound alcoholic. In studying the Bible one day shortly after I was saved, I ran across Matthew 6:33. I had lost almost everything that I had ever possessed, but as I applied this scripture to my life, God began to restore the material things that I needed until I now have much more than I had ever had before.

Al Duren
*International Director
for FGBMFI*

April 4

Mountain Moving Faith

"...whosoever shall say unto this mountain, Be thou removed, and be thou cast into the sea; and shall not doubt in his heart...he shall have whatsoever he saith." Mark 11:23

The Holy Spirit had quickened this verse to my heart some years ago, and even today, He continues to encourage, challenge, and strengthen me with it.

At the age of twelve, I received Jesus as my Saviour, right in my Sunday School class. The night I was baptized in water, my testimony was "I want to follow Jesus." My twelve year old mind did not fully comprehend the significance of that statement. I've been learning ever since the price and privilege of that commitment. He has led me to serve Him in many places, including Jamaica, Canada, Uruguay, Argentina, and Mexico. My testimony still holds, I want to follow Jesus!

One day in the country of Argentina, I needed a miracle. God reminded me of Mark 11:23. I prayed, "Lord, I accept this. Now I ask You to respond not only to meet this present need, but as a token of what You are going to do through me in the future." Then I spoke that miracle into being. God responded—in many ways like the story of Elijah!

The prophet Elijah one day said to the evil King Ahab, "There will not be any rain except by my word." How could he be so bold? Elijah had heard a word from the Lord and spoke it forth. God kept His and Elijah's word.

He'll do the same for you, too. Dare to believe His Word, it works!

Wanda Fane
*PTL's April
Employee of the Month*

_____ April 5

Love Is...

"Love is very patient and kind, never jealous or envious, never boastful or proud, never haughty or selfish or rude..." I Corinthians 13:4-5

Having been hearing impaired for most of my life, I hated the world. I was bitter against anyone who could hear well. Little did I know that my greatest handicap was not my deafness, but the hate in my heart.

As a young man, I looked for an escape. Alcohol was an easily accessible "high," and one way to stop thinking about my problems, about the world that had treated me so unfairly.

Then one day, my girlfriend talked me into going with her to a church she had heard about. Angry at her for talking me into going, I fumed as I slid into the cushioned pew.

As the pastor started talking, I looked up to watch what he was saying. He shared that God was love, and that it was through His great love that He sent Jesus Christ to die for our sins. That night, I asked Jesus to come into my life, and every day I ask the Lord to help me grow more into loving others as He loves us.

And, yes, I still get mad and even a little bitter sometimes. But I always know where the answer lies. I get out my Bible and read the entire thirteenth chapter of I Corinthians, then I put it to the test.

Maybe you are dealing with a handicap in your life today...whether it is physical, mental or even spiritual. Let me assure you, as someone who knows, Jesus is the answer!

Eddie Holder
PTL Chief Photographer

April 6

Press Toward The Mark

"...forgetting those things which are behind, and reaching forth...I press toward the mark for the prize of the high calling of God in Christ Jesus." Philippians 3:13-14

An incident related by an evangelist when I was only fourteen was used by God to make the above the motivating verse of my life.

He told of a group of people trapped in a flash flood in a dry river bed. They spread out, joined hands and stretched its full length grabbing securely onto trees at each side as the flood passed. The reason they were able to stand and not to be swept away was that they joined together to press against a rising current. The image of that scene was so engraved on my teenage mind, that of pressing together for the common good, and that verse so quickened my spirit, that I adopted it as my life verse.

It has become a guide, motivating me to stand against those things that seek to overwhelm or turn me away from the Lord's will. It also gives perfect guidance as to how that stance can be taken.

The formula is quite simple. First, forget what is past, don't cry over spilled milk. Secondly, reach for tomorrow, plan positively. Thirdly, don't doubt God's promises. Fourth, let Jesus be Lord of the past and future, just as we allow Him to be Lord today.

We should always remember, "Jesus Christ, the same yesterday and today, and for ever" (Hebrews 13:8).

Jack Hayford
Pastor/Church On The Way

April 7

Our Stronghold In Trouble

"The Lord is good, a stronghold in the day of trouble; and he knoweth them that trust in him."   Nahum 1:7

When our hearts are trusting in the Lord Jesus Christ, He orders every detail of our lives. Life is easy to live when you know He is your stronghold, the One you can strongly hold onto.

The Lord became a stronghold for me in a most embarrassing situation fifteen years ago. My husband was speaking at a camp and I was asked to teach a class of young people. It was a challenge I was looking forward to and wanted to succeed at. However, before I could fully enjoy the beauty of the experience, bitter and severe criticism was made about the make-up and jewelry I was wearing. I was heartbroken. I had only wanted to uphold Christ and do the right thing. When the criticism was repeated to me, I sought comfort and direction from the Lord.

Directing me to this verse, He assured me He knew the intentions of my heart, how I desired to please Him in all things, and all the hurt and disappointment was wiped away.

The incident brought to mind many questions about make-up and jewelry. I pondered, "Was I dishonoring His name by wearing it? Was I emphasizing the adorning of the outward man more than spiritual development?" After digging through the Scriptures, I was satisfied in my heart when I read the story of the beautiful Queen Esther and her year-long marriage preparation. Although my beauty regime is considerably shorter, I've realized God judges all our intentions.

Anna Hayford
Pastor's Wife

April 8

Not Being Sick Is Not Health

"And the disciples were filled with joy, and with the Holy Ghost." Acts 13:52

The ultimate heresy is boredom; the boring church is a sin in my opinion. It's not boring being "Jesus People." Church is where people are converted, healed, filled with joy. Church is a time to let God meet your needs, an hour when God blesses His people. Church is exciting! Christians should be like an artesian well, bubbling up and blessing others.

When life does its worst to you, you can say, "You meant it for evil, but God meant it for good" (Genesis 50:20). You can be sure of God's good intentions toward you, not only when you're in trouble, but when you're well and doing fine. There is something beyond just being well and whole, it means you go out and look for trouble for Jesus. There's a little old gal, well up in years in our church, who ministers to prostitutes and drug addicts in the worst tenderloin part of Seattle. When somebody mugs her and grabs her purse, they find a note that says: "I'm real sorry you had to do this. You must be in real trouble. If you need help here's my phone number, or better still, here's my address; come and see me." She's had people come and see her, and through her they've come to see Christ.

We evangelicals and Charismatics have sound doctrine, but rotten Biblical lifestyle. We must show faith, hope, love, and joy to the unconverted or they won't be hungry and thirsty. Joy means you dare to be selfish, you do the thing you love to do. So find the place you can't wait to get to and give it your all!

Bruce Larson
Author/Teacher

April 9

Forgive Yourself

"....he hath sent me to heal the brokenhearted." Luke 4:18

I was just sixteen when it happened. Within a matter of minutes, I saw my best friend's mother die and heard the laughter of my little sister and two little brothers turn into screams and moans. I saw their bodies cut and broken and I was to blame. I was driving.

In the months that followed, I was filled with depression and overwhelming feelings of guilt. I contemplated suicide but didn't know the easiest way to go about it and I couldn't justify putting my parents through any more pain.

I was a Christian and, little by little, Jesus began to heal me emotionally. But it wasn't until I was filled with the Holy Spirit that I realized through His power I had to forgive myself. I had to stop hating myself for what I felt I had put my family and the other family through, even though it was a no-fault accident. I had to start seeing myself as God saw me—loved and forgiven.

Jesus said "neither do I condemn thee" (John 8:11), and "there is no condemnation to them which are in Christ Jesus" (Romans 8:1). I realized that Satan was my accuser (Rev. 12:10). And he is your accuser. He loves to dump guilt on us to keep us from believing in God's forgiveness and finding healing through that forgiveness.

Whatever reason you're holding onto to hate yourself or feel guilty about, give it to Jesus. Accept yourself because He accepts and loves you just the way you are. Let Jesus heal your broken heart. I know He can, because He healed mine.

Paulette Prewitt
Pharmacist

April 10

The Prince Of The House Of David

"If David then call him Lord, how is he his son?" Matthew 22:45

The simple answer is: Christ is David's Lord because He is God. Christ is David's son because He became man through the virgin Mary, and the virgin Mary was of the house of David.

A few years ago, I had the privilege of visiting in the Holy Land. What a joy! Especially to visit Bethlehem where Jesus was born. And then Nazareth, where Jesus grew up. And, of course, Jerusalem, so famous because it was there that Jesus taught, preached, ministered and died.

But, (and here comes the discord in the great symphony), there was no room for Jesus in the inn at the town of Bethlehem. And later, they chased Him out of Nazareth; and still later, they nailed Him to a cross at Jerusalem.

It grieves me to think that the Lord Jesus was rejected in places that meant so much to Him. However, praise the Lord, there is one place where He would rather be accepted than anywhere else, and that place is in our hearts.

It was Stanley J. Peterson who said, "If there is room for the Lord Jesus in your heart, then it was worth it for Him to be rejected at Bethlehem, Nazareth, and Jerusalem."

Oh, dear friend, will you say now, " Come, Lord Jesus, come in today, come in to stay, come into my heart, Lord Jesus." Amen!

J. Herman Alexander
Evangelist

April 11

He Gives His Peace

"Be careful for nothing...let your requests be made known unto God. And the peace of God... shall keep your hearts and minds through Christ Jesus." Philippians 4:6-7

This is such a powerful and true promise. No matter what happens during the course of the day, this scripture provides the strength I need.

First of all, it says don't worry about anything but "by prayer and supplication with thanksgiving let your requests be made known unto God...." We are to pray to God with thanksgiving and leave the problem to Him. What a relief! He takes all our problems from us, and asks us not to worry about them. Secondly, and here's the promise I really like, if we do that, He'll give us His peace, the one beyond understanding. It's not only the peace of heart that tells us we'll someday be with Him, but peace of mind that tells us He's here now—here to take our worries and problems and to help see us through the day.

One of the most beautiful things about being a Christian is enjoying the peace of God in my life. I guess I enjoy this scripture so much because it reminds me of how simple it is to receive His peace. This peace satisfies our hearts and our minds. Jesus said, "Peace I leave with you, my peace I give unto you; not as the world giveth, give I unto you. Let not your heart be troubled, neither let it be afraid." His peace is truly "a peace that passes understanding."

Terry Steen
Accountant
PTL Voices

April 12

Drink From God's Fountain

"If the Son therefore shall make you free, ye shall be free indeed." John 8:36

I have been a Christian for over forty-four years, but that doesn't mean that I allowed Jesus to be Lord of my life for this entire period. Thirty years ago, I was given one year to live and at that time I yielded my life over to God's perfect will and surrendered to His calling for my life. I was a highly successful corporate executive and everything I purposed to achieve was realized in my life. Since letting God be truly Lord of my life, I have been actively engaged in counseling broken homes and broken lives related to alcoholism.

Our ministry is a ministry of love. There is no greater power than the power of love. Until I learned how to love without expecting any love in return, my life was not really effective for Christ. I Corinthians has become almost a textbook in our ministry, verse 4 of chapter 13 tells us, "Charity (love) suffers long, and is kind; charity envieth not; charity vaunteth not itself, is not puffed up." Only the love of Jesus can quench a thirsting soul and fill that emptiness with His overflowing love. The love and mercy of Jesus can heal the inner hurts, guilt complexes, bitterness, rebellion and unforgiving spirits. All of these are a self-created prisons that holds an alcoholic in a vice. Jesus paid the ransom price for freedom with His very own life. He can set any prisoner free.

Rev. Hugo C. Zerbe
Chapel of the Woods

April 13

Are You In Church?

"Not forsaking the assembling of ourselves together, as the manner of some is."
                                        Hebrews 10:25

Assembling for worship or fellowship with other Christians on a regular basis is so important to nourishing your walk with God. The writer here takes the time to say, and I'll give you my own free translation, "Don't skip church, as some do!"

My mother and father raised me, along with nine other children, in a strong spiritual atmosphere. All of us attended church every Sunday, and we were encouraged to pay attention and really get something out of it. And even when I left home and started my career as a race car driver, I always kept up with church attendance and the habit of personal prayer that I'd been taught.

Race driving is a tense and tiring occupation. By the time I was through racing on a Saturday night, I'd just want to dive into a motel and sack out. But before turning in, no matter what part of the country I happened to be in, I'd find a phone book or ask somebody where I could find a church in the area. And except for rare occasions, you'd always find me there on Sunday morning.

Let me urge you, if you possibly can, to get into a good church fellowship, and be faithful to attend services. Get to know the pastor and your fellow members. If you're shut in, ask someone to visit you regularly. You need the love of Jesus that other people can give. Reach out today and make sure that you receive the help you need.

Bobby Allison
Stock Car Driver

April 14

He Knows You

"Yea doubtless, and I count all things but loss for the excellency of the knowledge of Christ Jesus my Lord..." Philippians 3:8-9

Many Christians today discuss how Christ lives in their hearts, but live like He's cut off in heaven, apart from their daily routines, almost as if He is not a living reality at all. The fact is, however, that Christ living in us is the blessed privilege afforded to everyone who seeks intimacy and relationship with God. When Jesus breathed into us the Holy Spirit, He gave us all that He is. Without understanding His reality in us, we walk without His power, joy, peace and love.

When we know Him and enjoy His fullness within us, our horizons are so broadened that we can move in the power of the Holy Spirit and accomplish things beyond our natural abilities. His indwelling gives us a basis for confidence, assurance and boldness.

Many people who are the best in the world at what they do are often motivated out of fear that someone younger, stronger, or better will replace them. We need not live in fear if we realize that God has uniquely created us for a specific purpose. Our confidence is in His divine will for our lives. He knows what's best for us at all times. We should trust Him completely and cultivate an even deeper relationship with our Lord.

Take time to get to know Him, He knows you.

Steve North
Singer

April 15

I Learned To Follow

"Trust in the Lord with all thine heart; and lean not unto thine own understanding. In all thy ways acknowledge him, and he shall direct thy paths."   Proverbs 3:5-6

Each time I am faced with a problem or an obstacle, God reminds me that if I'll only trust in Him and not yield to fear, or trust my own intellect, He will show me what to do. My human nature is to figure out why, when and how, but when I have trusted in Him instead, my loving, heavenly Father has shown me His amazing grace and mercy. He guides me step by step when I ask.

This wasn't always true in my life. I married at a very early age, never asking the Lord's choice. This was the beginning of many heartaches and hard times. After a terrible divorce ordeal, I realized I was a mixed-up woman, filled with pride, self-pity, selfishness and lust. I repented, confessed my sins and asked Jesus to forgive and cleanse me. I stood on Jesus' promise, "...him that cometh to me I will in no wise cast out" (John 6:37). He filled me with his joy and forgiveness. Soon after this, He opened up a singing career for me.

More and more the Lord impresses on me that I cannot do anything without Him. At one time, I lost the use of my voice for six months. I could not sing a note and had difficulty speaking. Then the Lord showed me this verse in John 15:5, "...without me you can do nothing." When I fully realized this verse, the Lord healed me completely. Now I fully see a connection between these two verses—trust with all thine heart, without me you can do nothing.

Jean O'Dell
Singer/PTL Hostess

April 16

The Lord Directs Our Steps

"A man's heart deviseth his way: but the Lord directeth his steps."   Proverbs 16:9

When I came to the Lord at twenty-five, I wanted to begin "doing something for God" right away. I had been a music major in college, so I reasonably asked, "OK, Lord, where do you want me to start singing for you?" I suggested the Billy Graham telecasts, my personal preferences, but I was open to anywhere He might lead.

The Lord merely told me, "I want you to be a wife to your husband," which wasn't exactly what I had expected. After I had read all the right books on marriage, I tried again. "Now, Lord, about my music..."

"I want you to concentrate on being a good mother to your children, now," was the only response I got from Him. So I tackled that task, unable to understand why God wasn't using my talent to minister to people. When I would remind Him that I knew how to sing, and was perfectly willing to use my voice for His glory, the Lord would assure me by saying, "I'll take care of it in My own time."

I was thirty-seven before God opened the door for me to minister publicly, and then it was through writing! He had me use a talent I didn't even know I had, without my ever studying for it, so you know that any writing skill I have is totally from the Lord.

It doesn't matter how old you are, or what skills you have or don't have, when God's time is right, He'll open doors for you. That way it will truly be *His* ministry through you!

Joyce Landorf
Author

April 17

God's Keeping Power

"Oh, the joys of those who do not follow evil men's advice, who do not hang around with sinners...But they delight in doing everything God wants them to..."   Psalm 1:1-3

For so long, I really wondered whether I even had a testimony or not. My life as a Christian seemed so blase. I grew up in a Christian home, got saved as a child (I must have gone to the altar at least ninety-nine times, just to make sure!), surrendered to full-time Christian service as a teenager, attended a Christian university, married a girl who had also been a Christian since childhood, taught in a Christian school, traveled in a Gospel group and, several years ago, came to work at PTL. How ordered can anyone's life be, right?

It all seemed so tame and boring compared to the "exciting" testimonies. I couldn't "wow" people with a drug addiction story, or a life of crime, or even an out-of-the-body death experience.

"Nothing is more boring than a basic good-guy Christian testimony," I always thought. "Nobody wants to hear about a life spent in the church. They want to hear a little sin, a little scandal mixed in."

During one of the moments when I was wondering if I had missed anything by trying to serve God since childhood, I discovered Psalm 1. I also began to realize that the best things take time to grow, even Christian testimonies. And I've been amazed, since then, to see how many other "boring" Christian testimonies there are, people like Bill and Gloria Gaither, Jim Bakker, and Jimmy Swaggart. I'm now persuaded, maybe the greatest testimony is not just God's saving power, but also His keeping power.

Darryl Hicks
PTL Producer/Writer

April 18

Until His Return

"Being confident of this very thing that he which hath begun a good work in you will perform it until the day of Jesus Christ."
Philippians 1:6

One day I discovered that the Lord had placed a call on my life and soon realized that it could never be fulfilled without His direct workings in my life. My associations with many other servants of the Lord let me know that I must expect God to keep His Word. Anything I would undertake in His name must be done in selfless, sincere effort. At the time, many of them simply didn't understand the scope of the investment God had in me. We have all had cause to rejoice because of the scope of it. If the Lord is going to fulfill our faith, He must be allowed to be the author of it.

The Lord has placed His authority in us. We need to always remember, however, that it must be His working in us, rather than our doing for Him. He is the Master of life, and He offers to fulfill His life in us.

For over twenty-nine years now, I have allowed this precious Saviour to have total control in my life. How blessed we are to be His children. But we must know, too, that in order to fully enjoy the divine benefits, we must completely surrender our all to Him, making a total commitment to Him.

Soon after my conversion experience, I began preaching. For eighteen years, I ministered in crusades in forty-four nations. He has never failed to confirm His Word in reality and power in helping the multiplied thousands. I will maintain until He returns.

Quentin Edwards
Pastor/Author

April 19

Transforming Evil For Good

"Giving thanks always for all things unto God and the Father in the name of our Lord Jesus Christ." Ephesians 5:20

At the close of World War II, I was preparing to become an attorney. This seemed to me to be the safest and surest method of acquiring wealth. During that time, at my grandmother's loving insistence, I attended church with her in an old barn. One night God spoke to me in an inaudible voice and told me I should change my life or be prepared for great suffering. His gentle, but firm message reached me, and I surrendered my life to Him. Instead of the stuffy, restricted life I had expected, He has given me a life full of joy and freedom. Serving Him has become increasingly satisfying over the past 35 years.

One of the most loving things God has revealed to me is that if I trust Him, He will take all things that happen to me and make them work for my good. He has proven that He is able and willing to take any event—past or future—and use it to help me and to build His kingdom. Throughout Scripture He has proven His ability to use even Satan's accomplishments for His own purpose. The crucifixion of Jesus was the supreme example. Satan did his worst and God used it to redeem us.

As I praised God for everything that had ever happened to me, in obedience to His command, He began to use my past to bless me and to help others. As I shared this with others, they began to praise Him for their own lives, even the unhappiness. Joy replaced their sadness and often changes took place in their circumstances. God honors His Word.

Merlin R. Carothers
Author

April 20

Kept From The Evil One

"I pray not that thou shouldest take them out of the world, but that thou shouldest keep them from the evil." John 17:15

In pro football, I realized success beyond what I'd ever dreamed. In fact, football became my god. I quit studying the Bible, I quit praying, I quit associating with Christians. In college, during January of 1958, I changed my major from Religious Education to Physical Education. I wanted to be popular with my teammates, so I began to compromise my beliefs to get the attention that I craved. It would be twenty years before I would change my major back.

During my football career, one sports writer described me as "without doubt, one of the wildest, slickest, toughest athletes ever to grip a football." Eventually I got so empty, having football as my god, I turned to making money. In one year, I made a million dollars. I never had any trouble earning a living, and it seemed I could get rich overnight and lose it practically as fast. Still, I felt so empty, there was a void in my life. I had so much pride and ego.

In January of 1978, I got turned round and made Christ the major of my life. I found that He is the man He says He is. And Jesus is alive and well and does everything today that He did when He was here in the flesh. One day the Lord brought to my attention this verse in John 17:15. He let me know, if I followed, He'd keep me.

Harold 'Hayseed' Stephens
Former QB/N.Y. Jets
Evangelist

April 21

Freely Received, Freely Given

"And as ye go, preach...Heal the sick, cleanse the lepers...cast out devils: freely ye have received, freely give." Matthew 10:7-8

Because this is exactly how we live, these verses are significant to me. Whether I am in the supermarket, the bank (where three tellers were baptized in the Holy Spirit when I got locked in accidentally one day), in the gas station, or in the Aleutian Islands, I am always expecting God to open a door for me to preach, heal, cleanse, raise, and cast out, because I have been given so freely of His love, His power, His healing, and His Spirit.

God orders my steps and uses me in a miraculous way wherever I go. One day I got to preach to five women in a ladies' apparel store when I went in there to look for a coat. One lady was a Moslem, one British, one French, none of them were saved. God is sending us all over the world now and we are happy to let the Holy Spirit fulfill this scripture in our lives.

In recent years, I began to see how God was sending me places and using me wherever He sent me. The culmination came in 1977 when He sent me to the Aleutian Islands in Alaska. I argued with Him and told Him, "Why don't you send an evangelist like Billy Graham or Jimmy Swaggart?" When I arrived there and found myself in a rocking chair holding and ministering to a 23 year old young man who had not been held since he was seven, God asked me, "Now wouldn't Billy Graham look funny doing this." I realized that His call is always specific to each need and I trust Him to be in control.

Billie R. Deck
Bible Teacher/Counselor

April 22

Christ: Head Of The Home

"Husbands, love your wives, even as Christ also loved the church, and gave himself for it."
Ephesians 5:25

After nine years, our marriage had fallen apart. All the pieces lay broken at our feet. My wife had moved out and we were about to begin divorce proceedings. At that time, neither of us had a personal relationship to Jesus Christ.

One day I was sleeping and our little son came into my bedroom to wake me up. Wanting more sleep, I told him to turn on the nearby TV set. I was drifting back to sleep when I realized the show on the air was talking about marriage problems...talking about my problems. I woke up and began to pay close attention. The PTL Club was on and Tammy and Jim were explaining how to solve marriage problems according to the Word of God. I heard them read, "Husbands, love your wives, even as Christ also loved the church..." I examined my own heart and knew I hadn't loved like that. Then, they threw another one at me: "...men ought to love their wives as their own bodies..." (Ephesisans 5:28). I began thinking about that all day.

At 5 a.m. the next morning, the Lord woke me up. I was so depressed and low I was looking up at my feet. I sobbed and cried out, "Lord, I can't solve my problems." Up to now, I'd bragged I was self-sufficient and needed no one.

I remembered what Jim had said and prayed, "Jesus, come into my heart and save my soul." I then felt the calm, peace and serenity only Jesus gives. He started mending my torn marriage from that day. Now we have experienced a complete healing and are living with Him as the head.

Dave Dentino
Saved through PTL

April 23

My Husband, A New Creature

"Therefore if any man be in Christ, he is a new creature: old things are passed away; behold, all things are become new."
II Corinthians 5:17

Our marriage had apparently come to an end. I thought there was no hope—but I hadn't reckoned on the work of the Holy Spirit in both our lives.

After my husband, Dave, experienced the peace and joy only Jesus can give, he called me up one day and said, "Will you help me make Christ the head of our home and life?" I was stunned. He shared from the Bible, "Submitting yourselves one to another in the fear of God" (Ephesians 5:21). Then Dave asked me to forgive him for not loving me as he should have. I doubted his sincerity, thought it was just a ploy to get me to come back home. After about five weeks, I saw it was real. Dave was a different person. He had become a "new creature" in Christ that the Bible talks about, "...if any man be in Christ, he is a new creature: old things are passed away; behold, all things are become new" (II Corinthians 5:17). The love Dave showed toward me saved our marriage and drew me to experience Christ's love in a new and special way. Jesus Christ saved our marriage.

Now we are a part of PTL's outreach from Greenville, North Carolina, to help others who are having problems in their marriage; we are helping them put Christ in their marriages and making HIM head of their homes. From a broken marriage, we have learned to help others heal their marriages based on the Word of God and the love of God.

Debbie Dentino
Saved through PTL

April 24

Live For The Lord

"...yet surely I know that it shall be well with them that fear God, which fear before him."
Ecclesiastes 8:12b

Every new day brings with it opportunities to experience God more fully, to love Him more deeply, and to realize the depth of His love for us. We can live in victory having power with God when we are obedient to everything the Lord speaks to us. We hear His voice clearly through His Word.

I've found the easiest time to experience close fellowship with the Lord is during the troubled and perplexing trials when nothing is going right. Trouble tends to draw you closer to God because that's when you are aware of your need for strength. When things are going good, it's more difficult because we delude ourselves that we don't need help. How mistaken we are. We should prepare in time of peace for the time of war; in other words, we should fortify ourselves with faith for future victories.

Singing with the PTL Singers gives me an opportunity to be a channel of God's blessing to others. I feel used of God to help others see and feel His love for them. Many times lives are changed as a result of that ministry in song. I'm reminded over and over again, the benefits of a yielded life.

Living for the Lord is a most fulfilling lifestyle, and I pray continually that the Lord will give me boldness and opportunity to bring the Gospel in song to His people.

Terry Bradford
PTL Singer

April 25

I Have Chosen You

"You did not choose me, but I chose you to go and bear fruit that will last. Then the Father will give whatever you ask in my name."
John 15:16 (NIV)

Thirty years ago, the Lord Jesus revealed Himself as my personal Saviour. I was sitting under a tree reading the New Testament, when the Spirit of God convinced me of my misery and that I was a sinful man. With that knowledge, He also made me aware of His sacrifice on the cross. I read, "Herein is love, not that we loved God, but that he loved us, and sent his Son to be the propitiation for our sins" (I John 4:10). Instantly I believed and felt my life flooded with peace and joy.

For years I had tried to follow my religion, but I had no relationship with God. I lived in the frustrations of a complex nature, always unsatisfied and anxious. My thirst for God made me seek Him in churches and once even at a retreat in a monastery. In the Air Force, a friend gave me a New Testament. As I was reading it one day, Jesus met me. A brand-new life began for me that day.

Later, at a prayer meeting, I asked God to give me a confirmation on my desire to serve Him and I prayed, "Lord, I do not want to be called into Your service by a man, but by YOU." A prophesy was given that began with the words: "It is not you that chose me, but it is I who called you..." From that time on, I was sure of my calling to His service and realized the answer to my questioning about the vocation He had given me was all part of His eternal plan.

Roland Cosnard
Host French PTL

April 26

The Total Trust Commitment

"Trust in the Lord with all thine heart; and lean not unto thine own understanding. In all thy ways acknowledge him...." Proverbs 3:5-6

The key to living a successful Christian life is found in a total trust commitment of all that I am, and all that I am not, to the grace of God. Great peace and confidence is mine as I daily realize that I do not have to rely on my own wisdom and strength. To acknowledge Him in everything is to recognize that, in His sovereignty, God knows what is best for my life, and He is vitally interested in enabling me to reach my fullest potential in Him.

The daily encounters of life and challenges of the ministry have caused me to realize that total reliance on Him liberates and empowers me to become all that He has intended.

It was my privilege to come to a personal faith relationship with Jesus Christ through the influence of wonderful Christian parents, who introduced me to the Saviour as a young child. In the nurturing process through the years, I have struggled with temptations and failures that are common to humanity. However, my testimony is not of an outstanding deliverance or radical conversion experience, but of the sufficient and sustaining grace of God. And, even though God is not finished with me yet, as long as I put Him first in all things, He will perform His Word in my heart.

You, too, can have the assurance of peace, joy, emotional stability, and complete provision as you trust completely in the Lord.

Paul R. Gaehring
*Dean Of Heritage
School Of Evangelism*

April 27

Impossibility? God's Possibility!

"And he said, The things which are impossible with men are possible with God."
Luke 18:27

God's Word is truth. There are many things in life that we can speculate on, whether they are factual, credible or not, but the Word of God, indeed, God Himself, is a *fact*. His eminence and authority are above human scrutiny. He is the necessary ingredient to a life of contentment and fruitful ministry.

Man can't save himself, it is impossible. It takes God. Man can't heal himself. Man can't do anything for himself, it is impossible. Thank God, though, that through His Holy Word, we can be born again, we can have the Holy Spirit, we can be real, we can be set free, we can be delivered and made whole by His divine intervention. We should be eternally grateful that those things that are impossible to man are quite possible with God.

However, all these blessings are the benefits rendered to loving obedient children of a mighty, loving Heavenly Father. He dwells in our hearts by faith. Keeping faith alive is easy. Just follow these two principles: First, READ AND STUDY THE WORD OF GOD, because faith comes by hearing the Word (Romans 10:17). Second, PUT INTO PRACTICE WHAT YOU READ IN THE WORD, or exercise your faith.

Some people exercise their faith, others revel in foolishness, putting God to foolish, selfish tests. Still others presume on His mercy, acting impulsively and without wisdom. But the Word of God declares "the just shall live by faith," faith in the God of the impossible.

Kenneth Hagin, Jr.
Evangelist/Author
"Word of Faith"

April 28

Key To Christian Living

"The Lord redeemeth the soul of his servants: and none of them that trust in him shall be desolate."   Psalm 34:22

In 1925, when I was only eight years old, I heard a ladies duet sing, "He's Coming Soon." Suddenly, I realized I didn't know Jesus personally at all. It was like in Revelations 3:20, where the Lord says, "Behold, I stand at the door, and knock: if any man hear my voice, and open the door, I will come in to him, and will sup with him, and he with me." I opened the door with a simple child's prayer and began my walk with Jesus. That wonderful walk has never ended nor been interrupted.

One day I felt overwhelmed by fast moving changes and all the moral decay of the world. As I sought God for a key as to how a Christian should live in this problemed world, He directed me to Psalm 34. The instructions from verse 1 are, "...bless the Lord at all times...." We're to praise Him at all times, not just when things are going good.

Verse four tells us to turn to the Lord when we're filled with fear, "I sought the Lord, and he heard me, and delivered me from all my fears."

We have a promise of His absolute protection from physical harm in verse 7, "The angel of the Lord encampeth round about them that fear him, and delivereth them." He promised to feed us daily, "The young lions do lack and suffer hunger: but they that seek the Lord shall not want any good thing" (Psalm 34:10). He reminds us we will never be comfortless in verse 22, "...none of them that trust in Him shall be desolate."

Vep Ellis
Pastor/Musician

April 29

A Less Stressful You

"...yield yourselves unto God, as those who are alive from the dead, and your members as instruments of righteousness unto God."
Romans 6:13

We spend too much of our time pretending we have our lives together. We dress for the part, drive the right car, and live in the right house. Get out of the notion that you have to wear a mask. Christians, especially, should stop trying to live up to what they think others would want them to do. Christ made you, He knows you! Stressful living is living up to the expectations of others.

Once you recognize that you are living stressfully, try to meet regularly with close Christian friends to have a covenant relationship. A covenant relationship is when you stop going through life pretending that things are always right, that you are living up to what is expected of you, and that you never have a problem. It is important to meet with a group of other believers and have a chance to say, "I really blew it this week." You need someone that will pray with you and help you overcome your problems. One way to be more honest is to yield more to Christ.

One problem area for most Christians is jealousy. Jealousy is Satan's way of coming between husband and wife, mother and daughter, the in-laws, jealousy creates stress. If someone confesses they have jealousy in their life, don't condemn them. Invite them to confess their sin, and according to I John 1:9, "If we confess our sins, he is faithful and just to forgive...and to cleanse us... ." God wants us to have more honesty and more people praying for our weakness.

Don Osgood
IBM—Teacher Of Leaders

April 30

Don't Stay In The Valley

"Yea, though I walk through the valley of the shadow of death, I will fear no evil: for thou art with me...." Psalm 23:4

Like so many others, I have "walked through valleys"—the death of loved ones, loneliness, unfulfilled dreams, disappointments and many other deep valleys. However, I have learned that, because God is with us, we do not have to stay in the valley—we can keep walking.

In Israel, a friend of mine and I were discussing great men of the Bible. We mentioned David and the lasting impact of his Twenty-Third Psalm. He asked, "Would you like to see the valley of the shadow of death?" I did not know it really existed. The next day we went there; it was gloriously beautiful. I spent four hours walking through that valley. I saw the "still waters," and the "green pastures." The "valley" became very real to me. It was the inspiration for my book, *Victories In The Valley*.

When going through trials, it is comforting to rest in the words of the fifth verse where God gives us the promise, "Thou preparest a table before me in the presence of mine enemies..." God is assuring us we will triumph over our enemies whatever and whoever they might be. When faced with the death of a loved one, or with the specter of our own death, we can rest assured that He accompanies through the "valley of the shadow of death." Further, He assures us of being in His presence throughout eternity, and now, in this present time, "...goodness and mercy shall follow me all the days of my life: and I will dwell in the house of the Lord for ever" (v. 6).

Charles L. Allen
Pastor

May 1

Christ, Our Stabilizer

"Yea doubtless, and I count all things but loss for the excellency of the knowledge of Christ Jesus my Lord."   Philippians 3:8

The "All-American Boy," that's me. For years I was called that in Hollywood and across the country. Anyone, from any age bracket, could come to see or hear Pat Boone without reservations about the quality or tone of the performance. But just when I was so busy being "wholesome" and charming the socks off of everybody, subtle violations, even exploitations caused the very foundation of my success to crack. My marriage and family relationships were in serious trouble. I had allowed the Hollywood lure to get to me. I thought I had "arrived" as an entertainer. This success nearly blinded me, distorting not only my marital communication, but that intimacy with my Saviour as well.

Having been raised in a Christian home, I enjoyed, as some have said, "a clean-cut, story book upbringing, laced with academic and athletic success." I've also experienced the joys of worldwide fame, hit records, movies, travel, command performances and the like. And most decidedly, I've faced near bankruptcy and disillusionment.

Priority is so important, vital, if we as children of God are to know His perfect will for us. We can experience His stabilizing, renewing, victorious presence in our lives daily. I must admit, the Lord Jesus Christ has truly been our stabilizer when priorities were not in order in our family. In the times that our marriage was nearly destroyed, and my career almost ruined, the Lord Jesus called us closer to Himself and renewed us. Now our lives are centered in Him alone.

Pat Boone
Singer/Actor/Author

May 2

Everlasting Love

"The Lord hath appeared of old unto me, saying, Yea, I have loved thee with an everlasting love: Therefore with loving-kindness have I drawn thee."   Jeremiah 31:3

When I experienced the magnitude of God's love, it revolutionized my life. The Lord Jesus has indeed called His people as loved friends. We are precious, unique, and special to Him and He demonstrates His love for us continuously.

Participating in this love relationship is the foundation of life itself. He is all magnificence, all beauty, all truth and all goodness. He wants us to see through the distresses of life, that He is a good God who gives us good. We must purpose in our hearts to let nothing separate us from that love.

The intimacy, desire, and expressed love between the Lord and His bride in Song of Solomon 2:14, "Let me see thy countenance," and "Let me hear thy voice," shows how hungry He is for our fellowship and love. He wants His love to permeate our beings, transforming us into His likeness.

The Lord also wants you to know He loves you with an everlasting love. He is calling you right now into the embrace of His perfect love. You can consider yourself a "Loved Person," not because of circumstances or associations, but because God loves you: perfectly, totally, and eternally.

Take the love of God as a coat and wear it. Say to yourself, "I am a loved person," and believe it. You are!

Marie Chapian
Author/Ladies Speaker

May 3

The Mystery Of Jesus Working

"Now unto him that is able to do exceeding abundantly above all that we ask or think, according to the power that worketh in us."
                                    Ephesians 3:20

This verse is dear to me because God has done much more for me than I ever expected or deserved. Ephesians has always been my favorite New Testament book because it reveals the mystery of Jesus working in and through His Body, the Church.

In Ephesians 2:5, we read, "Even when we were dead in sins (He) hath quickened us together with Christ, (by grace ye are saved)." This emphasizes the grace of God, we were like dead men and He quickened us, made us alive in Himself. Then He goes on and tells us the truth that we are even one with Him in heavenly places. "And hath raised us up together, and made us sit together in heavenly places in Christ Jesus" (Ephesians 2:6). In verse 10 of Ephesians 2, He declares it is God Himself who has made us what we are and has given us new lives and even made plans long ago that our lives should be spent helping others, "For we are his workmanship, created in Christ Jesus unto good works, which God hath before ordained that we should walk in them" (Ephesians 2:10).

My love for these wonderful messages of Ephesians has increased as the Holy Spirit progressively awakens my spirit to my position with Christ in heavenly places. The overriding theme of Ephesians (and indeed, the entire New Testament) is about the wonderful power of Christ at work in us and through us, and the Lord's desire to minister through His Body, the Church.

Ken Sumrall
Author

Every Home—God's Church

"As for me and my house, we will serve the Lord." — Joshua 24:15

Our home is a converted church building. It was my old home church when I was growing up. When the congregation decided to build a new building, the Lord led me to buy the old wooden structure and remodel it into a house.

In a sense, our family is in church all the time. Not just because of the building itself, but because Jesus Christ is acknowledged as the Head of our household and my wife, four children and I have all dedicated our lives to His service. Part of our service to Him is having regular Bible studies and prayer and sharing times for large gatherings of forty to fifty people.

Not every house can accommodate that large a gathering, but every household can receive Jesus Christ as its Head and welcome the Holy Spirit as their lifetime guest. It is our desire to see every home in the world become dedicated to the service of Jesus Christ; everyone saved, filled with the Holy Spirit and delivered of all sickness and disease. We just can't keep the Good News of Jesus Christ to ourselves, not with all the miracles the Lord has done in our lives as individuals and as a family.

Make the decision today that you and your house will serve the Lord. As you begin to study God's Word and pray together as a family, you will experience the reality of God's power, wisdom and love.

Hosea Prewitt
Layman

May 5

No Flowery Words

"...there is a friend that sticketh closer than a brother."   Proverbs 18:24

I have to say the Lord and I go back a long way. Without a doubt, I know Him to be a friend who has stayed beside me through the very hardest times in my life.

One of those times was the day a neighbor rushed into our little country store with the news that our four children had been in a car accident. Several of them had severe concussions and were not expected to live. If they did pull through, it was uncertain whether they would ever be the same.

Praying friends and neighbors lined the halls of the hospital. Their love and concern meant so much to my husband Hosea and me. But it was the ever present nearness of the Lord Himself that held me up through the darkness of those days and replaced the fear in my heart with the light of His hope.

One by one they recovered completely. Today, I see each one as a living miracle. Perhaps, the most dramatic being our daughter Cheryl who was crowned Miss America 1980. That's really hard to believe if you had seen her as a little eleven year old girl with over a hundred stitches in her face, cracked back, and a leg crushed and two inches shorter than the other. God supernaturally recreated and lengthened her leg.

Jesus has been my closest Friend through so much. I talk to Him just like I talk to other friends; not with flowery words but just my little simple ones. Let Him be your Friend too, and He will see you through every trial.

Carrie Prewitt
Wife/Mother

May 6

Fire From Heaven

"Jesus Christ the same yesterday, and today, and for ever."   Hebrews 13:8

Early in life I was very opposed to the moving and working of the Holy Spirit even though I was a Christian. But, through a miracle, God changed my heart and mind.

Called a child prodigy, I got an executive ulcer by the time I was in my late twenties because I was so successful early in life. Burned out, I was dying and went to some religious leaders for help. They told me, "If the doctors can't help you, we can't." I asked if God could help and they replied, "The healing business was only for the first generation church."

Knowing I was dying, I wanted to see India one more time with my family. In India, in a little village, a national wanted me to preach at a convention. I was ministering to about ten thousand people and dying at the same time.

As I preached to them, something strange happened. The people in the congregation could see fire fall on me and knew something had happened. It was a replay of Acts 2:3 "...cloven tongues like as of fire...sat upon...them." Filled with the Holy Spirit, I preached forty-five minutes in an unknown tongue. At the same instance, the Lord gave the interpreter the gift of interpretation and as I'd thunder out a sentence, he'd thunder the interpretation. The power of God was all over us. I gave the altar call in the Spirit and over one hundred Hindus came forward. I also was marvelously healed. Since then God has moved in me and through me within the Charismatic movement in the Untited States.

Dr. Joe Maas
President World Wide Faith

May 7

His Spirit Abiding With Our Spirit

"Howbeit when he, the Spirit of truth, is come, he will guide you into all truth...he will show you things to come."   John 16:13

I grew up in church and was faithful to go every time the church doors opened. I paid my tithe, was faithful in attendance, but ended up sick in body and so head-over-heels in debt I didn't know what to do. I was confused because I had not been taught how to use the Word of God over the circumstances of life.

Through these problems, I began searching the Scriptures and applying them in my own life. I found out I was thinking wrong and acting wrong because I had the wrong confession. I was always confessing "the devil said this" and "the devil said that" and my time was taken up with what the devil said. Suddenly, I realized the Word of God can work for us today and does work for us today.

Jesus said, "...when he, the Spirit of truth, is come, he will guide you into all truth...." This is a clear declaration by Jesus that the Spirit of truth would reveal things that He could not share with the disciples at that time. Later, Jesus said, "To him the porter openeth; and the sheep hear his voice: and he calleth his own sheep by name, and leadeth them out. And when he putteth forth his own sheep, he goeth before them, and the sheep follow him: for they know his voice" (John 10:3-4).

When you hear the voice of the Good Shepherd, the Spirit of truth abides in you and teaches you all things. The Spirit of God guides you in all truths and teaches you things to come. The wisdom of God is built into your spirit by His Holy Spirit.

Charles Capps
Evangelist/Teacher

May 8

God's Light—Jesus In You

"But we all, with open face beholding as in a glass the glory of the Lord, are changed into the same image from glory to glory, even as by the Spirit of the Lord." — II Corinthians 3:18

There's a precious song that puts the message of this verse to music. It goes: "From glory to glory, He's changing me, changing me, changing me. From glory to glory He's changing me, the Light of God shown to the World!"

It's really something to realize the power of God's grace. He doesn't save us and then leave us in the condition He found us. If that were so, Simon would never have become Peter, nor Saul become Paul.

Nope! God didn't stop there. His abundant grace changed that hot-tempered fisherman and Christian-killing zealot into new creations (II Corinthians 5:17)-NEW MEN! He not only gave them new names but created in them new hearts—hearts that became mirrors of the indwelling Spirit of Jesus Christ.

God will do the same with any Christian who is committed to Jesus as Lord. Through us, He wants to manifest the person of Jesus Christ to the world. As our nature takes on the nature of Jesus, people will see the reality of God's love shining through us. Through us, they will see that Jesus really loves them in the same way the Father loves Him (John 15:9).

The gift of all gifts is to be chosen to radiate the image of Jesus Christ. Give the Holy Spirit full permission to change you from "glory to glory" into the Light of Jesus Christ—God's Light shining out to the world.

Mother M. Angelica
Abbess of Our Lady Of Angels Monastery

May 9

Foolishness Of Man

"But the natural man receiveth not the things of the Spirit of God: for they are foolishness unto him:....because they are spiritually discerned." I Corinthians 2:14

I was raised in a formal denomination and had always led a "good moral life." Because I was a moral person, it was extremely difficult for me to realize I needed God's love and forgiveness. Thinking I was a "good person" and didn't need all that "being saved" stuff, because of my self-righteousness, it was perhaps harder for me to see my sinful condition than a person who was down and out, or on drugs or living a violent, sinful life. I'm thankful that one day I saw the need to invite Christ into my life and that He then showed me the reality of Isaiah 64:6 which says, "But we are all as an unclean thing, and all our righteousnesses are as filthy rags...."

As a new Christian, one of the things that bothered me was, if the Christian way was the right way, why didn't more people walk in it? Then, the Lord led me to this scripture, "....the natural man receiveth not the things of the Spirit of God....", and I realized a truth. Until a person becomes born again and has his life transformed, he simply cannot understand or receive the things of the Spirit and they appear as "foolishness" to that person. Added to this understanding was an understanding of Christ's words, "....Father, forgive them; for they know not what they do..." (Luke 23:34). When the Lord brought my attention to this verse, it helped me to love rather than have a condemning attitude toward the natural man.

Robert Silvers
Religion Editor
Saturday Evening Post

May 10

Sweet Surrender

"...I am come that they might have life, and that they might have it more abundantly."
                                                John 10:10

I have such a burden for entertainers, they're seeking peace and joy in the next contract, the next mansion, the next relationship—and it never happens. Real peace, real joy are found only in Jesus; I know, I had it all—eight gold records, lots of money, fame and such emptiness of heart I didn't want to live.

I was a rough kid from the streets of New York. I had a little group, we sang in subways and tenement hallways; that was the start of Dion and the Belmonts. People loved our hits of the 50's and 60's: "Teenager in Love," "The Wanderer," "Ruby Baby," "Abraham, Martin and John." I traveled the world, had plenty of money and no joy or peace. But, by the grace of God, He had His hand on me.

I had a neighbor who was out washing his car. I noticed he had this big smile, and I saw joy in him. He started telling me about Jesus like He was a friend he really knew. From that neighbor, I learned about the "abundant life." "...I am come that they might have life, and that they might have it more abundantly" (John 10:10).

Since I've come to know Christ personally, the "abundant life" has swept through my family. My parents, sisters and brothers have this joy and peace. One sister lived in a methadone center for ten years, now she's like a saint—so full of peace. Jesus said, "Peace I leave with you, my peace I give unto you: not as the world giveth..." (John 14:27). Surrender to Him for rest, joy and peace.

Dion
Singer

_____ May 11

Building On A Firm Foundation

"Therefore whosoever heareth these sayings of mine, and doeth them, I will liken him unto a wise man, which built his house upon a rock...."
Matthew 7:24-29

This passage comes at the end of the Sermon on the Mount as Jesus was summing it all up and said, "If you do these things that I taught here, then you have a good foundation, just like a man that built his house on a rock and a great storm came with wind and rain, and the house stood. The storm didn't have any effect on it. But the guy that built his house on the sand didn't have a good foundation, and the same storm hit that house and it fell." So there is a big difference. One falls and another stands. I feel like it depends upon our foundation.

The foundation is the most important thing, because if you build a beautiful house and you don't have a good foundation, then it won't stand the storm. And so, if you have a good foundation, it will stand. The foundation is more important than the house, if I may say it that way. They are both important, but the foundation comes first. Of course, all these teachings of Jesus, here in the Sermon on the Mount, they are summed up in those verses. If you keep the sayings of Jesus, you're building on a firm foundation. If you don't, you're building on the sand. The sands of time, instead of the Rock of Ages. And that's it. I've thought a lot about it and preached a lot about it and it's ultra simple, but it's very important. I've attempted to follow this to build on truth and honesty and just old-fashioned dedication to God.

Rev. James Thompson
Pastor, Christian TV
President

May 12

From Glory To Glory

"And all of us, as with unveiled face...are constantly being transfigured into His very own image...from one degree of glory to another."
II Corinthians 3:18 (Amplified)

We need this "change into His image" if we are to successfully "run the race" and, in the end, arrive at our "goal." Each day as we press into His presence and have fellowship, communion and exchange of life, His Spirit touches our spirit, and we are changed, taking on a little more of His nature. From each entering—from Shekinah glory to Shekinah glory—"old" drops off and all things are made "new."

We enter this, "Special Presence of Shekinah glory," by praise, singing, thanksgiving, clapping, dancing, leaping, praying in the Spirit, and so on. In this entering with unveiled face, the ears of our inner man are sharpened, and God is able to bring revelation and power into our life through the revealed Word.

In this scripture, there's no need to be discouraged about present abilities, or events, because of the progressive anointings of Christ within. Our lives can become more effective every day as these anointings allow the ministry to flow forth with ease and great power, completely in His control and provision.

How completely God has planned our development and growth processes. It is almost like a metamorphosis from one nature to another, just like the caterpillar to butterfly. Experience every day's lessons and heed His instruction and grow from glory to glory.

Rev. Chuck Flynn
Pastor/Teacher

May 13

The Book Of Remembrance

> *"And a book of remembrance was written before him of those who reverenced and worshipfully feared the Lord, and who thought on his name."* Malachi 3:16 (Amplified)

This is a verse given to me many years ago. At first I didn't fully understand its meaning, but as the years have gone by, I have found pleasure in centering my conversation on Him. When I do, it brings Him pleasure and we are close and become one. Whether talking with a friend about Him over coffee in my kitchen, or riding with my husband in the car, and our conversation turns to Him, the warm knowledge that God is listening and is pleased, and is writing about us as we talk, is a tremendous incentive to live wholly for Christ.

Because He knows our motivations and intentions, the Holy Spirit guides us into daily communion with God. Even in our thought life, we are cautioned to think on things that are "honest, just, pure, lovely, and of good report" (Philippians 4:8).

If only we would praise and honor Him in our daily conversations. What wonderful tribute to be chronicled as one who spoke with tenderness though authoritative, confidence though tempered with humility, and honesty seasoned with wisdom.

One thing I have found in serving the Lord, that every good desire and aspiration we have in Him, God begins to bring it to pass in our lives. As we flow with Him, in His timing, we see it. But first, all must be surrendered to Him, even our speech. Remember it's all being recorded. Honor Him with upright conversation.

Mary Ann Flynn
Bible Teacher

May 14

The Battle Is Not Yours

"...for the battle is not yours...Don't be afraid or discouraged...Believe in the Lord your God, and you shall have success!"
II Chronicles 20:15-20 (LB)

He who knows the end from the beginning can be trusted to strengthen, establish, and settle us in any of life's experiences. Complete trust in the God of all Ages will produce a confidence and maturity unsurpassed by human reasoning. Trust in our abilities alone results in hurt feelings, crushed lives and tense situations. We must let Him go before us and produce in us effective, productive, ministry. "...You don't have to fight...(we only need to) stand quietly and see the incredible rescue operation God will perform..." (verse 17). When God fights our battles, the victory and "spoils of war" are extremely rewarding.

Recently I've come to appreciate more fully, "the incredible rescue operation God will perform." I was in India with the Mark Buntain Ministries for a Christmas presentation. The first night the United States Consul from the embassy was in the audience. He invited me to lunch the next day and complimented me on the service he had enjoyed the night before. Our lunch date was on Friday, but on Thursday night my purse was stolen, and I lost all my money, my passport, and visas. Realizing I had a friend at the embassy, I went over early Friday morning and explained my dilemma. He was so kind, everyone there helped me, and in two hours I had everything I needed for my seven week, around the world trip. What a tremendous blessing! I will remain faithful to my God who is ever faithful to me.

Lillie Knauls
Singer

May 15

Running For Jesus

"Teach me to do thy will; for thou art my God; thy Spirit is good; lead me into the land of uprightness."   Psalm 143:10

Many were shocked and surprised, some even angered over the President's decision to boycott the Summer Olympics in 1980, but I'm convinced that God allowed the boycott to halt America's ever increasing obsession with sports. We have almost made it an idol god. I should know because, for many years now, I've been involved in the sports arena as a runner and Olympic competitor. But all glory belongs to God, and we must learn to walk in obedience to His will, in unity.

All along, during this incident, the Lord had been speaking to my heart, that "a nation divided against itself cannot stand." Whether or not we realized it, we were dividing ourselves to our own destruction. So when asked to respond on behalf of the athletes, at the President's request, I let the media know that we were not there to bring division among athletes or go against our President's wishes, or to be disobedient or rebellious, but that we had to renew the trust and love that was needed for the family of America. Only God can renew that.

Those statements brought to mind a commitment I had made earlier in life, to give the Lord my *all*. My entering the Olympic competition for the fourth time was in absolute obedience to Him. God is very creative. He, the Creator, works through us for His pleasure. Everything I've been able to do has come from my being obedient and saying yes to the Lord, even running, if I can minister His goodness.

Madeline Manning Mims
Athlete

May 16

Pressure Off Me, On Him!

"He is the source of your life in Christ Jesus, whom God made our wisdom, our righteousness, and sanctification and redemption."
I Corinthians 1:30 (RSV)

I am nothing outside of Jesus. The day these words moved from my head to my heart, I was free. Jesus gives me my salvation, my holiness, my righteousness and my wisdom. He gives all of this because of His grace, not because of anything I do or am. This takes all the pressure off me to do anything good to earn His favor. I have finally realized that anything good I do is really Jesus doing it. In verse 31 of I Corinthians 1, we're told, "...let him who boasts, boast of the Lord." This means I must praise Him and thank Him for living in me and through me. The more I recognize Him, the more He can do. When I take any of the credit for something good in my life, I am really disregarding Jesus in my life.

I was raised in a Christian home, accepted Christ as Saviour at a young age, but didn't let Jesus be the Lord of my life until many years had passed. I went to church for social reasons rather than spiritual reasons. I finally reached the point where my marriage and family were almost lost, then I reached out to Jesus. My husband and I reached out to Him at the same time and for the next couple of years, we spent all our time getting to know Jesus more and didn't think of our problems. One day we realized we had been given a new marriage, a new family and a new life. He did that because we were concentrating on Him instead of our problems. "For it is God who is at work in you, both to will and to work for his good pleasure" (Philippians 2:13).

Dana Cadwell
*PTL's May
Employee of the Month*

May 17

Exceeding, Abundant Life

"Now unto him that is able to do exceeding abundantly above all that we ask or think, according to the power that worketh in us."
                                    Ephesians 3:20

Since I became a Christian, I have been living the "exceeding, abundant" life. It's so exciting to live for Jesus—the life of trust, the life of faith.

My faith life began because of a golf game I was playing in Nashville. I noticed this fellow golfer with a nice countenance. In a conversation, I discovered he was a minister. He invited me to his church and I politely declined, saying, "I don't believe in speaking in tongues, healing and all that stuff. It was only for the early church."

However, I did go to his church. I learned the truth of "Jesus Christ the same yesterday, and today, and for ever." By reading Hebrews 13:8, I learned the Holy Spirit baptism was for me personally. I was filled with the Holy Ghost and I have never been the same.

When my wife became pregnant, we agreed in prayer to have a boy. We wanted a son to go with our daughter, Sarah. We said, "Lord, you name him." Later, I was ministering in the hill country of Texas and the Lord said, "Ray, your son's name is 'Adam.'" While our son was being born, my wife sang in Holy Ghost language...singing to Jesus. We named him "Adam" as the Lord instructed us.

The Lord is so good, He blesses in so many ways. The abundant life, the overflowing life, the joy unspeakable life is found in Jesus Christ.

Ray Peterson
Recording Star

May 18

The All-Providing Saviour

"Who forgiveth all thine iniquities; who healeth all thy diseases; who redeemeth thy life from destruction...crowneth thee with lovingkindness and tender mercies..." Psalm 103:3-5

I was raised in a Christian home, attending and participating in church at an early age. However, the teaching that we were subject to did not emphasize a need for personal commitment to Christ. I went away to college and became active in a church and again was under a teaching that did not emphasize a personal commitment. It was not until I was married and joined my wife's church that I realized, through the teaching of that pastor, that I had not accepted Jesus Christ as Saviour and Lord. When I did that, I found a significant change in my life had occurred.

It was many years later when the Lord, through a series of circumstances, brought my wife and me to the place where we were ready to say, "Lord, if there is anything more that you have for us, we want it." Although we had never heard about the baptism of the Spirit, we were led into it through reading the Word and related books on the baptism. Since that time, our Christian life has been further enriched with this added dimension.

After I had received the baptism in the Holy Spirit, the Lord began dealing with me about my use of aspirin and antacids. I was one of those who would take these medications at the first sign of headache or fuzziness. It was this and other related healing scriptures that the Lord quickened to my heart, that delivered me from depending on medication, instead of on the healing power of prayer.

Jay H. Montgomery
PTL Vice-President
Facilities Division

Practice The Presence Of The Lord

> *"...the children of men (who) put their trust under the shadow of thy wings...shall be abundantly satisfied and...drink of the river of thy pleasures."*   Psalm 36:7-8

I was going along fine without God; I had enjoyed all the success I'd tried to attain, achieved all I thought I wanted to achieve. But then, I noticed I had such emptiness and a huge vacuum inwardly. Success didn't fill my insides. I started seeking what would fill that empty inside place and found out it was God. I asked Jesus inside and, sure enough, He did fill the empty places. The Psalm says, "He will abundantly satisfy," and I found He did.

Sometimes I get too busy to do what He wants me to do, and when I do that, I miss out. I'm the loser when I forget to bring Him into that deep relationship He desires to have with us. I want to be really, really in love with Him, bring Him into every part and every moment of every day. To achieve this, I have found it's very important to read His Word very early in the day. When I read the Word slowly and take to heart what He's saying to me through the Word, I find it stays with me all day. He'll recall some word or thought that I've fed on to bless me, rebuke me, or encourage me sometime in that day. How we are in the morning is how we are all day long, we keep hearing His Word all day. That's living in the Spirit, hearing His Word and heeding His Word all day long. As we praise Him and thank Him, He draws us closer to Himself. If we allow Him to speak to us and minister to us in this way, we grow and prosper daily.

Donna Jean Young
Actress/Comedian

May 20

Wisdom In Winning

"He that goeth forth and weepeth, bearing precious seed shall doubtless come again with rejoicing, bringing his sheaves with him."
                                            Psalm 126:6

Just think, it is possible—in our generation—to win the world to Christ! Our generation, more than any previous generation, has wonderful tools at our disposal—radio, television, computers, and a vast availability of the printed word.

And it is not only a possibility to win the world for Christ, it's our responsibility. All of us, working together can make it a reality. Many, doing a little can accomplish great things. We have the potential for turning the world upside down and ushering in His Coming! That's exciting!

Our Saviour is our source. He said, "All power is given unto me in heaven and in earth. Go ye therefore, and teach all nations..." (Matthew 28:18-19). He commissioned us to evangelize the lost. We have the resources to do it. Our Source is our resource, a Source who has all power, a Source who can, and has already once, turned the world upside down.

The Lord promised us joy in obedience to His command to win souls. And there's such joy in winning souls to Him; there's wisdom in winning the lost to Christ. For Proverbs 11:30 reminds us, "The fruit of the righteous is a tree of life; and he that winneth souls is wise. In bringing souls to Him, we reap great benefits, great joy, and great wisdom.

Vern McLellan
PTL World Missions Director

May 21

A New Song

"I waited patiently for the Lord...and he heard my cry. He brought me up...out of the miry clay, and set my feet upon a rock, and established my goings." Psalm 40:1-2

I was born into a preacher's family and raised in a Christian home. I had always loved the Lord, but it wasn't until I suffered a serious breakdown that I came to know Jesus as He really is.

In a pit of depression, the Lord taught me some very basic facts. The agony which I was experiencing did not come upon me suddenly. It took years to form my wrong thinking and living patterns. Consequently, it took time to heal and reestablish new patterns. Only Jesus has the true remedy to heal a broken mind and spirit. I knew by following His Biblical prescription for living, I could regain sound emotional and mental health. When I accepted the fact that I needed to know the truth about me and my situation, He responded to my desperate cries. The Holy Spirit helped me accept the teaching from God's Word and showed me where I needed to change and how to change. He transformed my life! I had to come to the place where all I had been taught must become a personal reality. That proved to me that a "horrible breakdown" *can* become a "beautiful breakup" when we let Jesus transform us from our own destructive "self."

He renews our minds through the principles of His Word and the ministry of the Holy Spirit with our spirit and life. The words of Psalm 40:3 became true in my life, "And he hath put a new song in my mouth, even praise unto our God: many shall see it, and fear, and shall trust in the Lord." He has redeemed my pain and sorrow.

Pat Ansite
Author/Speaker

May 22

Created In His Image

"In the beginning was the Word, and the Word was with God, and the Word was God. The same was in the beginning...." John 1:1-3

Too many people don't know where they have come from, and most don't know where they're going. As Christians, we should know where we have come from and especially where we're going.

From the beginning we were made in the image of God; nothing else was ever made in God's image. Not angels, not fish, not fowl, not the animal kingdom, only man was made in the living image of our great God.

Since we're made in His image, we're more important to Him than our own children are to us. His love is so great our every move is important in His sight.

He's doing everything for us for the furtherance of His Kingdom so he can have the joy of our fellowship.

As God's sons, made in His image, we are inheritors. He has great rewards for us. If we have sense enough to revere the rewards that are temporary—money, prestige, houses—why not work for the rewards that are permanent? I'm His son—I want my rewards *there* much more than the rewards *here*.

So, sons of God, get your eyes on the inheritance, disdain the temporary rewards and give your all for the rewards of the Kingdom.

Demos Shakarian
Founder FGBMFI

May 23

Salt and Light

"and it shall come to pass, that whosoever shall call upon the name of the Lord shall be saved." Acts 2:21

There's a human dilemma going on in the lives of ten percent of the population of this country. Many people are out of balance. We call this situation mental breakdown or neurosis. It is caused by stress and produces insomnia, inability to eat, or sharp contrast in personality. But by God's grace, we are learning the scriptural approach to dealing with these pressures.

As the Body of Christ, we must learn to show those suffering from stress-related illnesses, how Christ would react. We should show compassion, understanding, and speak the truth in love. Christ's love demonstrated in our lives will make His love and healing available to their lives.

When Jesus spoke to the woman at the well (John 4:7-30), He lovingly expressed the truth to her. She confessed her sins to Him, and the opportunity for redemption was offered to her. Christians, too, are in the redemption, rebuilding business. Our love and concern for others should motivate us to lay our lives at another's feet.

In Matthew 5:13 & 14, He said, "Ye are the salt of the earth," and "Ye are the light of the world." Without His love, our "salt" loses its savor, and the "light" goes out. Both become useless. Fears, insecurities, and unforgiveness are broken and cast away when we call on the Lord and receive His love and forgiveness. We can love ourselves and others as well.

Dr. Fred Gross
Psychologist

May 24

We Are Ambassadors

"Now then we are ambassadors for Christ, as though God did beseech you by us: we pray you in Christ's stead, be ye reconciled to God."
II Corinthians 5:20

"Ambassador" is the key word in this scripture, and it's the only place it is used in the Bible. Other scriptures deal with our oral proclamation, but ambassador has to do with totality of life. It is living your life in an unfriendly, hostile and unfamiliar environment. As Christians we can expect something of this same treatment. At the least, we are in an environment that does not reflect our Christian lifestyle.

I refuse to withdraw from that lifestyle or to retreat from society or reality and am very critical of the 20th Century evangelical monasticism. We are called to involvement, and not withdrawal, except for periods of rest and renewal.

As ambassadors of the King of Kings, we are to represent Christ in life, sometimes in places where Christianity is not a part of the culture, and demonstrate a Gospel that's not just vocal, but lived out in caring, compassionate love—love that is true to our Lord's example.

The description of the incarnate Christ by John is that "...the Word was made flesh, and dwelt among us" (John 1:14). There is no substitute for living out the Gospel. Computerized witnessing, computerized faith, beaming the words down by satellite is no substitute for loving, caring Christians who speak the words of Jesus and live out His compassion. It is this demonstration of our commitment that makes the Gospel believable and creditable.

Stan Mooneyham
President World Vision

Holy Exchange

"To appoint unto them that mourn in Zion, to give unto them beauty for ashes, the oil of joy for mourning, the garment of praise for the spirit of heaviness..." Isaiah 61:3

The Lord offers us an exchange: the beauty of deliverance and freedom for the ashes of despair and depression. We often go through our ash heap, an ash at a time, and call it prayer. We ask forgiveness for something Heaven has no record of. We'll not receive the oil of joy until we give up mourning.

Mourning itself is not a sin, but a vehicle to get us from one situation to another. The sin comes in when we refuse to go to another place or release ourselves from mourning. It's natural to mourn when we're disappointed or lose loved ones, but as we obey and offer "sacrifices of praise," even in these difficult times, we find ourselves being ushered out of circumstances and into His presence.

The third promise in these verses, "the garment of praise for the spirit of heaviness..." is worthy of note, too. We refer to the spirit of heaviness as a mood, but the Lord never intended Christians to be motivated by moods. Rather, we are to rule over our emotions bringing them into total alignment with God's Word.

Let go of the ashes in your life, praise the Lord continually, be obedient to His instructions, and you, too, will realize how valuable this Holy exchange can be. Know too, that you can rely on His faithfulness to perform His Word.

Iverna Thompkins
Bible Teacher

May 26

Joy In The Word

"For whatever was thus written in former days was written for our instruction...by endurance and encouragement...we might hold fast and cherish hope." Romans 15:4 (Amplified)

I have observed a change in the philosophic atmosphere of secular colleges and universities during my years of teaching. When I was a student at the University of California, the popular philosophy was one of automatic progress. They believed they could work out their own problems and didn't need Christ. After two world wars and the events that have followed, this has been replaced with a philosophy of despair. The feeling is, "If the bomb doesn't get us, pollution will." But the Scriptures give us hope. God is a faithful God who keeps His covenants and promises. Jesus will come!

Our hope is quickened as we search the Scriptures. Receiving the baptism in the Holy Spirit has made Jesus very real to me. He's also given me new joy in the Word. In the Hebrew this is called, "simchat Torah," the delight in the study of Scripture. Many people never read the Bible, they don't know what joy, encouragement, blessing and hope they are missing. Humanistic, destructive theories taught in major seminaries destroy this "simchat Torah." The purpose in all my teaching is to help restore it.

I have just completed thirty-six years of teaching in Bible school, during that time I have enjoyed God's wonderful blessing and provision. I have found His promise in Romans 15:13 to be true, "May the God of hope fill you with great joy and peace as you trust in him, so that you may overflow with hope by the power of the Holy Spirit" (NIV).

Dr. Stanley Horton
Prof. Bible, Theology

May 27

Let Go And Let God

"But what things were gain to me, those I counted loss for Christ...and do count them but dung, that I may win Christ." Philippians 3:7-8

Retired at thirty-nine, I was at the top of the corporate world ladder. I had achieved all my goals: a good wife and family, a sailboat, extensive travel experiences, had made millions, and was a financial success. In short, I had all the natural man could desire. But because none of us is complete until we have experienced God, I had a Damascus Road encounter with Christ and accepted Him as my Lord. Soon afterward, I was to experience this truth as well: "But what things were gain to me, those I counted loss for Christ."

Everything was new to me, so I joined a wonderful Christian fellowship. I began to grow and finally to serve. Part of that maturing process included receiving the baptism in the Holy Spirit. With the Spirit of God living in me, I found the power to free myself from the worldly trappings. I also learned this truth: God doesn't remove our talents when we come to Him, He utilizes them for His glory. Our basic skills bloom more fully under Christ's leadership. Before, it was a working, sweating, do-it-yourself everyday grind. Now Christ is doing everything through me, every day is an adventure. I've entered into His rest.

Priorities are so important. When they are ordered by the Word of God, we have victory. Philippians 4:13 says, "I can do all things through Christ which strengtheneth me." We must realize that Christ gives His ability for every task.

Dan Boone
Consultant

May 28

Contentment For Single Adults

"...I have learned, in whatsoever state I am, therewith to be content."   Philippians 4:11

The "all-American single" is supposed to be happy, competent and successful. Yet, with many single adults there is a war going on between aloneness and loneliness. I know, because I am single. Through the years, I have claimed this scripture in my life and it has produced joy. I am not crusading for some kind of "singlepower." For some, singleness is temporary, for others it may be permanent. But one must accept marriage if it comes, or singleness if it stays.

Now, I do not view myself necessarily as single, but as a person. Therefore, I have an identity as well as self-respect! I am a person of value-dignity-worth.

Whether I am married or single is not the point. I think of myself first as a Christian, second as a person, then third as a single adult. In a humorous way I say concerning marriage, "I had rather want what I do not have, rather than have what I do not want!" In all seriousness people need to release themselves to the Lord God and trust Him with their marital status.

Total commitment in everything, including my marital status, came for me as I let Jesus be Lord of my life after accepting Him as my personal Saviour. I am not a college professor who happens to be a Christian. I am a Christian who happens to be a professor. As I understand it, "Saviourship" is when I get Jesus, and "Lordship" is when Jesus gets me. Therefore, I know, single or married, I can have the anointing power of the Holy Spirit in my life.

Dr. Jim Towns
Professor, Stephen F. Austin State University

May 29

The Exhilarating Life

"Trust in the Lord with all thine heart; and lean not unto thine own understanding."
Proverbs 3:5

I have been through many deep waters but God has never failed to lead, guide and direct me when I have trusted fully in Him and leaned not unto my own understanding. When making decisions we have to learn to trust the Lord all the way, not just for part of the way.

During my college days, I strayed from God even though I was born again. When I arrived at college, I quickly got acquainted with night life, partying, drugs, alcohol and living in a deep pit of sin and shame. Although the life of sin may look glamorous and exciting to someone who has never been in it, it is neither glamorous nor exciting to the person caught up in the cycle. It takes ever increasing amounts of alcohol and drugs to get high and the excitement is not to be compared to the wonderful excitement of living for God and waiting with expectancy to see what He will do next in our lives.

When I grew tired, even sick of the sinner's life and turned from my own understanding to fully live for Him, then I knew not only excitement but also joy and peace which you can have only in Jesus Christ. Now I know the truth of: "...in him we live, and move, and have our being..." (Acts 17:28). That's where the really exciting life is, in Him!

Beverly Glenn
Singer

May 30

Abide In The Vine

"If ye abide in me, and my words abide in you, ye shall ask what ye will, and it shall be done unto you." John 15:7

Everything we need for a productive, fulfilling life is found in our Lord Jesus Christ. His Holy Word gives us absolute direction, teaching us how we can participate in His divine nature and live effective lives to His glory on this earth. The only condition for enjoying this lifestyle is that we stay in constant fellowship with Him or "abide in Him," as paralleled through this passage.

I found the Lord four years ago. At thirteen I was introduced to drugs and when they got the best of me at seventeen, I turned to drinking. By the time I reached twenty-three, I was at the end of the road. I was so depressed with life I didn't want to live. But praise God! He saw me and sent someone in my path to tell me about salvation and the love of Jesus. I found the true "Vine."

Without God's Word in us, we die on the vine, much like unpicked fruit that spoils from neglect. Through the Word we are fed and ministered to. As we search the Scriptures, we gain knowledge, wisdom, and power from God. When the Word of God abides in us, we are confident that what we ask in His name, we shall receive.

Study the Word, meditate on its teachings, commit its principles into actions as a lifestyle. It pays to stay in relationship with the power source, learn of Him first, then cling to Him.

Sheila Wong
PTL Staff

May 31

Walk Uprightly And Hang On!

"...the Lord will give grace and glory: no good thing will he withhold from them that walk uprightly."   Psalm 84:11

All through school, I was the fat ugly duckling. Year after year, I put up with the cruel remarks and cold shoulders from classmates. But I had one thing I held onto--my faith in Jesus.

Among my world of school peers, I walked alone. I didn't fit in. In fact, any excuse was enough for me to stay home from school and escape the pressures. It wasn't easy to face rejection, but I knew my life with Jesus was not a game, and therefore I never wavered from walking uprightly before Him.

Today, I can look back and know that God has abundantly blessed me. He gave me the willpower to shed those excess pounds, and going to school at PTL was the beginning of a new life. Now I work here, and God has opened so many doors, given me so many friends, and so many opportunities that were just daydreams before.

Many Christians go through trials like I did, where serving the Lord seems almost fruitless. But this verse is for all of us. If we walk uprightly, God is going to bless us!

Put God to the test and see if He doesn't perform His Word in your life and turn your daydreams into realities. Whatever you do, don't get discouraged. God's timing is not always our timing. But if you wait on Him, you'll find His grace and goodness!

Lauri Braaten
PTL Photographer

June 1

The Sin-Bearing Shepherd

"But he was wounded for our transgressions, he was bruised for our iniquities: the chastisement of our peace was upon him; and with his stripes we are healed." Isaiah 53:5

This verse is so special to me because I am so amazed that Jesus, who was flesh and blood just like you and me, was willing to be so obedient. For Jesus was so moved by love, He was willing to be oppressed and afflicted. Verse 7 describes this so vividly, "He was oppressed, and he was afflicted, yet he opened not his mouth: he is brought as a lamb to the slaughter, and as a sheep before her shearers is dumb, so he openeth not his mouth."

Of his own choice, Jesus "made his grave with the wicked, and the rich in his death; because he had done no violence, neither was any deceit in his mouth" verse 9 tells us. Jesus made His soul an offering for sin as He bore our sins on Calvary and now He makes intercession for us in Heaven.

During a time of personal devotion, I was reading in Isaiah and was totally caught up by the overwhelming compassion exhibited by the Master in this text. What a tremendous security in knowing that God's love is so great, that He would lay down His life for us. He loves us so much, that He sticketh closer to us than a brother.

We can also remember the words in I Peter 2:25, "For ye were as sheep going astray; but are now returned unto the Shepherd and Bishop of your souls." For as Jesus was led to the cross, He was as a sheep going to slaughter, but through his death and resurrection, He is now the Great Shepherd guiding and protecting us.

Roger Bradley
*PTL's June
Employee of the Month*

He Alone Satisfies

"Delight thyself also in the Lord; and he shall give thee the desires of thine heart."
Psalm 37:4

Delighting ourselves in the Lord, making Him our satisfying portion should be the objective of every sincere Christian. Taking pleasure in our mutually beneficial relationship with the Lord Jesus Christ is a way of life, not simply a nice sounding cliche.

It is remarkable how everything fits into proper order when we joyously put God first in our lives. Even the worst of trials seem to turn out for our good. Why? Because it is a fixed law of God. He promises in this very passage to provide, not only our needs, but the desires of our hearts, when we put our relationship with Him before all else.

When our hearts are in tune to God's order, His teachings and principles; when, indeed, we relinquish our "all" to Him, then our motives and desires are in line with the nature of God. Our desires are no longer selfish, vindictive or damaging.

This scripture is a practical, legal contract with God. He said, "If you will delight yourself in me, if you will make it your business to joyously put Me first in your life, then I will make it my business not just to answer your prayers, but will give you the desires of your heart."

For over fifty-three years, I have been preaching the Gospel. The Holy Spirit has made me to know the truth of these verses. God's Holy Word and exalting Jesus is my life's work because I realize He alone satisfies.

Howard P. Courtney
Bible Teacher

God's New Creature

"Therefore if any man be in Christ, he is a new creature: old things are passed away; behold, all things are become new."
II Corinthians 5:17

I was nineteen years old when I got out of the Navy after World War II. Alone, and no place to go, I rented a room from a widow who took in a few young fellows whom she considered her mission field. She'd get out her Bible after the evening meal and tell us about Christ and read to us from the Scriptures.

In two weeks, I'd heard enough to know I should be born again. Soon, I wanted a Bible of my own. I realize, now, that this desire was God's way of wooing me into a deeper relationship with Himself. But where would I buy one? I didn't even know where to go to get one. So I asked my landlady to help me.

My new Bible became my most prized possession. I had to learn how to read it, too. I thumbed around in it awhile until one day I found II Corinthians 5:17, "Therefore if any man be in Christ, he is a new creature: old things are passed away; behold, all things are become new." Praise the Lord! I'm glad I did. Since that day way back in 1945, it has blessed me and still blesses me daily.

I'll never be able to plumb the depths of my relationship as a "new creature."

Even though we are surrounded by ever increasing decadence, and immorality, we should be extremely grateful to God to have been made new creatures in Him. God, by His grace, has made us new, not perfect, but new.

Olan Hendrix
Director of ECFA

June 4

Changed Into His Image

"And it shall come to pass, that whosoever shall call on the name of the Lord shall be saved." Acts 2:21

I started training as a skater at thirteen. When I was sixteen the San Francisco Bay Bombers asked me to skate with them.

We skated fast, made good money, traveled to Japan, Puerto Rico, Hawaii and it was nice, but all through those years, I had such an emptiness. The more you have, the more you want. At the age of twenty-nine, I began to say, "What's happening, I have a car, beautiful home, money and friends but I'm so unhappy?" Someone said to me, "You should give your life to God." I thought I would have to be a nun and I didn't want to change my lifestyle.

I began to search and seek and one day I went to church and heard the Gospel for the first time in a church in New Jersey. I realized I couldn't get to God by being a nun, but through saying, "Jesus forgive me and come into my heart and change my life." I was shown in the Bible where it says, "And it shall come to pass, that whosoever shall call on the name of the Lord shall be saved."

In Roller Derby, my life was the opposite of what I believed. All of a sudden the Holy Spirit let me know what I was saying, that I was a Christian who should be showing love, gentleness, and meekness; and what I was doing in Roller Derby was punching, hitting and shoving. These were two directly opposite actions. In 1973, I left the Roller Derby.

I enrolled in Bible college and through prayer and Bible study my life changed. Christ and His Word are what keeps us.

Judy Arnold
Former Queen of Roller Derby

Worship Him For Who He Is

"But seek ye first the kingdom of God, and his righteousness; and all these things shall be added unto you."

Matthew 6:33

It has become crucial in my life that my prime objective is not to worry about possessing material things, but to seek to develop His character in my life. I have found it to be true: if I first seek the Lord, He will care for the needs of my life.

Too often, in our permissive society, we hear, "If you'll do this, God will do that." It's like a balancing game or barter system. However, I do realize that there are fixed laws in God's Word, and giving is one of them. But we must be sure that our motivation and intentions are aligned with the nature of Christ. Our sole purpose for living is to enjoy relationship and communion with the Lord Jesus Christ. When we are diverted by selfish desires for gain, our Christian growth and development are hindered, and our view of who God is, is dimmed. We should seek Him because we want more of Him, not because we want more from Him materially.

We must remember that our basic reason for being here is to get to know Him personally and to develop His character and divine nature in us. As disciples, our witness is so important to others who want to know about the one true God.

He is God, King of Kings and Lord of Lords. We should seek Him because of our need for salvation, deliverance, healing and spiritual hunger to get to know the Creator God. Our motives have to be unselfish to worship Him in holiness.

Kevin Hofer
Singer

Finding The Right Gear

"Come unto me, all ye that labor and are heavy laden, and I will give you rest."
                                                    Matthew 11:28

I was a pastor for twelve years, fitting neatly into the mold and guidelines of pastoral work. Then God called me out of pastoring to go out into the highways and minister to the trucker. A big rig highway chapel was completed in 1978 just for truckers. I have been on the highways, in truck stops and terminals taking the message of Jesus, the "Headlight," to all who will listen ever since then. "Come unto me, all ye that labor and are heavy laden, and I will give you rest," can be paraphrased uniquely to truckers in this way: "Come unto me, all you truckers who are pulling hard and overloaded, and I will shift your load on me."

Although unconventional, the trucking ministry is much needed. The long uphill pull can drag you down and stall your motor if you can't find the right gear. Jesus, facing the highest hill ever known to man, carrying the heaviest load, was reaching for that right gear with "sweat as great drops of blood." He found it when He said to his Father, "....let this cup pass from me: nevertheless not as I will, but as thou wilt" (Matthew 26:39). With this, He hauled for the top. At the instant the cross was in position and His head went down, the words, "But as many as received him, to them gave he power to become the sons of God, even to them that believe on his name" (John 1:12), took on their full meaning. These words are as permanent as though cast with lead in hardest granite.

Chaplain Sam Rust
Trucker's Chaplain

Hearing And Receiving

"Hear, O my son, and receive my sayings; and the years of thy life shall be many."
                                       Proverbs 4:10

I was saved and had been hearing God's Word for thirty-eight years, but I had never really had victory through Jesus or really received what God was saying. Then, one day, while I was studying God's Word, this portion of Scripture, "...and receive..." jumped out at me. It was quickened by the Holy Spirit.

Then I discovered the Bible is full of many wonderful scriptures promising long life, prosperity in every area and real victory through Jesus Christ. The Holy Spirit emphasized to me—the Scripture must be received by faith and not just heard and not acted on.

One of the things I heard by faith is Psalm 90:10, "The days of our years are threescore years and ten; and if by reason of strength they be fourscore years, yet is their strength labor and sorrow; for it is soon cut off, and we fly away." This is a promise of long years. In Psalm 90, verse 12 was another important scripture, "So teach us to number our days, that we may apply our hearts unto wisdom." Not only will we have many days, but the Lord will show us how to spend those days wisely.

About five years ago, I received the baptism in the Holy Spirit, He showed me the importance of total commitment to Christ. For the first time, I was *receiving,* not just hearing the Word. Romans 10:17 says, "So then faith cometh by hearing, and hearing by the word of God." This receiving has helped me tremendously in my life in Christ.

Maurie Deming
Captain, Eastern Airlines

June 8

Days Of Harvest

"Say not ye, There are yet four months, and then cometh the harvest?...Lift up your eyes, and look on the fields; for they are white...to harvest."
John 4:35

We are living today in that great day of the harvest that Jesus tried to make His disciples realize would occur in the end time. We—His present day disciples—must realize there are not four more months to the harvest. Now is the time! Today is the harvest!

In Amos 9:13, we read of the Lord's prophecy that the "plowman shall overtake the reaper...." That's what is happening in Japan today. People are responding as quickly as we plant the seed. At one meeting, 3,500 responded to the invitation to accept Christ as Saviour in answer to our prayers.

One evening at a meeting in Korea, 15,000 people attended. We finally had to bar the doors to keep out more because of safety reasons. A year ago there were 275,000 believers in Korea, today there are 425,000. A tremendous harvest is being reaped.

God is raising up people in these last days to help bring in the overwhelming harvest of souls for His glory. Nothing on earth can stop God's moving in these end times.

Spiritually, the nation of Japan is ready to explode in revival. II Corinthians 4:7 tells us, "...we have this treasure in earthen vessels...." This treasure is Jesus, Jesus in us—His earthen vessels. Break open your vessel, let "The Treasure" shine forth! This *is* the moment!

Bob Houlihan
PTL Japanese Outreach

June 9

What Time Is It?

> *"And it shall come to pass at the same time when God shall come against...Israel, saith the Lord God, that my fury shall come up in my face."* Ezekiel 38:18

Want to know "The Latest Word On The Last Days?" I have written a book that outlines it all as I have learned from the Word of God. As I see it, Russia will attack Palestine, America intervenes, and both nations annihilate each other militarily, reducing both to third-rate powers. This military vacuum will dictate that another power must assume the reigns as leader of government. That power is the European Common Market. It will emerge as the most powerful force in the world, and out of this will come the one-world ruler, the Anti-Christ. Even today, powerful money systems and forces are working to bring this one-world system to reality.

Many are concerned, therefore, as to the fate of the believers. Will the Rapture take place before, during, or after the Great Tribulation, as the seven-year period is named? After reflecting on all these schools of thought and much study, the Lord has revealed to me an alternative. I've become a "Pre-Wrath" Christian. I distinguish between wrath and tribulation because there is nothing wrong with tribulation, we are made by it, our faith purified by it. More than likely it will take tribulation to ready the church for the coming of the Lord. Tribulation will wean us from the world, detach us from the worldly influences, and allow us to get our eyes on the Lord Jesus as our only hope. To know how to handle tribulation spiritually, every Christian must prepare Himself in the Word. We should not be afraid of perilous times.

Dr. C.S. Lovett
Author

June 10

Sick With Love

"My flesh and my heart faileth: but God is the strength of my heart, and my portion for ever."   Psalm 73:26

At a time when my heart was cold, and I was putting the Lord second in my life, the Lord brought the 73rd Psalm to my attention. The preceding verse 25 asked the question, "Whom have I in heaven but thee? And there is none upon earth that I desire besides thee." It was so intensely personal that it caused me to weep. It was the answer to all my questions, all my problems, it is the "bottom line." No matter what my spiritual temperature happens to be, these verses minister to my soul.

Forty years ago, when I accepted Christ and arranged for water baptism, a relative asked me, "Are you going to get *dunked* in front of all those people?" As I said, "All those people won't matter. This is a personal thing between me and the Lord," the whole earth seemed to stand still. At that moment I came alive. I think every angel in heaven shouted, "Gotcha!" An awareness of God's love for me came to me with such exquisite clarity, it was like pain. I was "sick" with love.

I prayed, I Chronicles 4:10, "....Oh that thou wouldest bless me....and enlarge my coast, and that thine hand might be with me, and that thou wouldest keep me from evil, that it may not grieve me..." As God increased His ministry through me, I became aware of temptations I had never confronted before. The most subtle of all temptations is to start believing your own publicity. Any evil, obvious or subtle thing won't keep me from Him.

Ethel Barrett
Author/Speaker

June 11

For Our Good

"And we know that all things work together for good to them that love God, to them who are the called according to his purpose."
Romans 8:28

I'm not a psychiatrist or sociologist. I am a bereaved parent who has been walking wounded but recovered by the grace of God. I know the pain of losing a child, and I have learned, with Jesus Christ, to forgive death for taking my child too soon, and forgive life, for the supreme hurt. To bury a child is to see a part of yourself, your eye color, dimples, sense of humor, being placed in the ground. It is life's hardest and most pathetic experience, and must, therefore, be the hardest with which to deal. In reality, when children die, not only are we mourning them, we are mourning that bit of our own immortality that they carry. Only God can help you overcome this loss.

Everyone talks about being victorious Christians. But how can you be victorious without a battle? For years, God and my religion was a protectorship, duty, not relationship. I was practically "born on a church pew." But through this traumatic experience, and five arduous, torturous years wondering why me, God granted me divine grace and loving mercy, and I realized that shock is the sponge to absorb the impact of crisis. God truly cares, and every situation can be a growing opportunity.

My husband and I lost our fifteen-year-old daughter to leukemia, and at the time of death she was ready to go to be with the Lord, though we tried to hold her back. Our acceptance freed both of us to receive that peace that passes all understanding.

Beth Jameson
Author

June 12

God Is For Us

"What shall we then say to these things? If God be for us, who can be against us?" Romans 8:31

Heaviness from problems facing us each day sometimes presses us out of measure until we get the distorted view that God is part of our problem. The reverse is true, however. God is *for* us.

We look on problems as the enemies of our soul. There's a possibility that we may lose sight of the fact that God is part of the solution, never part of the problem.

Over and over again in the Scriptures, Jesus talked about His concern for us, His desires for us, His hopes for us. His concern for us is always linked together with the thought that He is for us wholeheartedly. If we got our minds clear on this point, it would give us a more ready access to the Father. We must understand that God is working out His will in us, both for His good and for our good.

"God be for us..." covers all the hurting, testing, and troublesome times. If our understanding of God is focused on the simple fact that He is for us, we will not experience self-condemnation or drag ourselves through the debris of life.

In life, we often experience unfortunate events, troubles we have no control over. According to Romans 8:1, there's no reproof, reproach, or rebuke in God's love toward us.

Get this into your mind, heart, and understanding. God is working His will in your life. God knows, God loves, and God cares.

Rev. Richard Dortch
Illinois Superintendent
Assembly of God

June 13

Healing Of Attitudes

"Ye have not chosen me, but I have chosen you, and ordained you, that ye should go and bring forth fruit..." John 15:16

I was chosen by Jesus on December 17th of 1974. I came into His kingdom because of the persistent prayers of a black girl named Ruth. Completely unknown to me, her whole church prayed and fasted, off and on, for three months. Because of the faithfulness of this church group, my blinded eyes were opened. James 5:16 tells us, "....The effectual fervent prayer of a righteous man availeth much." Because of their faithfulness, God healed me in one night of a violent temper, filthy mouth, drugs and drink. Not only have I been freed of these soul binding habits, but freed to help my brothers and sisters.

The Lord says, "...I have ordained you, that ye should go and bring forth fruit..." (John 15:16). His ordination on my life has been to use me with a life-giving message that has healed many marriages. My ministry is one of healing attitudes between men and women toward one another. The "healing of attitudes" differs from "inner healing" as the attitude depends on the conscious choice of the individual. The Lord who chose me and ordained me has also promised I would bring forth fruit, "....and that your fruit should remain..." Because my Father changed our personal lives first, attitude healing is a reality rather than a concept and we have been able to share this to the healing of many.

Treena Kerr
Teacher/Writer

June 14

God Can Do The Impossible

"...With men this is impossible; but with God all things are possible." Matthew 19:26

"It's impossible for you to go back to China!" Many people made that statement to me before my husband and I left for China in October 1979. How could I return to a country where I'd faced severe persecution like the horror of being brought before a firing squad.

But my dream and heart's desire to reach China for God were stronger than any fear of what man might do to me. There are 42 million Chinese in the Free World and over one billion in Red China and all must know that Jesus loves them and died for their sins.

For braving a trip to my homeland, God blessed my life with another "impossibility." I found the now 83-year-old doctor who had delivered me and given me to my adoptive mother. The doctor had accepted Christ. As you probably know, in the Orient, family ties are respected and treasured. Ever since God had given me the burden to minister to the Chinese, I wanted desperately to meet my natural mother and tell her the salvation message. This doctor had been able to locate her and now I am planning a second trip to China to find my mother.

Truly, God can do the impossible. My husband and I are believing God will open the doors of Christian television to the Chinese people of the world. It may look humanly impossible now, but wait and see what God will do. Will you pray with us that all will hear the Gospel of Jesus Christ and believe on Him?

Nora Sung
Evangelist

June 15

The Great Commission

"Go ye therefore, and teach all nations, baptizing them in the name of the Father, and of the Son, and of the Holy Ghost."
Matthew 28:19

A few years ago, the Great Commission found in Matthew 28:19 challenged my heart to work full time for God with my wife, Nora. At that time, I owned four factories with 2000 people working for me and had formed thirteen corporations.

My fellow-businessmen only wanted more and more money. Money was their god. Then I noticed the "Sunday Christians" at my church who served God on Sunday and lived their own way during the week. Like my wife, God had given me a burden to witness to the millions of Chinese people all over the world, especially those in Communist China.

So I gave up everything-the factories, the corporations-to minister for the Lord. Since the Chinese are very clanish people, God gave me a plan to reach them. If the Chinese people in the Free World could hear the message of salvation, thousands of Chinese Christians could then spread the Gospel to their families in Communist China. These thousands of believers already speak the language and dialect of the country.

I believe when the Free Chinese are saved, endued with power from on high, and travel to tell their families, mainland China will hear about Christ. You have been commissioned by God to witness to your family and city. Have you accomplished that task?

S.K. Sung
Businessman/Minister

June 16

Your Reasonable Service

"I beseech you therefore, brethren, by the mercies of God, that ye present your bodies a living sacrifice, holy, acceptable unto God, which is your reasonable service." Romans 12:1

Doing my best in the Lord's service has become a way of life for me. I love being in His service. Realizing that He has given us special abilities, equipping us for effective ministry is the foundation on which I've built my witness.

Just in the past year, I've changed the flavor of my ministry. The Lord has shown me how the "Show Biz" emphasis damages the spiritual life. So, I've moved from the more commercial, entertaining aspect of ministry to a more inspirational demonstration of His love.

Now, I feel I am using my talents for His purposes rather than just furthering my career. Being involved more and more in the show business circles has opened my eyes to the futility of serving for any purpose but to glorify God. We must seek to glorify Him, alone.

Ministering to the spiritual needs of people is the main purpose of my music. If I can create an atmosphere of praise and worship, and bring people together through a positive attitude toward God and each other, I'm in the center of God's will for me. I've met people who don't really believe in God or they don't think Jesus is for real, but a myth instead. What a blessed privilege to be a channel of His love and declare to this generation that our Lord is not a myth, but a tremendous gift. It is my reasonable service.

Teddy Huffam
Singer

June 17

The Interceding Shepherd

"Seeing then that we have a great high priest....Jesus the Son of God....without sin. Let us therefore come boldly unto the throne of grace...." Hebrews 4:14-16

For me, the three most important books in the New Testament are the Gospel of John, Hebrews, and Revelation. In the first, Jesus Christ is my Good Shepherd, in the second my Great High Priest, and in the third I want to throw myself at his feet because He is King of Kings and Lord of Lords.

It is wonderful to be in the Shepherd's flock, but, as a missionary surrounded and harassed by the powers of darkness, I find great comfort and constant assurance in this blessed passage.

Just to know that while I am being pressured from below me and around me, I thank God I am being protected and provided for from above. That is all I need to strengthen and keep me encouraged.

My Great High Priest, Jesus Christ, through the merit of His precious blood is interceding before the Father for me right now. He has never once failed to come to my aid immediately and effectively. Oh! How I love Him with all my heart!

God's wonderful Word is made real to me daily by the infilling of the Holy Spirit. I can personally assure anyone that, "...When the enemy shall come in like a flood, the spirit of the Lord shall lift up a standard (the Cross) against him" (Isaiah 59:19).

Certainly Jesus Christ is our protecting and interceding Shepherd!

Dr. Mark Buntain
Missionary

June 18

A Day That The Lord Has Made

"This is the day which the Lord hath made; we will rejoice and be glad in it."
                                       Psalm 118:24

Every day is determined by our mood in the morning and I have discovered we set our own mood. This scripture says the Lord made the world and created this day just for me.

Whenever I look around, I am sure to see the hand of the Lord. No matter what the circumstance, the Lord is in it. Therefore, there is cause to rejoice, to be glad, to be positive.

Expecting the best from each day is sure to result in positive rewards. If when you arise in the morning, hit the floor, rub your eyes, and say, "This is the day the Lord has made for me," you will hurry to work, and then look around you at lunch for the person you are supposed to meet.

By doing the above, you will add love and thoughtfulness to your day.

My eyes fell on Psalm 118:24 while reading the Bible one day. Immediately it said something to me and I wondered why I had not seen it before.

I had been raised among a people who saw a negative problem in everything. To my knowledge, we were not taught to anticipate the day, but rather to dread it by thinking, "Today would only be a good day if Jesus returned before sunset." No doubt about it, that would be a great day. But it does not subtract from the fact that this day can be a great one too.

James Lee Beall
Pastor

June 19

Special Gifts Through Strength

"I can do all things through Christ which strengtheneth me." Philippians 4:13

Having the experience of lifting more weight than anyone in the history of the world, I personally know what it is to be strong physically to the ultimate degree. Having experienced this particular gift, I also realize that no matter how much we have in a physical way, the only real strength comes from knowing God through Jesus Christ and having the guidance of His Holy Spirit. I found out long ago that I could do nothing really significant with only physical strength, but I can indeed experience the divine spiritual strength that, by far, overshadows my physical strength through a personal relationship with Jesus Christ.

Something else to remember is to never covet the gifts God has bestowed upon others. An entire lifetime can not only be wasted if you do not discover your own talents and develop them, but a great contributor to that waste can be the viewing of green fields in the other person's backyard. So many times we have all heard the "sour grapes" projected by those who will say, "If only I had his (or her) talents." An entire lifetime can be spent just observing others and being jealous of what God has given them and never looking within to find the generosity God has invested in ourselves.

We can all use the gifts that God has bestowed upon us to the best of our abilities when we gain our strength through Jesus Christ.

Paul Anderson
Olympic Weightlifting Champion

June 20

You Will Be Filled

"Through God we shall do valiantly: for he it is that shall tread down our enemies."
Psalm 60:12

As a Baptist minister for many years, I didn't realize that Jesus still heals, delivers and gives victory over our enemies. Suddenly, the truth of Hebrews 13:8, "Jesus Christ the same yesterday, and today, and for ever," became real to me. I knew you could take His Word literally. I discovered you can act upon His Word and that it is indeed true. "For we have not a high priest which cannot be touched with the feeling of our infirmities; but was in all points tempted like as we are, yet without sin" (Hebrews 4:15).

I also discovered that Matthew 5:6 was true, "Blessed are they which do hunger and thirst after righteousness: for they shall be filled." I received the truth of this verse and received the infilling of the Holy Spirit. I knew personally, if you hunger and thirst, you *will* be filled.

I was sick for nineteen years, and during this time, I continually talked of death. Then, I discovered Proverbs 18:21, "Death and life are in the power of the tongue..." and began acting on it. I started claiming, "...with his stripes we are healed," day after day and held firmly to that confession. I clung to the fact that God is faithful to His promises.

He admonishes us to "...be without wavering..." in Hebrews 10:23. So, I clung, without wavering from, expecting Him to do what He said He would do. God proved to be faithful and what the medical profession could not do, Jesus did!

Don Hughes
President Hughes Ministry

June 21

God's Way Works

"Likewise, ye wives, be in subjection to your own husbands; that, if any obey not the word, they also may without the word be won by the conversation of the wives."   I Peter 3:1

By the world's standards, I had a good marriage. But as I began to grow in the Lord, I realized I had some maturing to do in that area, too. My husband and I felt we were missing the Lords' very best.

You know, we always have the tendency to blame our mate when he is not treating us as we desire. But, Scripture helped me to see the part I played in getting the best, God's best, from my marriage. I decided to accept the challenge to do it, "God's way."

God's standard of excellence for marriage is: "So ought men to love their wives as their own bodies...no man ever yet hated his own flesh; but nourisheth and cherisheth it, even as the Lord the church" (Ephesians 5:28-29). When this standard is in operation, submission is no longer a duty, but a joy.

Being honest with yourself is often difficult. "...they may without the word be won..." should be translated, "a word." I realized it was not even necessary for me to "say" anything, but that my deeds and love with understanding would bring our relationship in line for God's blessing. It was exciting to then sit, and watch and let God bring us into His very best.

I dedicated my life to Christ when I was fourteen years old as the church sang, "I Surrender All." I realize now that it includes our marriages as well as our lives.

Karrel Hughes
Wife of Don Hughes

June 22

Dig In Your Heels

"But without faith it is impossible to please him: for he that cometh to God must believe that he is, and that he is a rewarder of them that diligently seek him."   Hebrews 11:6

This was my first memory verse after I accepted Jesus as Lord of my life. Its instruction and promise have seen me through many of the hard places I've had to walk over the years.

When God called me down from the mountaintop experiences of my conversion and right behind it, my baptism in the Holy Spirit, I found out the Christian walk was more than strolling through a primrose garden. But rather a pilgrimage through mountain ranges with valleys and peaks, deserts and rain forests, and everything in between. Sometimes the weather is so clear you can see where the climb takes you right up into God's throne room. But other times the fog is so thick you wonder if God even knows where you are.

Hebrews 11:6 always comes to my rescue during those foggy times. Like a compass, it helps me get my bearing again. I'm reminded that God is Who He is—He's God! And He rewards those who diligently seek Him! (See those two exclamation points!) God is not going to fail me. He is not going to fail you. What we've got to do is just keep seeking Him, in His Word, in prayer, in praise, in worship, in song, in hope. Keep seeking Him!

When it comes to faith in God, I believe in digging my heels into that circumstance, crossing my arms across my chest and saying "God is God, and He is able!"

Whatever circumstances you may be facing, face them with faith in God. Seek Him and keep seeking Him and know He will reward your diligence.

Hope H. Lippard
Writer/Dancer/Actress

June 23

To Become As One

"And when he had said this, he breathed on them, and saith unto them, Receive ye the Holy Ghost: Whosoever sins ye remit..."
John 20:22-23

After Jesus had breathed on His disciples, telling them to receive the Holy Ghost, the church was born. His first assignment to the new members of the Body of Christ was to forgive everybody. That assignment was for the whole church!

I believe that if the Church had practiced forgiveness throughout its history, as Jesus commanded, we wouldn't have all the divisions in the world that we have today.

But the Church, from the very beginning, failed to carry out that assignment. They didn't even want to forgive Paul!

Of course Stephen did, and his prayer changed everything. Saul of Tarsus, the greatest persecutor of the Church, became its greatest apostle. That's what forgiveness will do!

God is still interested in the unity of Christians, because where there is unity, there is power. I can see the Spirit moving the Body of Christ today to heal some of the schisms we've made amongst ourselves. Pope Paul prayed publicly for God to restore fellowship among Christians and asked Protestants to forgive Catholics for their part in the separation.

In this move of forgiveness, there is healing, and in healing, unity. It is this unity of God's children that is going to change the world!

David DuPlessis
"Mr. Pentecost"

June 24

Let Jesus Make You Whole

"But he was wounded for our transgressions, he was bruised for our iniquities: the chastisement of our peace was upon him; and with his stripes we are healed." Isaiah 53:5

To think He was lashed—and we were healed. What an exchange! It is so important that we receive the total healing God has provided us through this promise.

The most precious healing God has for us is spiritual—being united with Him in life eternal through salvation. But He doesn't stop there. No, God wants the fullness of His love and life-changing power made real in our everyday lives.

God created each person as a trinity, having three parts: spirit, soul, and body. In order to be a whole person, He wants us healed emotionally, physically and spiritually.

Even as Spirit-filled Christians, we can still be emotionally crippled. It is medically proven that a person's emotions are often the cause of their physical symptoms. Emotions like bitterness, fear, guilt (real or imagined), hate, depression, and unforgiveness. God wants to set us free from these types of destructive and negative emotions. Many times when we allow God to heal us emotionally, physical healing takes place.

God gave His only Son, Jesus Christ, as a ransom for us. The blood Jesus shed covers our sins and the stripes He received on His own body are appropriated to us as our healing. Give God your spirit, soul and body and allow Him to touch and heal each area in your life. Then you will truly become the person God created you to be—complete in Christ.

Betty Tapscott
Author/Inner Healing Teacher

June 25

Facing The Difficult

"I can do all things through Christ who strengtheneth me."   Philippians 4:13

This promise makes the challenges we face so reachable. It is our assurance from God that where our abilities stop, He'll take over. We are not limited by our humanness because God's supernatural power is always there as a reservoir of strength.

I believe this verse in totality. But the portion "all things" is especially meaningful to me. Without that inclusive word "all," my whole life would have been a complete disaster.

Twice in my life, difficult circumstances have placed me in a position to discover the truth of this verse. My father died when I was only eleven and then my mother died while I was in dental college. It was through the Lord's strength that I was able to remain victorious in my spirit and continue to face the future.

I finished dental school, and after studying abroad, God has allowed me to develop a large dental practice in Des Moines, Iowa. I have had the privilege of enhancing the smiles of many celebrities, including Jim and Tammy, Uncle Henry and others.

As in any profession, training and natural skill are important but, where they run out, it is such a privilege knowing that God is my superior advisor ready and willing to step in and help. A plaque on the shelf of my operating room reads: "God be in my hands and in my labors." It is my constant prayer along with God's promise that "I can do all things in Christ who strengthens me."

Dr. James E. Boltz
Dentist

June 26

His Temple

"And every man that striveth for the mastery is temperate in all things."   I Corinthians 9:25

There is hardly an American who has not heard all the cute little commercials and jingles advertising this brand of cereal or that candy bar. They are quite skillful in persuading people to buy their products. Well, that's what the free enterprise system is all about. However, anyone who is serious about good nutrition, will realize that many of the products contain processed white sugar whose vitamins and minerals have been stripped away, leaving empty, sickness-breeding calories.

While we are in these mortal bodies, we are responsible before God to be good stewards over our health and physical well-being. After all, what affects the physical will eventually affect the emotional and spiritual as well.

I've often said, we are killing ourselves with our mouths. In 1975, I was living the "good life," eating rich, fattening foods, drinking too much, and not resting properly. As a result, I came down with acute pancreatitis. I would have never had that disease if I had been watching my diet and taking care of the temple that God had given me.

We are the crowning glory to God's creation. He has very wonderously made the intricate, detailed and precision machine we call our bodies. It is in this body He chooses to dwell by His Holy Spirit. Be careful not to harm this precious temple. In it dwells the best heaven had to offer.

Dr. Donald Whitaker
Physician/Surgeon

June 27

Unashamed

"For I am not ashamed of the gospel of Christ: for it is the power of God unto salvation to every one that believeth...." Romans 1:16

As a young man when I accepted Jesus Christ and His call on my life to be a minister of the Gospel, I was met with great opposition by members of my family. They could not understand my desire to spend my life serving God.

They tried to discourage me from entering the ministry, but the new-found reality of joy, peace and love that Jesus brought into my life was stronger than all their arguments and persuasions. God's grace had saved me and I had to tell everyone I could that His grace was available for them, too.

Romans 1:16 describes how I believe Christians should feel about sharing the Gospel. Remembering my own salvation, it took someone willing to share Christ with me, for me, to know of God's love and how to receive it. When I accepted Christ, I was not ashamed of the Gospel. I needed the good news of salvation for the forgiveness of my sins and the power of the Holy Spirit to make me a new person.

If I do not share and live out the Gospel in sight of others, there is a possibility they may never discover God's love for themselves. In my many years of ministry, I've seen so many people like I was, who are hurting and lost with no hope, peace or love in their lives. I want them to know God offers all three through faith in Jesus Christ.

Roman 10:17 says faith comes "by hearing, and hearing by the word of God." I know that in sharing the Gospel, my faith is strengthened as well as the faith of those with whom I share.

Jack Mitchell
Pastor

June 28

The Power Of Positive Praise

"Whoso offereth praise glorifieth me: and to him that ordereth his conversation aright will I show the salvation of God."   Psalm 50:23

    The Lord is always aware of our daily needs, whether they are physical, material, spiritual or emotional. When we let the Lord Jesus Christ be first as true Lord of our whole life, our needs are met without struggle or anxiety. This passage, basically, is not a formula, but a principle that works. Multitudes have entered a new phase of their Christian walk as they also discovered the power of positive praise as faith in action!

    As soon as I acted on what this passage said, I found His salvation as well as entering into all His blessings. This verse taught me the power of the spoken word, praise, and confession. It is a sure cure for all forms of introverted personalities, depression, and discouragement.

    In the spring of 1955, my daughter Darlene's club feet were healed in answer to prayer. Being Jehovah's Witnesses, and ultra-dispensationalists, our acceptance of this miracle resulted in our being removed from fellowship from the movement.

    Some weeks later, while ignorantly visiting an Ukrainian Pentecostal church in New Hampshire, I had my first encounter with the Holy Spirit and His gifts. We were apprehended by Jesus and found our way into His Kingdom through the love and acceptance of these simple Russian believers. We began to honor God and praise Him in all situations. When we honor God in this way, He honors His Word in our lives.

Charles Trombley
Evangelist

June 29

Unlimited Mission Field

"...Go out into the highways and hedges, and compel them to come in, that my house may be filled."   Luke 14:23

My childhood could have been lived in darkest Africa because nobody ever told me about Jesus. I grew up in the ghetto, the inner city of Brooklyn. It's a different world and can't be compared with any other city in the United States. This is my ministry; to reach and love these kids for Christ.

People are moving out of the ghetto and graffito to the grass and green trees. We've set up a Sunday School for little kids and teens, to hit that specific age group. We started in a borrowed church and on day one, we outgrew it with one thousand and two kids in Sunday School. The ghetto kids are dirty and rough; people don't want to deal with them. But, I believe in those kids. We can reach two thousand kids and not go a mile away in the neighborhood. It's an unlimited field. If this were Africa, Christian leaders would say, "What a tremendous field!" Here it is, right in our own country—and it is a tremendous mission field! But people are saying, "Oh yeah, just kids."

We became aware that not a lot of material from publishing houses met the needs of newly saved kids—they were aimed at kids who'd grown up in Sunday Schools. We formed "Train Depot" and put out our own materials.

If you've been asking God for a mission field, look around your area. Chances are, you will find a special place and way to spread the Gospel like I did.

Bill Wilson
Youth Evangelist

June 30

Balance

"Jesus said unto him, I am the way, the truth, and the life: no man cometh unto the Father, but by me."   John 14:6

Balance is the key to life. Everything in life has to have a balance. When things are unbalanced, they're abnormal.

A checkbook has to balance, the ballast in a ship has to balance, and as far as we're concerned, we must have mental balance, emotional balance and spiritual balance. Jesus teaches in this verse that our ways and our life must rest upon truth to be balanced. When our life is based on truth, the better will be our way and the greater will be our life.

Truth not only is the foundation stone but causes the balance of life. Resistance to the devil is proportionate to our submission to the Lord.

Our confession has to be balanced with a confession of sin and confession of righteousness. To confess one without the other is unbalanced. Repentance without faith leads to despair, and faith without repentance is presumptuous.

Sin goes out of the life by the way of the mouth and righteousness is established in the life. Righteousness is in the life, when the mouth confesses what the heart believes. God is concerned with righteousness in our character because His will is to develop Christ's likeness in us.

Dr. Edwin L. Cole
Teacher/Evangelist

July 1

Strengthening Faith

"...and lo, I am with you alway, even unto the end of the world. Amen."   Matthew 28:20

As we see assassins at work targeting three world leaders—first President Ronald Reagan, then Pope John Paul II, and later President Anwar Sadat, it causes us to realize the accuracy of the scripture: "The earth also was corrupt before God, and the earth was filled with violence" (Genesis 6:11). That statement was recorded of Noah's day. But Luke 17:26 tells us, "And as it was in the days of Noah, so shall it be also in the days of the Son of man." You and I are living in the "days of the Son of man"—the last days before the coming of Christ.

How can we live daily in victory, in faith, in joy during these final days on earth? The Bible describes how David overcame the trials and tribulations that he encountered. And here we can realize that David was no pushover. While fleeing from King Saul, David led a motley army of 400 misfits—those "in distress...in debt...discontented." Yet David remained strong in his faith "...till I know what God will do for me" (I Samuel 22:2-3). When a jealous Saul tried to kill him, David resisted the urging of his men when a "perfect" opportunity came to slay the king. He showed mercy instead, and centuries later, you and I call David, "the sweet Psalmist of Israel." Our task is to be faithful to God. His promise to us is: "...lo, I am with you alway, even unto the end of the world. Amen" (Matthew 28:20).

Freda Lindsay
Christ For The Nations

July 2

Grin Or Growl

"As the fining pot for silver, and the furnace for gold; so is a man to his praise."
                                                        Proverbs 27:21

Praise is the catalyst that God uses to give us increase and to bring us through tough circumstances. Praise directs our focus on Jesus and His ability. We see His greatness, the greatness of God, instead of the greatness of the problems. Then the answers begin to flow our way. We can either "grin or growl." Praise keeps us grinning! Praise lifts us up, puts us on top. God is glorified, Jesus is exalted and the Holy Spirit is honored and given place to work in our lives!

I first discovered the practicality of praise when I needed healing from a tragic accident. Just shortly after I was saved, I was seriously injured in the first televised Hang Glider flight in the United States. Doctors told me I would be in a body cast for one year and then it would be two years before I could begin to walk. It was doubtful if I would be able to walk, even then, and a permanent disability was predicted.

My wife and I began praising the Lord. The Scriptures say, "...let us offer the sacrifice of praise to God continually, that is, the fruit of our lips giving thanks to his name" (Hebrews 13:15). Jesus healed me ninety days after the crash. My wife and I used a hammer and chisel and chopped the cast off. I was blessed, but the doctors nearly fainted. I was X-rayed and there was no damage found. Shortly after that I went into the ministry. I have been bragging on Jesus ever since.

Lenny D. Anderson
Pastor

_____ July 3

God Is Love

"He that loveth not knoweth not God; for God is love."   I John 4:8

Love, the most abused word in our vocabulary, is the most important. How easily we speak this word, insincerely, carelessly, or perhaps because it is expected of us. But I am persuaded that the central truth of the whole Christian Gospel is the fact that God, truly, "loves" us. Because He cares, we have hope and the expectation of living with Him throughout eternity.

To understand God's love, we must realize that it is not contaminated by human sensuality, nor is it dependent on fleshly enticements. The love of God is pure, powerful, merciful, tender, corrective, and extended to all who will desire it. It is ours for the asking and receiving.

To learn to love is to live life at its best. As a personal practice and reinforcement to my own "love walk" with Christ, I have read all five chapters of I John every day since 1965.

Every day I experience new depths in His love. I gain strength and reassurance in His promises. Loving others is no longer a chore. Fears of rejection and selfish gain are not a part of my personality, my only desire is to love without limits as I enjoy His enduring, unfailing love. Many years ago, a Sunday School teacher, godly parents, and a praying friend, demonstrated God's love to me by introducing me to the Saviour. His precious love continues to sustain me today. God is love.

Thomas A. Carruth
Bible Teacher

July 4

True Happiness

"Delight thyself also in the Lord and He shall give thee the desires of thine heart. Commit thy way unto the Lord...and He shall bring it to pass."   Psalm 37:4-5

The more I walk with the Lord, the more I realize that He is not seeking to always put us down, but rather He wants to lift us up. He wants us to prosper in everything that we do. I firmly believe that if you commit your life to the Lord, He can use you in a mighty way no matter how insignificant you feel your talents are. The key is to remain in submission and obedience to Him.

Being successful has always been important to me and I find that standing on this scripture has been a real key in obtaining the goals that I have set for myself.

I was saved at the age of nine, and received the baptism in the Holy Spirit at the age of nineteen. When I was twenty-one, the Lord called me to work at PTL. I have had many ups and downs in my Christian walk but I have found that the Lord is always faithful to bring me through the rough times.

Another verse that has been a bulwark is from Psalm 1, verse 2, "But his delight is in the law of the Lord; and in his law doth he meditate day and night."

As we meditate in His Word and let His Word become a part of our lives, we will be more able and willing to commit our ways to Him. As we delight ourselves in Him, He has promised to give us the desires of our heart.

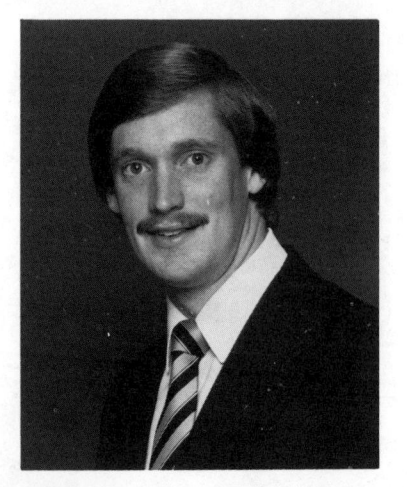

Walter Warren
Director of Cable Market

July 5

Receiving Exceeding Abundantly

"Now unto him that is able to do exceeding abundantly above all that we ask or think, according to the power that worketh in us...."
Ephesians 3:20

I have had many battles to overcome in my life and through them the Lord has turned tragedy into blessing far beyond my comprehension. No matter what we face or how large or small our dreams, God is able to do exceeding abundantly above any limits we ourselves set. Many times we tie God's hands because we set limits when He has no limits.

Recently, I suffered from a serious injury where both bones in my left leg were broken completely in two. I went through much suffering and came very close to losing my leg due to several complications. I was in a battle to keep my leg. When the doctor X-rayed it, he knew it would be about an inch shorter than my other leg if I did not undergo surgery. I knew the power of God and had seen many miracles. I told the doctor not to operate as "God would heal me." When I returned to work, I had a limp and had to use a cane. My leg was shorter than the other.

During our PTL Victory Parade in 1980, when I was very busy helping our guests at PTL, God stopped me right in the midst of all of the excitement and healed me through the laying on of hands by Charles and Francis Hunter. This was such a surprise to me, but God was there to "do exceeding abundantly above all that I asked or thought" in His perfect plan. God can do exceeding abundantly above all of your hopes, all of your dreams, all of your needs, all of your sufferings.

Nancy Hawkins Warren
PTL Producer's Dept.

July 6

Love Obeys

"If you obey my commands, you will remain in my love...My command is this: Love each other as I have loved you."
John 15:9-12 (NIV)

How much you obey shows how much you love. These verses tell us if you love the Lord Jesus Christ, you'll do what He commands you to do. His command is that we love. Not sensuously alone, or selfishly, but as He loves. The Lord says, "if you obey" you will "remain in His love." Obedience to someone is based on a meaningful relationship and mutual love and respect. It is a total commitment of heart and mind.

Continuing to describe this principle of a deepening, intimate relationship, the Lord promises joy. Complete joy comes with complete obedience.

If you want God to work in your behalf, the first step is total obedience. People often quote, "...you shall know the truth, and the truth shall make you free" (John 8:32), but the verse before it is seldom quoted. I feel the freedom promised in verse 32 is contingent upon obedience to the previous verse 31 which reads, "...If ye continue in my word, then are ye my disciples indeed." Continuing in the Word is obedience to the Word.

The Lord admonishes us over and over to "show love." According to the Scriptures the Lord is saying, "You show love and I'll do all in my power to help you."

Ernie Frierson
PTL Singers

July 7

No Fear In Love

"Beloved, think it not strange concerning the fiery trial...But rejoice...as ye are partakers of Christ's sufferings..."   I Peter 4:12-13

Going through. This phrase rings throughout all Christendom as a battle cry of perseverance. Indeed, we all need to learn the lesson of steadfastness, absolute confidence in the Lord Jesus Christ, and consistency in our behavior/attitude toward God. However, many Christians, because of hurts, disappointments, and the fear of rejection are living beneath their privilege as children of the King of Kings and the Lord of Lords, Jesus Christ.

Their suffering is very real, though a remedy exists. Feelings are neither right nor wrong, but they definitely *are*. The healing process begins by recognizing the root of our fears. The culprit is usually pride, or the desire to be accepted by our fellowman. The decision must be made, whether to gain our fellowman's acceptance, or be led by the Holy Spirit into a life-building, fulfilling relationship with the Lord Jesus Christ.

God's unfailing love is the cure. When balanced with a prayer time, study ritual, and positive confession, negative feelings can be overcome.

I know the power of God's love. I experienced it nearly twelve years ago in a rehabilitation center in Miami, Florida. I had been a one hundred dollar a day heroin addict and thegirlfriend of a gangster. One of God's precious witnesses prayed for me one night and I was delivered and saved. God's love alone dispels fears. He truly empowers.

Sandra Fatau
Singer

July 8

He Cares And Provides

"I have been young, and now am old; yet have I not seen the righteous forsaken, nor his seed begging bread."   Psalm 37:25

I was raised in a minister's home. I have heard so many lament they were "P.K.'s" and how they were so restricted as "preachers' kids,' but I never resented the restrictions. The spiritual benefits in our family and home were so abundant, I knew we were blessed of God.

I was the tenth of fourteen children in our family, and we all grew up during the Great Depression. True to the above scripture, we were never without food for our table. We were extremely poor, but my mother always set a good table.

My father initiated a love in our hearts for the Lord and for each other that has remained to this day. We were taught to truly trust the Lord, not only day to day, but in establishing life's goals.

We were constantly assured of God's good intent toward us, that whether there might be famine, trouble, or illness, the Lord would *never* forsake us.

This scripture has been my comfort and confidence. I *know* the Lord *will* provide. I wrote this concept one day in one of my songs, "Consider the Lilies." And it's a truth we can rely on, "...as the Lord clothes the lilies and feeds the sparrow," He will just as certainly care and provide for us.

Joel Hemphill
Singer/Composer

July 9

Delight In Him

"Delight thyself also in the Lord; and he shall give thee the desires of thine heart. Commit thy way unto the Lord...and he shall bring it to pass."   Psalm 37:4-5

The very first time I ever read Psalm 37:4, I really believed it and have tried to live it.

I came from a broken home, my parents divorced when I was only four years old and I was raised by my grandparents. The greatest desire of my heart was to have a Christian husband, children, and a happy Christian home of my own.

I accepted the Lord at the age of 15. The love message won my heart. When I heard from a pulpit that Jesus loved me, I responded. The verse that so revolutionized my entire being was I John 4:10.

I began to design my life according to the Word of God. God can't do it by Himself, He needs cooperation from us. I seriously desired someone to share my life. I searched in the right places for that special person. I found my husband in the house of God.

We see so much flaunting of immorality that husbands and wives being unfaithful is accepted. From the day of our marriage, Joel and I have loved each other exclusively. This is God's perfect plan, His perfect plan to create mutual respect and trust. Loving my husband is a part of delighting myself in the Lord.

I have a happy Christian home, three children who love the Lord as we do. We're working together for the Lord. This is greater than I expected, greater than I deserved, but the Lord honors His Word. He gives you the desires of your heart.

LaBreeska Hemphill
Singer

July 10

You're In His Sight

"Greater love hath no man than this, that a man lay down his life for his friends." John 15:13

One day my dog Nikky, a beautiful German Shepherd, and I spent two days in the cool mountains. When we returned to the hot valley, Nikky was exhausted and sat in the shade of a horse trailer and rested. He had a right to be tired, he'd walked fifty miles and I'd ridden it on horseback. I decided to exercise my other horse. I knew Nikky was tired so I told him to 'stay!' I climbed on and began to lope across the field. After I'd gone a half mile, I glanced over my shoulder and there was Nikky, running with all he had in him, to keep me in his sight. At first I got mad because he'd disobeyed, but then I realized he loved me so much he just had to keep me in his sight.

That day, Nikky rode a horse for the first time, because he'd run so hard in the heat he couldn't walk anymore. I laid him in the shade of the horse trailer and put my hand on his shoulder and said, "How's it going Nikky?"

He looked at me a long moment then he closed his eyes and died. As I sat beside him crying that day, the Holy Spirit whispered to me, "Lee, just like Nikky broke his heart to keep you in sight...so Jesus broke His heart on Calvary so He could keep you in His sight throughout all eternity."

My friend, today, let's take time to thank Jesus for the terrible price He paid for you and for me—to keep us in His sight.

Lee Robbins
Singer/PTL Host

July 11

Sing His Praises

"For in him we live, and move, and have our being." Acts 17:28

The Lord used music to speak to people all through the Bible. I use music to speak to people about God. My co-writer is the Holy Spirit. I like to have my music minister to the spirit. I try to stick very close to the Scriptures with lyrics. I want my songs to bring life—the new life of the Holy Spirit.

School is always on—school is never out spiritually. We are always learning and being renewed. God's Word renews us. We're commanded in Romans 12:2 "...be ye transformed by the renewing of your mind...."

The first time I was ever in church was when I was thirteen years old. A fellow up front was playing guitar and singing, "When He Reached Down His Hand For Me." The words of that song ministered to my heart.

I wanted to go forward, but hesitated, finally the evangelist invited me. I not only went up, I went up to the platform and started singing, "Coming Home." And I started a ministry of song as soon as I got saved.

And song *does* minister. Recently, I received a letter from thirty teenagers in Australia who had bought one of my records. They asked the meaning of the words, and said, "We want to find what makes you happy." I answered their questions and sent my song albums, "Seed of Abraham," and "Whole Lot Of People." Back came this reply, "Praise Jesus, He's real!" They listened to the songs, read my letter, and all thirty were saved.

David Ingles
Singer/Musician

July 12

A Servant's Heart

"...whosoever will be great among you, shall be your minister: And whosoever of you will be the chiefest, shall be servant of all."
Mark 10:43-44

These beautiful words of my Lord are becoming a way of life for me. Every time I read them I am impressed with the simplicity and wisdom they express. These words of Jesus state a fact which many Christians haven't yet discovered and many others have never tried. It is so easy to get into the game of "one-upmanship." Worldly success is measured in terms of outdoing someone else and racing up the promotional ladder to the top. But that goal is never what one thinks it will be. The "top" is so often disappointing and the victories hollow and empty. Often the victors are possessors of nothing more than ulcers, heart attacks, and broken families in the end.

In God's kingdom, the quickest way up is down. God does not hold us accountable for how we measure up to the competition. He doesn't even consider that, He does hold us responsible for how we measure up to His example of service to others. The prime prerequisite for being Sons of God is that we have a servant's heart. The more we become like Jesus, the more willing we are to serve others. There is release from bondage in that. We don't have to be constantly "checking our score" or worrying about who is outdistancing us. Rather, we can begin to rise to our own potential in Him. For years I have noticed, even in the church, the jealousy prevalent over those who had the "chief seats in the synagogue." Christ said, "...whosoever shall exalt himself shall be abased; and he that shall humble himself shall be exalted" (Matthew 23:12).

L. Calvin Bacon
Pastor

_____ July 13

A Just God And You

"Give therefore thy servant an understanding heart to judge thy people, that I may discern between good and bad...."   I Kings 3:9a

One of the most neglected areas of Christian understanding today is the justice of God. God *is* a God of love, and that's how most of us know Him. But He's also a God of justice. God was so pleased with the above prayer of Solomon for wisdom because it evidenced a concern for the kind of discernment that would bring justice to God's people.

Scripture speaks much of justice. This fact has been somewhat obscured by our familiarity with the King James Version of the Bible, in which the word for "justice" is most frequently translated "judgment." The Psalms are full of promises that God will some day administer perfect justice. Justice in ancient days was often sold at a premium to the highest bidder, a practice not altogether dead in our country today. Promises are made by God to free prisoners in the Old Testament, and Jesus echoed these promises as part of the Good News He preached personally. The depth of God's concern for justice has considerable bearing on my ministry with prisoners. If justice was a vital concern for God, it ought to be for me also, just as much as love and compassion.

We as Christians cannot reflect all of the Spirit of God and be unconcerned with human justice issues. We as Christians can't live life in a cocoon, merely satisfied with our own piety and spirituality, ignoring the demands of justice in society. That's why I'm trying to focus attention on the plight of prisoners.

Charles Colson
Prison Evangelist

July 14

Hide The Word In Your Heart

"Thy word have I hid in my heart..."
Psalm 119:11

Because I have hidden the Word of God in my heart, the Holy Spirit brings to my remembrance, the verses that I need at the time I need them for effective ministry. It is such verses as: "I can do all things through Christ which strengtheneth me" (Philippians 4:13); "...with God, nothing is impossible" (Luke 1:37); "Come unto me, all ye that labor and are heavy laden, and I will give you rest" (Matthew 11:28); "Cast thy burden upon the Lord, and he shall sustain thee" (Psalm 55:22) that have kept me during times of distress and temptation.

Recently I experienced circumstances so distressing that I could not feel the love of God. It was through the Word hidden in my heart and the fact that God's Word is truth that I realized God loved me, whether I could feel it or not. It was with childlike faith I accepted the verses that said over and over, "I Love You." They sustained me during this time of drought.

God is also saying to you today, "I have loved you with an everlasting love: therefore with loving-kindness have I drawn thee" (Jeremiah 31:3).

The Word of God is our only road map to heaven. Study it, heed its instruction and live in victory. Meditate on its passages regularly, and commit yourself to its lifestyle. Hide its principles in your heart.

Ellen Baker
*PTL's July
Employee of the Month*

July 15

God's Love

"For God so loved the world, that he gave his only begotten Son, that whosoever believeth in him...have everlasting life."   John 3:16

Being in the Salvation Army is my way of showing my love for Jesus Christ. God is too big for my small heart, too big for what He really means to me. We live in a world of pain and suffering. We live in a world where millions of people face hunger daily, where disease is rampant and hope is in short supply. The Gospel is the answer to these problems, we have to deal with people and the circumstances in which they are living. If they are hungry, we have to feed them; if they are naked, we have to clothe them; if they are oppressed, we have to free them; if they are in danger of life, we have to protect them.

We must put our love for God into action. "Soup, soap and salvation" is the slogan of the Salvation Army. This means we put our love for God to work. We find an expression of this in I John 4:9-10, "In this was manifested the love of God toward us, because that God sent his only begotten Son into the world, that we might live through him. Herein is love, not that we loved God, but that he loved us, and sent his Son to be the propitiation for our sins." God loved and He expressed that love. What He did was send His son to earth, for our sakes, cause Him to die on a cross, for our sakes, and then He raised Him from the dead again, for our sakes.

Eva Den Hartog, Major
Officer Salvation Army

July 16

He Will Comfort You

"And I will pray the Father, and he shall give you another Comforter, that he may abide with you for ever."   John 14:16

For years I'd wanted more of God. Then in 1964, I met Lovenia James, a lady who has become a dear friend of mine. She told me about the baptism of the Holy Spirit and God filled my hungry heart.

Being filled with the Spirit allowed me to know Jesus more intimately and gave me a clearer, more meaningful understanding of His Word, the Bible.

His Holy Spirit was not only a guide and helper, but I found out what a wonderful comforter He can be.

I'd suffered two great losses in my life through the deaths of loved ones. My first husband, the founder of an insurance company, passed away and later I married a rancher who died a few years afterward.

The comfort of the Holy Spirit within gave me courage and cheer to go on living my life and serving God in an even greater way. Since I've experienced sorrow and grief, I am now able to share with other widows about His overcoming power.

To anyone who has lost a loved one in death, I say, count your blessings for the good years. Don't dwell in the past, but stay busy in the Lord's work because there's so much to do before He returns. And keep looking forward to that grand reunion in Heaven.

Eleanor Foster
Laywoman

_____ July 17

He Makes The Difference

"We are troubled on every side, yet not distressed; we are perplexed, but not in despair."
II Corinthians 4:8

God promises He'll take care of us. He commands us that though we are troubled we're not to be distressed, and even though we're perplexed by our circumstances we are not to despair. Anything about any of us that's any good is Jesus. Everything I have or am is because of Jesus, from my head down to my toes. I can never begin singing without saying, "Lord, give me the anointing of the Holy Spirit." HE makes the difference, if there be any magic in us, it's the Holy Spirit.

In April of 1975, I was rushed to Mayo Clinic and given only one year to live. My pastor and I planned my funeral. I asked to be buried in the churchyard and he was working through the red tape involved. Then, the Spirit of the Lord came and washed all the heart disease away. Two years later, I had a heart examination and doctors found the new by-pass arteries working fine and amazingly the formerly clogged arteries were also functioning.

I received a second chance at life. I don't care what people think of me anymore. I'm me and it's all you're gonna get! I learned if I place God first in my life, it's O.K. HE must like what I'm doing. The Lord says, "...we dare not make ourselves of the number or compare ourselves with some that commend themselves...measuring themselves by themselves, and comparing themselves among themselves, are not wise." Later, He says, "But he that glorieth, let him glory in the Lord. For not he that commendeth himself is approved, but whom the Lord commendeth" (II Corinthians 10:17-18).

Vestal Goodman
Singer

July 18

Four Steps To Mending Marriage

"He that covereth his sins shall not prosper; but whoso confesseth and forsaketh them shall have mercy." Proverbs 28:13

The Lord helped me put together four steps that will narrow the distance between troubled couples. The first begins with faith in Jesus. Calvary bridges gaps. I've seen over three thousand couples having trouble in their marriages, but I've never seen distance that Calvary can't bridge!

After faith in Jesus, a couple needs to face the issues. Sometimes it's easier to hide or cover the issues that are dividing them. The Scriptures address this in Proverbs 28:13, "He that covers his sins shall not prosper; but whoso confesses and forsaketh them shall have mercy." Once we face our situations, we've overcome our biggest fear. Then we can find the courage, through faith in Jesus, to face and solve the issues dividing.

The third step is forgiveness. We have to forgive! You really are the one who hurts the most when you can't forgive. A faith in Jesus gives us the grace to forgive others and is what helps couples find the forgiveness they need.

The fourth step is flexibility. Although you have forgiven, there will be tension and pressure points. Here you have to be flexible with each other and meet each other's needs. Paul gives us a good thought filter in Philippians 4:8, "...whatsoever things are true, whatsoever things are honest, whatsoever things are just,...are pure, ...lovely,...of good report; if there be any virtue,...any praise, think on these things."

With these four steps, there is no such thing as a hopeless marriage.

Dr. Richard Dobbins
Marriage Counselor

July 19

Self-sufficient Through Christ

"I have strength for all things in Christ who empowers me—I am ready for anything and equal to anything through Him...."
Philippians 4:23 (Amplified Version)

During my nearly twenty years as a pastor, and as a graduate trained Counseling Psychologist, I have observed in a one-to-one counseling rapport the devastating effect of a negative self-image. I have found that many people suffer severe ego-damaging experiences in early childhood and never seem to recover. I further found that the usual psychological approach to therapy was slow, cumbersome, and frequently simply did not work over an extended period of time.

Through prayer and the adaptation of scriptural principles, I discovered a definitive path to a self-image recovery. By directing the patient lovingly to an in-depth awareness of God's Word and the person of Jesus Christ, a new self-image emerged, complete in Jesus' name.

Simply stated, my "Can't do patients" became "Can do Christians." I discovered that finding and following God's plan for one's life is the soundest and most lasting way to the vital ingredient of self-confidence, it is also the best way to keep the feeling of self-confidence growing. It's great to discover, for yourself and others, that one can step from a defeated, self-condemning person to an "I can do all things through Jesus" person.

The mixture of God's Holy Spirit, His Holy Word, and the principles of psychological healing is a great spiritual discovery. Truly the Bible is the greatest psychological manual in the entire world of humanity.

Earl J. Banning
Pastor

July 20

Faith—A Lifestyle

"As ye have therefore received Christ Jesus the Lord, so walk...Rooted and built up in him, and stablished in the faith, as ye have been taught...with thanksgiving." Colossians 2:6-7

I was very fortunate to be raised in a Christian environment by wonderful parents. At an early age, I received the Lord Jesus Christ into my heart—*by faith.*

Over the years, I have learned that while faith is essential for receiving salvation, it is also essential in receiving all the fullness of life God has for us. It was *by faith* that we came to Christ. It is by being *established in faith* that we continue to grow in Christ.

The broad principle for our life is to search the Word of God, find His promises for us, and act *in faith* to believe these promises. Remember how simple it was to receive Christ once you decided to accept Him? That decision was an acknowledgement of your faith.

Now as a Christian, you still have choices to make. You can accept (in faith) the promises of God's Word. Or you can reject (in doubt) God's promises. It was the simplicity of faith that opened the door to your salvation. It is that same uncomplicated expression of faith that will open the doors to your healing, prosperity, and receiving of God's Holy Spirit.

Begin to "root and build up" your inner spirit by feeding on God's Word. Think faith; act faith; walk faith, and you will begin to see God's power in your life as you have never seen it before. Make faith your lifestyle.

Major Richard L. Engel
Air Force Pilot

July 21

Women Are Special People

"Whose adorning let it not be that outward adorning...But let it be the hidden man of the heart...a meek and quiet spirit, which is in the sight of God of great price."   I Peter 3:3-4

We are instructed in Proverbs 16:3 to commit our way unto the Lord and He will establish our paths. As I dedicated my walk in life to the Lord, He led me into a very unusual and previously all-male environment—military aviation.

It is a profession that by nature is extremely unfeminine. The clothes, equipment, and peer groups are all designed for men. As a woman, I had to deal with my self-identity in Christ. Through prayer and studying scripture pertaining to women, God led me to a deeper understanding of what is truly important and precious to Him—the heart.

The virtuous woman described in Proverbs 30:10-31, shows a woman who is not only a cherished wife and beloved mother, but one who is creative, industrious, and even enterprising. But above all, she is a woman who's heart is towards God (v. 30).

Society pushes us to prove ourselves equal or even superior to men and yet at the same time advocates exploitation of women through fashion and our entertainment media. One way or the other we are expected to measure our worth according to the recognition we can gain.

It is when we know our worth in Jesus Christ that we realize we are already special people—in His sight. The adorning of our hearts with the spirit of Jesus Christ is how we will discover true fulfillment as women. Check out your heart's reflection in the mirror of your soul and see if you are wearing Jesus Christ.

Connie Engel
Wife/Mother/Pilot

July 22

He Added All These Things

"...seek ye first the kingdom of God, and his righteousness, and all these things shall be added unto you."   Matthew 6:33

This verse in Matthew 6 was one of the first verses to "come alive" for me when I was newly saved. I did most of my work of singing in Las Vegas-type night clubs. Four months after I became a Christian, the Lord gave me the faith to trust Him for a better way of life and I gave up the night club dates. At the time, I feared our standard of living would go down, but my love for Jesus was so strong I didn't care. How wrong I was—God had a wonderful surprise for me and quite the opposite happened. He showed me that, if I would take care of His business, He would take care of my business. He has proven faithful in "adding all things" for ten years now.

Another wonderful verse the Lord has made real to me is II Corinthians 5:17, "...if any man be in Christ...old things are passed away...all things are become new." It's true, God has added all new things. The things I used to love, I now hate and the things I used to hate, I now love. I had fame, fortune, children, a good marriage, health, a career; but I was unhappy, unfulfilled, unsatisfied, not wanting to live but scared to die because I knew I wouldn't go to heaven.

I was in this condition one June morning in church when my heart cried out to God, "God, don't pass me by!" He replied, "Wanda, walk with Me." For the past ten years, He's given my life purpose and direction. I know I'll go to heaven when I die.

Wanda Jackson
Country/Gospel Singer

July 23

An Instrument Of Harvest

"...I will make thee a new sharp threshing instrument...thou shalt thresh the mountains, and beat them small, and shalt make the hills as chaff."   Isaiah 41:15

I was on a Dutch freighter in a stormy, treacherous sea making my first missionary journey when God gave me this verse. Traveling in Africa, I didn't know or understand the African and everything seemed scary and harsh. I was afraid. God led my heart to this verse, "...I will make thee a new sharp threshing instrument...." I thought that meant that God would put into my hand some special gift, but no, God was saying I would be a threshing instrument. He has used me as the cutting edge in His harvest field. I believed it, God acted on it and in one country alone we registered over 10,000 decisions.

The Lord promised, "thou shalt thresh the mountains...." Jesus spoke of our mountains of struggle, trial, tribulation and suffering; but He said, "I will thresh your mountains and beat them small." And the whirlwind of His Spirit shall scatter their residue to the corners of the earth.

I stand boldly on God's Word and declare: anyone can come out of the hot oven of trial and triumph victoriously through Jesus Christ. Christ *is* our strength, Christ *is* our victory. The Scriptures encourage us, "I can do all things through Christ which strengtheneth me" (Philippians 4:13). Stand on this scripture, take Christ at His word. You *can* do all things through Christ. You *can* be His sharp instrument of harvest.

Paul E. Olson
New Day Ministries

July 24

By His Power

"...Not by might, nor by power, but by my spirit, saith the Lord of hosts."
Zechariah 4:6

From the moment of my conversion, God began preparing me for full-time service. I have always sought to live His will and have never strayed from the Lord. I am continually amazed and thankful for all the blessings of God.

This challenge to all who are involved in Christian service, success and fruitful ministry depend on your ability to "rest" in His strength and allow God to be God in all things, giving Him glory for the miracle He performs, great or small.

I began preaching when I was sixteen years old. Before my first revival, I prayed every day, read my Bible every day, really sought the Lord, asking Him to use me and bless the revival. In one night, fifty people found the Lord and many others were filled with the Holy Spirit.

After that night, I didn't continue praying and reading the Bible like I should have, and the following week no one was saved. It seemed like nothing was happening. I got down on my knees, crying out to God, "Why have you let me down, Lord? I came all the way from Kansas City to here in Texas." I finished praying and lifted my head and looked up to see on the wall a plaque with the words from Zechariah 4:6 written on it. I said, "Yes, Lord, my eyes are open." I learned that God does the work, and He blesses human instrumentality, but only when the person gives the glory to God.

Tommy Barnett
Pastor

_____ July 25

My Guilt Was Lifted

"Being justified freely by his grace through the redemption that is in Christ Jesus."
Romans 3:24

It is possible to let your life waste away to nothing. I know, I did it. I started mainlining heroin when I was twenty. My boyfriend wanted me to see what a big thrill it was. You think you can just try it once, but you can't. First thing you know, you're hooked. It can happen to anyone. When I was twenty-five, my parents asked me to move out of their home. My born-again Christian uncle kept in touch with me. One night he invited me to dinner. He put me in front of a mirror and made me look at the waste I'd become. He said, "Look at what you've done to yourself, the waste you've become. Go to the Walter Hoving Home, they can help you." I was skeptical, I'd tried rehab programs and psychiatrists. I sneered, "What can Christ do for me?" I grew up never hearing about Jesus or salvation. I didn't know He died for everyone in the whole world, including me.

My uncle began praying for me. When you pray for someone, things happen. During that next week, I lost my job, I lost my apartment and I lost my boyfriend. I went to my uncle on a Saturday and said, "OK, I'll go the Walter Hoving Home." By Monday I was there.

I felt so much guilt! I was weighed down with it. I read Romans 3:23 and learned of God's promise to us, "For *all* have sinned, and come short of the glory of God;" then the next verse gave the wonderful provision for guilt, "...justified by His grace...," I was relieved of guilt. Jesus can relieve you of your guilt just as He did it for me.

Stephanie Pappas
Former Walter Hoving Home Resident

July 26

All Things Become New

"Therefore if any man be in Christ, he is a new creature: old things are passed away; behold, all things are become new."
II Corinthians 5:17

This scripture has challenged me to look at my own personal life and action. It has motivated me to evaluate my lifestyle. Am I, in fact, "a new creature"; have "old things passed away and *all things* become new"? Are these principles active in my life? Hearing other people use this verse in their testimony before I was born again brought me under great conviction.

However, after confessing my sins and repenting, this scripture defines my personal feelings and experience.

As a child nine years old, I gave my heart to Christ and decided I would be a missionary. During my teen years, my attention was diverted and I became an agnostic. I married at twenty and two months later committed my heart and life totally to Jesus Christ. I joyfully determined to follow and serve our Lord and Saviour, Jesus Christ. I have done so the past thirty-three years.

The purpose and plan of God became more clear and revealed with each passing year and I rejoice in the words of Jesus. One other scripture that has blessed me also is Titus 3:5, "Not by works of righteousness which we have done, but according to his mercy he saved us, by the washing of regeneration, and renewing of the Holy Ghost." He continually gives fresh new conviction in our hearts in our encounter with Jesus Christ.

Gerald Derstine
Pres. Gospel Crusade

July 27

Willing Clay

"Therefore if any man be in Christ, he is a new creature: old things are passed away; behold, all things are become new."

II Corinthians 5:17

I was twenty-seven when I accepted Jesus Christ as Lord of my life. I had grown up knowing about God and that He loved me. But, it wasn't until I met Jesus personally that I began to see the marvelous power of God become a reality in my life.

Before accepting Jesus Christ as Lord, I lived for myself. Now that I know Him, all I want to do is serve Him and have my life count for Him. Accepting Him has made that huge difference in me.

When Jesus is number one in your life, the old things that seemed so important before become insignificant. God's forgiveness through faith in Jesus Christ washes away your past. *All* things become new! Being alive takes on a different meaning—a life-changing meaning!

Jesus is in the business of changing lives and giving them new meaning and purpose. He is the Master Potter whose skilled hands can mold and shape our hearts and lives into beautiful vases and vessels to be filled with Him. All we have to do is be willing clay.

If there is anything in you that resists the movement of the Holy Spirit in your life, confess it to Jesus. Ask Him to remove all your known and unknown areas of stubbornness so you will be more yielded to the touch of His hand. Then place yourself in His hands and let Him begin making all things new in you.

Casey Enda
Housewife

July 28

Parents As Prophets

"And ye fathers, provoke not your children to wrath: but bring them up in the nurture and admonition of the Lord."   Ephesians 6:4

The Lord has blessed our ministry with delinquent girls. We see girls rehabilitated from sadness and sin into vibrant, new lives for His glory. Like any other ministry, one must be called of the Lord. Without the definite knowledge my wife and I had been called and chosen for this work, there would have been times of overwhelming discouragement. When you are positive the Lord has put you in a ministry, you can be positive the results are in His hands.

We know and have experienced the fact that anyone can be rehabilitated and born anew in Jesus Christ. We have former murderers in our home, former prostitutes, former lesbians, former drug addicts—and we realize—in God's sight, they are pure and reborn because of His work on Calvary. The Lord's invitation is universal, "...him that cometh to me I will in no wise cast out" (John 6:37).

The needier the soul—the more eager a person is for the Saviour. We shared the Word with fifty women prisoners at Rikers Island. When we invited them to make Christ Lord of their lives, forty stood to accept Christ.

Parents should be very careful how they speak to their children. Too often they're prophets when they say, "You're going to end up in prison." They're right, but they've taken the wrong approach. The Scriptures warn, "...provoke not your children to wrath: but bring them up in the nurture and admonition of the Lord."

John Benton
*Author/Head of
Walter Hoving Home*

July 29

He Wonderfully Comforts

"What a wonderful God we have—he is the Father of our Lord Jesus Christ...source of every mercy...the one who wonderfully comforts and strengthens us..." II Corinthians 1:3 (LB)

When girls first come to the Walter Hoving Home, we are with them—to comfort them while they make the adjustments of being there. Many are coming off drugs, many are hysterical and upset. We sit with them and pray with them and try to help them understand how precious they are to God.

Our girls range in age from ten to fifty. Since 1969, we've had about three hundred girls through our home. We try to give them a sense of balance to their lives. Psalm 119, verse 71 states, "It is good for me that I have been afflicted; that I might learn thy statutes." We teach that anyone can learn from their afflictions and troubles. We teach them pride. When a girl cooks a good meal and others appreciate it, it does so much for her to know she is appreciated. We give them responsibility and they don't let us down.

Memorizing scripture is a very important part of our program. God promises,"...my word...shall not return unto me void..." (Is. 55:11). God's Word changes us in the inner man where it counts. When you memorize Scripture, you always have it. God uses the Word to work in our lives—it doesn't return void.

II Corinthians 1:4 tells us, "when others are troubled, needing our sympathy and encouragement, we can pass on to them this same help and comfort God has given us." That's the reason we have afflictions and troubles, so we can help and understand when others are going through the same problems.

Elsie Benton
Wife of John Benton
Walter Hoving Home

July 30

Grace Abounding

"And God is able to make all grace abound toward you; that ye, always having all sufficiency in all things, may abound to every good work." II Corinthians 9:8

My wife, Wanda Jackson, and I were saved together June 6th, 1971. We were at a point in our lives where we had just about everything the world could offer. We had everything except inner joy and peace of mind. Then a young preacher came and shared three important truths with us. 1. It doesn't matter who you are, you need Christ in your life. 2. It doesn't matter what you have—you will never have "abundant life" until you know Christ. 3. You don't have to give up or change anything to come to God—come just as you are. These three truths helped us to know we needed Jesus in our lives. We dedicated our lives to Him in a little church shortly after realizing these truths.

The only explanation for the many beautiful things we have is "by the grace of God." Many times He has performed miracles and has supernaturally met our needs. Not only has He met our needs but there has been enough left over to give to others. The words of Psalm 37:4 have proven true in our lives, "Delight thyself also in the Lord; and he shall give thee the desires of thine heart." In Matthew 6:33, the Lord promises if we seek Him, He will provide our material needs, "But seek ye first the kingdom of God, and his righteousness; and all these things shall be added unto you." The secret is in seeking Him first, making Him first choice in your life.

Wendell Goodman
*President Wanda Jackson
Evangelistic Association*

July 31

Joy In My Soul

"I will sing of mercy and judgment: unto thee, O Lord, will I sing."   Psalm 101:1

It is possible for one to possess joy in the soul without realizing that joy is there. In the past years, I have signed autographs by the thousands, sometimes with a personal message to a fan. Always, after signing my name, I write Psalm 101:1.

We know when there is joy in the heart, when all goes well, when obstacles, trials and testing are on the decline, the heart feels happy. That does not mean there is joy in the soul. There is also joy of the mind. When the mind has made plans for material success and those plans are achieved, the mind can be filled with joy. Sometimes God will not get the glory from our success, which may keep the joy in the soul from developing to its fullest.

Joy in one's soul cannot be obtained. Joy in one's soul has to be lived out through hard trials, heavy burdens, broken promises, broken spirits, sorrows and sadness. The heart can feel the pain and the mind can feel the pressure, but the soul which thrives not on circumstances can feel the peace of God. He'll never leave you, God never forsakes, and God remembers His Word and watches over it.

This is when the joy of the soul can sing, "His eye is on the sparrow, I know He watches over me." This is "soul singing." When I can say, "Ability, musicianship, shut up and get out of the way, my soul wants to sing," I am truly a soul sister in more ways than one. Jesus has put a song in my soul. Praise God, there is joy in my soul.

Willa Dorsey
Concert Gospel Artist

August 1

More Than Conquerors

"Nay, in all these things we are more than conquerors through him that loved us."
Romans 8:37

Many productive, useful years are wasted as people continue to deny their need for the Lord. When turmoil strikes, disappointments arise, they forget His love, resist His comfort, and disregard His direction. What a waste! Yet, I can identify with this attitude completely, because for forty years I roamed around in this world trying to find out what love really was. Then the Lord came into my life, and all the fallacies of Christianity taking away everything were dissolved. I received everything of real value, peace of mind, fulfillment, security, and dedication to the "lover of my soul." All the other, material gain, notoriety, and pride in accomplishments seemed trivial to the joy of having Jesus as my Lord!

It is so important, too, for us to know how to maintain this victory we have in Christ. First, we must defeat Satan by getting ourselves together as individuals. Second, we must get involved with and care for others, our families, our neighbors, classmates, working companions, and so on. We must bring them to a saving knowledge of the Lord Jesus Christ. This will unify the "Body of Christ." It will be this unity that defeats Satan ultimately, he's not used to it. By standing united, realizing our power and authority, submitting our all to Christ, we can resist Satan's deceptions. Remember, we are already victorious. We are more than conquerors through Christ.

Rosey Grier
Actor/Football Star

August 2

Crucified With Christ

"I am crucified with Christ: nevertheless I live; yet not I, but Christ liveth in me...I live by the faith of the Son of God...who...gave himself for me." Galatians 2:20

Many years ago, when I was only a child, I remember going to an old outdoor revival meeting. I can remember only a few things about that night, but one thing has remained in my mind all these years. The preacher used Galatians 2:20 as his text. He gave us a way to remember this reference in Galatians, he said to think of two electrical systems; a 110 circuit system and a 220 circuit system. He emphasized the 220 is the most powerful. Thank God, that stuck with me. Christ living in me is the most powerful!

This scripture deals with life through death...we live as Christians because we die to sin. When we accept Jesus as our Saviour and Lord, we are "passed from death unto life." This passage teaches that the Christian life is a dual one and even though Christ does live in us, we have to continue to live in the world and be human. As I live my life here on this earth, I sometimes fall and make mistakes, but whenever I feel discouraged, I always remember, "I live by the faith of the Son of God...." Christ reminds me that the chance to live in Christ is an individual choice that man must make while he yet lives on this earth. When he turns to Christ for life, his motives change. He becomes a "new man," the old man dies. The new man lives "...through Christ...."

Johnny Cook
Tenor
Happy Goodman Family

August 3

Fulfilling All Righteousness

"...for thus it becometh us to fulfill all righteousness... And Jesus, when he was baptized, went up straightway out of the water...."
Matthew 3:15-16

Although I have attended church for as long as I can remember, it wasn't until my early twenties that I totally surrendered myself to God and to His purposes for my life. While I began to feel a desire to be baptized, I longed for each step in the Lord to be realized in me to its fullest depth, and I began to seek the Lord for a greater understanding concerning water baptism.

He brought me to the above scriptures and, as I meditated upon them, the Holy Spirit caused me to realize that although Jesus had never committed a sin against the Father, He had yet to "fulfill all righteousness," and with His baptism the time came when Jesus, the man, surrendered Himself wholly and completely to God's eternal purpose for His life. It was with that surrender that the Holy Spirit descended upon Him and His ministry and His walk toward the cross began.

He could have chosen to live a blameless life without going to the cross, but in that moment, He committed Himself before both God and man to do His Father's will, even unto death, that He might bring life to us all. He fulfilled *all* righteousness through surrender and obedience and I realized that I, too, must identify with Jesus in TOTAL commitment unto death of every area in my life in order that I might be a source of His resurrection life to those around me.

Linda Ivey
*PTL's August
Employee of the Month*

August 4

A Guaranteed Protection

"After these things the word of the Lord came unto Abram in a vision, saying, Fear not, Abram: I am thy shield, and thy exceeding great reward." Genesis 15:1

I can remember a time, several years ago, when I felt every time I stood up, I had nothing to say that would interest people. I was going through a terrible spiritual depression.

Unfortunately, I had been scheduled to speak at a huge university in Tulsa, and I was really nervous. There's something intimidating about standing in front of a university crowd. You feel they're all a bunch of big brains and forget they're people with emotions and needs like everyone else.

I got down on my knees and said, "Lord, I'm scared to go out there. I can't do it." Somehow this scripture came into my mind, and suddenly it hit me that God was telling me, "Look, I'll protect you. If someone jeers, laughs, heckles you, or asks you a question you don't know the answer to, it's O.K. I'm your protection. Don't worry about it."

The Lord also assured me that He was my exceeding great reward and said, "You are important to me. Not just because you're an evangelist, but because you're My son, My child, and I love you."

What a tremendous thing to know, that nothing can separate us from God's deep, protecting love. It's that great love that is going to shield us in every situation we find ourselves. No matter where we're called, we can go forth in all confidence!

Leighton Ford
Evangelist

August 5

The Wonderful Faithfulness Of God

"For this my son was dead, and is alive again; he was lost, and is found...." Luke 15:24

I know the wonderful reality of this verse: "...he *was* lost, and *is* found...." Twenty-three years ago, my husband and I separated, he kidnapped my three-year-old son. All through those lonely years, I never gave up the search, spending a lot of time traveling to large cities, calling every Lane in the book hoping they knew my son. For twenty-three years I got a "no" answer.

A church group in Detroit organized a bus tour to PTL. I used my last $50 to come on the tour. At the motel room the first night, I did what I'd done for years and started to call every Lane in the book. My first call, I explained, "I'm a mother looking for her son, have you every heard of Larry Lane?" Amazingly, she had. She gave me his address and phone number and I called him. I heard his voice for the first time in twenty-three years. The Lord is still in the miracle working business, the son I never expected to see traveled all night and met me at PTL the next morning.

Then I saw how wonderfully faithful God has been. My son is Pastor Larry Lane, a Baptist preacher. I had worried he'd be an alcoholic or drug addict but Praise God! He's a wonderful Lord, it's the greatest thing to hear my son is a Christian who'd been praying for me all these years. I know the truth of, "...the earnest prayer of a righteous man has great power and wonderful results" (James 5:16-Living Bible).

Laura Lane
Praying Mother

August 6

Listening Heart

"Not forsaking the assembling of ourselves together, as the manner of some is: but exhorting one another; and so much the more, as ye see the day approaching."   Hebrews 10:25

When the pressures of "end-time" living get you down, you can know that there is loving support from the Body of Christ. God uses other believers to give us the will to recover when we sometimes find it hard to pray for ourselves.

You, too, may be called to be an instrument of God's peace. Become a dynamic help when a friend or neighbor is in trouble. Listen to them, allowing them to vent their frustrations. Then gently encourage them to commit their problem to the Lord. Give them the Word of God to nourish their seeking hearts. Then pray positively for and with them.

It is so important for us to take time out of our busy schedules to be available to one another. The love bond that links us with our Heavenly Father can also help us to strengthen the brethren. We need to dispel fears that plague so many by becoming part of each other's lives. Fear, another byproduct of these end times, is sin. An intimate relationship with the Lord will combat fears. I John 4:18 says, "There is no fear in love, but perfect love casteth out fear; because fear hath torment. He that feareth is not made perfect in love."

Bringing this comforting, sufficient God to our troubled friends is the best we can offer. We must have a listening heart, a sympathetic ear, practical prayers, and a comforting word from God that says, "If God be for us, who can be against us?" (Romans 8:31).

Vi Azvedo
PTL Vice President of Counseling

August 7

Love Fervently!

"...see that ye love one another with a pure heart fervently."   I Peter 1:22

Loving each other "fervently" applies to husbands and wives. Most arguing between couples is for leadership. God knows how we function best and in His wisdom he decreed the husband leader. Leadership shouldn't be overbearing but with "fervent love." Lordship in the home implies sensitivity. Women want understanding, particularly when they're being babyish, stubborn, and unreasonable. That's when they need tenderness.

A man functions best when his wife praises him. Too many wives say, "Oh, I can't do that," and they become their husband's critic instead of his cheering section. Most criticism grows out of a wife's pride. A woman can grow in the skill of noticing her man. Ask God to open your eyes.

I made my days miserable over my husband's thrown down socks. Every morning, I engaged in a mental harangue with myself because he didn't pick up his socks. I'd eventually do it, but I resented it. One day he invited me along as he flew to a remote area to deliver a baby. There, the wife and her mother were crying and fearful, the husband distraught. Within minutes, my husband took control of the situation. As I saw the burden he took on for others, I said, "Lord, I'm your handmaiden—I'll take on the burden of picking up his socks." After that I did it joyfully, where before pride kept me from doing it willingly.

I only know what I've learned by experience and I have learned God's Word is truth. The cement of the Holy Spirit can restore marriages and relationships.

June Nichols
Counselor

August 8

God's Good Intentions

"And we know that all things work together for good to them that love God, to them who are the called according to his purpose."
                                                      Romans 8:28

This statement: "...all things work together for good to them that love God...," has proven to be a concrete and sound foundation philosophy upon which to build a strong life and character. When we are going through great trials and face what seems to be overwhelming problems, it often does not appear any good could ever come out of the situation. But, if you stand on the Word and claim God's good purpose, you will eventually find His Word to be true.

During World War II, I was told that my injuries were so extensive that I would be a paralytic for the rest of my life. I refused to accept this and I stood on God's promise. Within eighteen months I was walking again.

A further wonderful promise is given to us, His children, in II Timothy 1:9, "(God) Who hath saved us, and called us with a holy calling, not according to our works, but according to his own purpose and grace, which was given us in Christ Jesus before the world began." Here God lets us know of His good intentions toward us even "...before the world began." Again in Ephesians 1:4, He assures us of His love and good intentions, "According as he hath chosen us in him before the foundation of the world, that we should be holy and without blame before him in love...." So Praise God, He loves us now and He loved us from the very beginning, at the foundation of the world.

Dr. Lee Thomas
Pastor

August 9

Equipped For Every Task

"Then said Jesus to them again, Peace be unto you: as my Father hath sent me, even so send I you."   John 20:21

    It is encouraging to know that, as a believer in Jesus Christ, God has totally equipped us for every task. Just as God sent Jesus forth with all the authority and power of the Father, Jesus sends us forth with that same authority and power.

    In every situation Jesus confronted, He had the weapons of spiritual warfare to conquer the enemy. He conquered death, disease, depression, and any other device sent by Satan to hinder God's work.

    We should begin each day by putting on "the whole armor of God," explained in Ephesians 6:11-17. From our spiritual helmet of salvation down to our Gospel-shod feet, we can stand against the enemy of our soul,"...and having done all, to stand" firm!

    In this last day, we need to take up the weapons of our warfare which "are not carnal, but mighty through God to the pulling down of strongholds" (II Corinthians 10:4). We must exercise our authority in Jesus Christ and use the sword of the Spirit—God's Word—"against principalities, against powers, against the rulers of the darkness of this world,...spiritual wickedness in high places" that wrestle against us (Ephesians 6:12).

    As we grasp the provision of God's power through faith in His Word, we will become "Overcomers" in our circumstances. No strategy of the enemy will be able to defeat us (Isaiah 54:17). And with Jesus, we know that when the battle is over, the victory belongs to the child of God.

Tim Bagwell
Pastor/Evangelist

August 10

Compassion For Souls

"Delight thyself also in the Lord; and he shall give thee the desires of thine heart."
Psalm 37:4

God's will is a frightening thing to some people because they believe God may force them to do something they don't want to do, or go where they don't want to go. I believe that is contrary to the Word of God. This Psalm says, "Delight yourself in the Lord and He will give you the desires of *your* heart." It doesn't say the desires of His heart. It says, *your* heart. The prerequisite to the fulfillment of that promise is that we delight ourselves in Him. We must put Him first in every area of life.

Several years ago at Bible college, our teacher asked, "What do you want to do when you get out of school?" Several students stood and said they wanted to do whatever God wanted, be missionaries, pioneer churches or go anywhere on earth. I stood and said, "I want to make records, sing to thousands of people, sing on television and travel all over the world." I was a new Christian and many probably thought I was on a tremendous ego trip, but that was not the case. I simply had a very clear idea of what I was equipped to do, what I wanted to do, and my motives were right—I had a burden for souls. God had given me compassion for people and a desire to tell about Jesus in any way possible.

I recognized my abilities and realized that through the communication of music I could best fulfill the burden of my heart-to share Jesus with others.

Dallas K. Holm
Singer

August 11

Called By Thy Name

"...Fear not for I have redeemed thee, I have called thee by thy name; thou art mine... When thou walkest through the fire, thou shalt not be burned." Isaiah 43:1-2

I was a prodigal daughter who returned to my Father's house from the secular world of music, and I walked rejected by those closest to me. There was mental frustration in the transition of being a successful songwriter in country music, on the Nashville scene, and writing my first Gospel song. God blessed the song to become a means of opening up a ministry. I also learned to trust Him for my finances totally. Some of my own family turned away and walked with me no more, but, the comfort of hearing Him say, "Child, I have called thee by thy name, thou art mine," was the sustaining power that helped me walk through that "fire" not to be burned.

Before each great trial in my life, He brings these scriptures so strongly to my heart, and I draw near to Him, then He does the work to conquer my enemies. The peace of knowing He knows our earthly name, our worth, our weaknesses, and still loves us with a deep, abiding love, passes our finite understanding.

For the past seven years now, I've been reunited with my Lord, and I have found that success is not the answer for a lonely, desperate life, away from Jesus Christ.

There is hope for mankind through Jesus Christ our Lord. He knows us personally and seeks relationship with us. Jesus is coming soon; we must prepare now to see Him face to face. He has provided for us to know Him. Remember, He knows us and has called us.

Betty Jean Robinson
Singer

August 12

Esteem Others

"...in lowliness of mind let each esteem others better than themselves." Philippians 2:3

I was raised in a Jewish home and was bar mitzvahed when I was thirteen years old. After college, I worked in Hollywood for such names as John Denver, Kris Kristofferson and Linda Ronstadt. My life became more and more empty. I hitchhiked around North America for three and a half months in a desperate search to find some meaning to my life. My wife and I ended up in a tiny Vermont town where God called us to Himself just as everything was falling apart in our lives and Candy was leaving to get a divorce. The reality of God and His love saved our marriage and our lives.

Often in "the ministry" I have a tendency to think in terms of serving God and doing great things for Him. Serving and doing are not as important as knowing God and allowing Him to change us on the inside. Oswald Chambers said, "God is not so much interested in what we do for Him as He is in who we are."

Because I am involved in music and drama—ministries that are in the public eye, I constantly have to remind myself of what is truly important. The important thing is not if I look or sound good, but if I'm manifesting Jesus in my daily life. Only by maintaining an intimate personal relationship with Him will I be able to truly think of others as more important than myself. In Matthew 7:22-23 people said, "...in thy name (we) have done many wonderful works." And Jesus answered, "I never knew you." They were sent from Him not for lack of works but because they didn't know Him.

Tom Green
Drama Coordinator PTL

August 13

Broken, Healed And Comforted

"The Lord preserveth the simple: I was brought low, and he helped me. Return unto thy rest,...for the Lord hath dealt bountifully with thee."   Psalm 116:6-7

When I was born again in 1972, the Lord gave me a whole new life. God saved and enriched our marriage. He delivered me from the occult, eastern mysticism, vegetarianism, and a jealous spirit. Early in my walk with Him, Jesus gave me a love for Psalm 116 and I memorized it. Many times the Lord has broken, healed and comforted me through this psalm.

One time I was completely broken when the doctors told me I would never have a child. My emotions were up and down, from the mountaintop of hope to the valley of unbelief. My fervent prayers were complicated by faithless confessions. While a guest on the PTL TV show, over three years ago, I shared with Susan Harrison the great desire I had for a child. She told me she had lost her little daughter, then her husband, before meeting Uncle Henry. I was so humbled and felt very small in the presence of God; I was speechless. As Susan was leaving the room, she turned to me and said, "God is going to give you a child." Between that time and the next time we returned to PTL, I had conceived! We now have a beautiful little daughter named Shoshanna...the Hebrew for Susan.

I thank the Lord, for He truly has "dealt bountifully with me," as He promised.

Candy Green
Actress/Singer

August 14

Feelings Don't Count

"...I know whom I have believed, and am persuaded that he is able to keep that which I have committed unto him against that day."
II Timothy 1:12

It took me awhile to learn that the Lord loves me as I am. I'd always been afraid of growing old, afraid of death. But, as I've become more mature in the Lord, I've been more willing to mature physically, to grow older.

When you're successful at something and the Lord says do something else—it scares you to death. I knew how to speak to hippies and relate to guys in bars, but when the Lord started telling me to speak at conventions and to Christians, I was scared. I found you have to be ready to be what you say you are—to be committed. I don't answer to anybody with my time but the Lord. One day I'll answer to Him and I want to say, "I was obedient."

A lot of people make the excuse, "I'm not good enough," when asked why they don't obey God. The truth is they're often too lazy or too afraid of being hurt. To do what Jesus wants you to do, you must put yourself out, expose your heart and do a lot of loving. Sure, sometimes you'll be hurt, but if you're committed the fear and feelings will be overcome. It's really HIS job and HE's promised to keep you.

Feelings don't mean a thing. When I was most successful and leading hundreds to the Lord, I felt the farthest from Him. People want the goose bumps, chills and thrills—disappointed if you don't feel tomorrow what you felt yesterday, but remember, "Jesus Christ (is) the same yesterday, and today, and for ever" (Hebrews 13:8). I see a rainbow or lightning and know there's power in God's promises.

Mike Warnke
Author/Bible Teacher

August 15

Remain Faithful

"Moreover it is required in stewards, that a man be found faithful."   I Corinthians 4:2.

I've traveled and ministered with my husband, Mike, for one and a half years. When the Lord first called me to minister in concert, I didn't feel confident He could use me. Then I remembered who Jesus had used—the twelve disciples who were weak men, Moses who couldn't speak—God uses weak and broken things to show His power. I learned, if God has a job He wants you to do, He'll help you do it.

I used to be ruled by my feelings—if I felt like ministering, I should. Once the Lord called Mike and me to minister in a little town of five hundred—three thousand came to that concert. I learned what difference does it make how you feel, don't question the Lord when He tells you to do something.

Another time when I didn't feel like ministering, I went along anyway and carried my guitar. The Lord gave me a beautiful song about His death and who was at the foot of the Cross and the words, "It is finished." It's required of us, as Christians, to be faithful even if we don't feel like it.

I used to worry how I looked to people, if my hair looked good, how my clothes were and I didn't like my mountain accent. Then one day I heard Mother Teresa say, "When I look at a person I see Christ." Now, when I look out over a crowd, I don't see the people—I see Jesus.

Rose Warnke
Singer/Musician

August 16

Lord As Well As Saviour

"And be not conformed to this world: but be ye transformed by the renewing of your mind, that ye may prove...that good...perfect, will of God."   Romans 12:2

I prayed and invited Christ into my life at the age of eight. But, for the next eight years, until I was sixteen, I didn't have the consistent witness of the Spirit in my life. While a sophomore in high school, I made a total commitment to Christ and He became my Lord as well as my Saviour.

God's wisdom comes to us through our spirits and Satan injects thoughts into our minds. If our brain programs our spirits, we die spiritually. "For to be carnally minded is death; but to be spiritually minded is life and peace" (Romans 8:6). If we allow our spirit, under the control of His Holy Spirit, to program our brains, then we have life and peace according to the Word. This is not a once for all decision, like salvation, but a daily process.

In Romans 12:1, we have another excellent principle laid down, "I beseech you...that ye present your bodies a living sacrifice, holy, acceptable unto God, which is your reasonable service." If we follow this concept, of presenting our bodies, our lives, wholly to God and day by day make a conscious yielding to Him, what joy and peace we will experience.

When you totally commit your life to Christ, let the Spirit control your brain and give your body as a living sacrifice to God, when body, mind and spirit are under His control, the result is a Christ consecrated, joy permeated life.

Karl Strader
Pastor

August 17

God Of The Impossible

"But as for you, ye thought evil against me; but God meant it unto good...." Genesis 50:20

All through the Old Testament we see God doing a special thing to convince His people: He's the God of the impossible. Sarah giving Abraham a son in his old age; God declaring David a man after His own heart. Joseph, thrown down a well by his brothers, falsely accused and thrown into prison and, finally, seeing God's overall plan declares, "But as for you, ye thought evil against me; but God meant it unto good...." God can take any plan against us and turn it to good, that's why He's the God of the impossible.

We must realize, what God guides, He provides. However, we must be sure of His guidance. The first step is a personal relationship with Jesus Christ. "...whosoever shall call on the name of the Lord shall be saved" (Acts 2:21). When you've accepted His death and resurrection, then turn your life over totally to Him. The third step is to spend time *daily* in His Word. I've been amazed through the years at His faithfulness to give afresh each day. The Word is ever new and vital. We're told, "Delight thyself also in the Lord; and he shall give thee the desires of thine heart" (Psalm 37:4). And lastly, make sure you have Christian fellowship. "Not forsaking the assembling of ourselves together...so much the more, as ye see the day approaching" (Hebrews 10:25). Struggles and hard places are like a blacksmith's anvil and hammer because they conform us into God's image. "...he also did predestinate (us) to be conformed to the image of his Son..." (Romans 8:29).

Lloyd Ogilvie
Pastor

August 18

A Call Is Given

"For whom he did foreknow, he also did predestinate to be conformed to the image of his Son, that he might be the firstborn among many brethren."   Romans 8:29

The Lord has been dealing with me very distinctly about this verse. The Holy Spirit is now getting individuals ready for the final revival. The final appeal has gone out to the nation, it has gone out to individuals, and it has gone out to the churches. This is the time for the "Body of Christ" to rise up as never before and be people of God, in every sense of the word.

The Holy Spirit is moving within the confines of the individuals, they are growing up, maturing, and "every joint is supplying." The glory of the Lord is going to be revealed. He is soon to come! The call is being given, right now. We can see so vividly Ezekiel 35 being revealed quickly. Every eye is turned toward the Middle East. Our responsibility is to pray, believe God, and demonstrate His power in this world.

God is saying to the nations, "You had better pay attention to My Word. I spoke to you thousands of years ago and you didn't take heed." This is the final appeal to both nations and individuals, to get aroused by the power of God's Spirit, because the glorious Church is now being readied, the grace of God is given without measure, and the time clock for humanity is slowly ticking to an end. We must be ready. Now is the time to get right with God!

America, stand tall and remain faithful to your task as a catalyst for world evangelism. And who is America? You and I are and we must accept our own responsibility.

Lt. Col. David Kithcart
U.S. Army (Ret.)
FGBMI Speaker

August 19

Baptism Of Kindness

"Charity suffereth long, and is kind; charity envieth not; charity vaunteth not itself, is not puffed up."   I Corinthians 13:4

The first Scripture I ever learned was the entire chapter of I Corinthians 13. I was twelve years old and very hungry for things of God.

I remember very clearly the close of a revival in our church and quite ignorantly asking the Lord for the gift of kindness (not realizing that it is a manifestation of the fruit of the Spirit and not a gift of the Spirit). That night, I went home a completely new person. God had granted my heart's desire—a baptism in love and kindness.

At the age of fifteen, I received the baptism in the Holy Spirit and immediately began to minister to others in camp meetings and tent revivals. I continued my evangelistic work for many years. The driving force in my life was and still is to minister kindness and love to those who are hungry for His presence.

In my subsequent ministry as counselor, there's not a greater channel for helping people in trouble. I've pledged myself to declare that God is love and, to fulfill God's will in our lives, we must receive and demonstrate the Love of God.

You, too, can experience strength, wisdom, and health from our Heavenly Father as you exercise His love and kindness to those around you.

Rev. Aubrey Sara
Associate Pastor
Heritage Village Church

August 20

Resist Resentment

"But they that wait upon the Lord shall renew their strength; they shall mount up with wings as eagles; they shall run, and not be weary...."
Isaiah 40:31

There is a constant conflict going on in the minds and hearts of God's people today. Christians and non-Christians alike have become involved in this struggle between the flesh and the Spirit. The Holy Spirit gently speaks direction to our spirits while Satan gains access to our flesh through the world. The good in our world and our perception of the role we have in the world can be distorted by suppressing our feelings. One of the most damaging is the harbored feeling of resentment caused by our failure to forgive.

Ten years ago I let resentment take complete hold of me and I had a breakdown. I even lost my voice. It's amazing how we allow seeds of bitterness and resentment to take root, grow inside us until they finally control us, blocking our communication with the Lord. If we could only learn the secret of forgiveness, our strength and emotional stability could be renewed.

I experienced God's faithfulness and received complete deliverance by the laying on of hands. The spirit of resentment was cast out and I learned new strength to resist this binding influence. For the past seven years, I've counseled several thousand people also bound by resentment. By God's grace, their lives were touched as they realized that only God's Word can peel away this bondage, dividing spirit and flesh, and they could live in a constant state of divine forgiveness as they forgive others.

Frank Dearing
Author/Counselor

August 21

We Are Victorious

"(For the weapons of our warfare are not carnal, but mighty through God to the pulling down of strongholds.)"   II Corinthians 10:4

It seems that every time God spoke to me a promise, things would look just the opposite. Before I caught hold of this scripture, I would think I didn't hear from God, and would give up. When I realized we are battling against principalities of darkness, and put the Word of God to work, no matter what the circumstances looked like, there would be a breakthrough.

Nothing in my life has ever come easy. I have had to pray, fast, and intercede for every blessing I've acquired, or so it seemed. But through it all, I've learned this great lesson—we are in a warfare, and we can't sit back and let the enemy rob us of what God has for us. We must put on the whole armour and use His Word to get effective results.

There are imaginations and strongholds, old mind sets, that will try to linger in our minds and hearts, keeping us from being open vessels for the Lord's use. But this scripture tells us, "With these weapons, I can capture rebels and bring them back to God and change them into men whose hearts' desire is obedience to God" (Living Bible).

Start using the authority our Lord left us. Speak the Scripture forth, and tear down strongholds that keep you or your family members alienated from God's blessings. We are victorious! Don't give up! Through God, you are an overcomer.

Connie Hager
PTL Activities Director

August 22

An Awakening Generation

"Behold ye among the heathen...wonder marvelously: for I will work a work in your days, which ye will not believe, though it be told you." Habakkuk 1:5

Someone once said, "What your mind can conceive, you can receive." As Christians, we are living in the greatest hour born-again believers have ever lived. There are no limitations of what God will do and plans to do in our lives. We have to realize our power potential is limitless according to Ephesians 3:20.

From God's point of view, He has given us an expanding ministry. When we feel we've reached our goals, then God reveals to us greater dimensions than we've ever dreamed.

Through God's power, the old saying, "The difficult we do now, the impossible takes a while," is true in the spiritual realm. I'll tell you why I *know* it's true. If God had told me in my early ministry I would be the president of a 5,000,000-watt TV station, I would have said, "Impossible!" If God had told me I would pastor the largest congregation in Montgomery, Alabama, I'd have said, "Impossible!" If God had told me the church would grow from 200 to over 3000 in four years, I'd have said, "Impossible!" But God is working a work in our day that we can hardly believe.

This is our day, as God's people, so lift up your eyes unto the fields of the harvest and go forth and reap and God will keep His promise to work a work you won't believe.

Coy Barker
Evangelist

August 23

Being Fully Persuaded

"He staggered not at the promise of God through unbelief; but was strong in faith...fully persuaded...what he had promised, he was able also to perform." Romans 4:20-21

In 1973, the doctor told me I had melanoma cancer, the worst form of skin cancer. I would have to go into the hospital for treatment. What the doctor didn't tell me, but told my husband, was that I had only a few days to live and he'd better get me a grave site. Up to that time I'd never faced a crisis in my life, never had a death in the family, no illness and no tragedy. I'd counseled with many people in their times of crisis but had never handled one of my own. It was the first time I'd had to exercise faith. I didn't realize it then, but it was critical I have faith if I were to live.

I began asking God, "Why?" Immediately the Lord started making me strong in the faith. The beautiful truths He taught me from I Peter 5:6-10 about "humbling myself" in verse 6 and "casting my care upon Him" in verse 7 helped me overcome the anxiety and insomnia I was having. I soon realized that the result of my experience with cancer would be used to make me perfect, stable and strong in God.

Finally, I reached the point of full persuasion. It was at that place my faith became confidence that He was bringing me through this for His purpose. When I entered the hospital, the doctors found the cancer gone. God had performed a miracle. I have enjoyed full health since that time.

Be fully persuaded in your own mind, God is the God of the impossible!

Donna Barker
Wife of Coy Barker

August 24

Anyone Can Be Saved

"and it shall come to pass, that whosoever shall call on the name of the Lord shall be saved."   Acts 2:21

Most of you have heard of the "Hell's Angels," probably the most notorious of all motorcycle clubs. For twelve years, I rode with several different bike clubs and three of those years were spent with the Hell's Angels. I always wanted to do my own thing. I was into drugs and alcohol to get myself high. While under the influence of narcotics and liquor, I would get arrested and put in jail for the mean things I did.

Praise the Lord, in October 1976, I gave my life to God totally. He took me out of sin and began to do a work in me. Now God is moving me back into prisons and jails to minister to the inmates. And God has also given me the opportunity to use my years of experience in bike clubs as a testimony for Him.

During my first appearance as a guest on the PTL Club, I met Gene Sullivan, a motorcycling evangelist. The two of us have combined our stunt driving and witnessing for Jesus at high schools and churches to tell young people how anyone can accept Jesus if they believe He died for their sins. Gene and I ministered in one South Carolina high school and the leader of a drug ring was saved.

You will most likely agree that no matter how sinful our lives have been, He still died so that anyone could call on His name and be saved.

Barry Mayson
Former Hell's Angel

August 25

Healing Through Strength

"I can do all things through Christ which strengtheneth me." Philippians 4:13

Not too long ago, the devil tried to attack me with arthritis in my knees, ankles, and wrists. I had been traveling extensively and driving sometimes 14-18 hours at a time to get to my meetings. I became physically run-down and the devil jumped right in and attacked me with this arthritic condition. I went to a specialist in my home town of Nashville, Tennessee, and he could do nothing but tell me to take 12 aspirin a day.

Because I believe that God uses doctors to heal as well as His miracle working power, I followed the doctor's orders. However, when the doctor told me he didn't think I would ever totally get over this condition, I looked him in the eye and said, "Doctor, I am a preacher and I believe in the miracle working power of God and by His power I will overcome this." He said, "Well OK, but just in case you don't do it, take the aspirin."

I left his office and began to rebuke the pain in each joint of my body as I walked out the door. This taking aspirin and praying went on for two months. I became disgusted with the aspirin, and one Saturday night, before I was to preach in Arkansas on the following morning, I told my wife, "I am not going to take any more aspirin, and I believe that God is delivering me from this pain and swelling in my joints." I went to sleep in the motel room where we were staying, and when I woke up the next morning, I felt like a new man. From that day to this, I have not had pain or swelling in my joints. I can run, jump, or do whatever I desire to do. That happened two years ago, and I give God all the glory.

Bill Baize
Evangelist

August 26

Blessed Be The Name Of The Lord

"...the Lord gave, and the Lord hath taken away; blessed be the name of the Lord."
                                  Job 1:21b

Hurt—are any of us immune to it? Grief—is there one among us who has not suffered loss? I suppose not, yet God has given His people a special ability to know He is present with healing, comfort, and strength when it is needed. Blessed be the name of our Lord. After two years of preparation for it, I experienced a very personal crisis for which I am eternally grateful.

For two years I had been directed to scriptures relating to death. I made notes of all the scriptures, thinking I would have the opportunity to share them with someone else. Then I started having dreams about death. The grounding in the Word with special preparation in death and grief was for me, and soon I received word that my son had drowned while on a trip with his father. We all go through stages of grief, some quickly, some slowly and a few get trapped in a stage not knowing how to receive what God has to offer. Stages of denial first, anger next, then bargaining, fourth depression, and finally acceptance.

I went through these stages in about twenty minutes. For God assured me that my son's death would cause many to come to know Him. I prayed the night before the funeral that the pastor would give an altar call at the funeral, and he, being an obedient servant, responded to the Lord without one word from us. Many were indeed saved that day, and I found myself sharing those scriptures with others that had come to comfort me. How thoroughly the Lord prepares us. Bless His wonderful name.

Mary Baker
Radio Talk Show Hostess

August 27

Trust in the Lord

"The Lord redeemeth the soul of his servants: and none of them that trust in him shall be desolate." Psalms 34:22

Unlike most preacher's kids, I never rebelled. The Christian faith was always real to me. My parents loved God so much it was transmitted to us. But while in college, I went through a time of testing. Every facet of my faith was questioned. But my beliefs came out on top.

I have always felt a certain amount of pressure to succeed because of what Dad teaches. However, as I get older, I realize that "Possibility Thinking" is that foundation that inspires us all to be all we can be.

Experiences have taught me that success isn't achieving fame and recognition, but taking any situation and making the most of it. Once in high school, I wanted the lead in a play. The drama teacher gave me a script. As I read it, I realized I couldn't do the role without compromising my beliefs. When the teacher asked me to audition, I explained it was contrary to my beliefs and asked for another role. She was dumbfounded and refused me. I was heartsick and broke into tears.

Dad said, "God gave you an opportunity to proclaim to all of your classmates that Christ is first in your life. You're a smashing hit with me." God is big. He can handle any problem. Problems are for testing. Remember, you never know if a boat will hold until the anchor is tested.

Sheila Schuller Coleman
Author

August 28

There's Always A Silver Lining

"If we live in the Spirit, let us also walk in the Spirit."   Galatians 5:25

The Lord saved me to serve Him. If the Lord can use me, He can use anybody. I was a very unlikely subject, and because of what I've been through, I want to minister to people going through divorce, those who've lost their children, those going through trials.

If the world can't see love and tolerance in Christians, we might as well hang it up. We have a responsibility to *live* Christ. Paul tells us in Galatians 5:25, "If we live in the Spirit, let us also walk in the Spirit."

We shouldn't tell a new Christian that the Christian walk is easy. Maybe if we knew all the trials when we started, we'd chicken out. We need to have faith regardless of the circumstances. "But without faith it is impossible to please him..." (Hebrews 11:6).

The Lord allowed Job to be afflicted to stretch his spiritual muscle. When I've had trials, it has stretched my spiritual muscles. Often we see wicked people enjoy a carefree life. God says, "I have seen the wicked in great power, and spreading himself like a green bay tree" (Psalm 37:35). But then in verse 38, the Lord reminds us, "...the wicked shall be cut off." Of the one who trusts Him, God says, "...the Lord shall help them, and deliver them...." No matter how random things seem, He does have a perfect plan for every single life.

Dale Evans
Actress/Singer

August 29

Don't Hold A Grudge

"Love does not demand its own way. It is not irritable or touchy. It does not hold a grudge and will hardly notice when others do it wrong."
I Cor. 13:5

Have you ever had your feelings hurt?

It's not a good feeling at all, and if we are not careful, the pain could come our way often.

In my line of work, I meet all kinds of new people every day of the week. And some are very kind, but every now and then, someone will come in just wanting to hurt someone or something.

I have found that I must always be praying for God's discernment, and when a bitter or unhappy person comes in, I want to be spiritually prepared for it. It is just human nature that if they hurt my feelings, I would, in my flesh, withdraw from them and they would not see Christ in me.

But, if I hold on to this verse, and not hold a grudge, I have a great chance of being able to witness to them and show them the Lord in my life.

It's easy to love our Christian friends, but loving others is a true test of our faith. Nothing is ever accomplished by reacting negatively to any situation. I have to do the things in life, no matter how hard, that work for the good. If we don't, we'll find ourselves in a state of confusion all the time.

If someone hurts you, get strength from this verse, then love them like Jesus does. You'll be happier for it!

Melvin Stewart
Recreation Director

August 30

He Will Crown You With Success

"If you want favor with both God and man, and a reputation for good judgment and common sense, then trust the Lord completely: don't ever trust yourself." Proverbs 3:4-5 (LB)

All that a man desires in his professional life is promised in these verses. He has favor with God and respect from the community. The next verse promises, "In everything you do, put God first, and he will direct you and crown your efforts with success."

I became a Christian when I was ten years old but had no growth in the next twenty years. When I finished my doctoral studies in psychology, I was faced with the reality that psychology alone does not solve man's basic problems. I made a deep commitment to Christ then. Three years later the Holy Spirit had free reign in my life. Without the fullness of the Lord in my life, I couldn't function adequately as a husband, father or psychologist.

When I opened my practice, I was told a Christian psychologist couldn't make it in independent practice. It was felt the moral values of Christianity would exclude me from success. We dedicated our practice according to Proverbs 3:4-6, and now, seven years later, the practice includes five full-time psychologists and offices in four cities and two states. I saw God fulfill His scriptural promises.

What Christ requires to obtain special blessing is to always trust and put Him first in our lives. Like all of God's blessings, it requires responsible actions of the believers in order to receive the blessing. God gives it to us if we are actively involved in following His will for our lives and trusting Him.

Michael A. Campion
Psychologist

From Suicide To Salvation

"Herein is love, not that we loved God, but that he loved us, and sent his son to be the propitiation for our sins."   I John 4:10

Jesus Christ reached out to me and gave me assurance I was dearly loved at a time when I was so bereft of love that I was seriously contemplating suicide. I was so definite about suicide that I had selected the day, the hour and the method. I had also purchased the first Bible I'd ever owned, thinking it was similar to buying a road map when starting out on a journey.

I began at the beginning in Genesis 1 and became more and more despondent. Finally, crying in despair, I asked the Lord to direct me to the smallest book of the Bible instead. He directed me to the most love-filled book of the Bible, I John. As I hungrily read, "Herein is love, not that we loved God, but that **he** loved us, and sent his son to be the propitiation for our sins," something wonderful happened. The darkness and despondency lifted and I was filled with a "joy unspeakable." Love, like a visible light filled my whole being and I suddenly understood that Christ dying on the cross had something to do with me. I realized too, that Christ rising from the dead was God's stamp of authenticity that Jesus really is who He claims to be, the very Son of God.

My life was changed for eternity as I came to the last verse of I John 5:20, "And we know that the Son of God is come, and hath given us an understanding, that we may know him that is true, and we are in him that is true, even in his Son Jesus Christ. This is the true God, and eternal life.

Lorraine J. Pakkala
Writer

September 1

Bathed In Love

"There is no fear in love; but perfect love casteth out fear...fear hath torment. He that feareth is not made perfect in love." I John 4:18

My dear friend, Diane Brady, who had been in the orphanage with me so many years before, loved me to Christ. I'd come to a point in my life where I felt life was hopeless and there was no joy or peace anywhere for me but in the needle. I'd been through men, drugs, money and even fame but was so very empty.

Then at one point, I'd been busted twice for drugs, had just had a baby boy and he'd been healed miraculously by God. Just out of jail, I was convinced the only important thing was my next hit of speed. I went into a building and ran face to face into Diane and she had this big, big smile. I figured she'd turned square. I wanted to get away from her and ran to the elevator; just as the doors shut, I shouted out my telephone number. She and her friends came, they were never pushy, never preachy but they just loved me. They loved, and loved, and loved me! They bought me food, paid my rent, got clothes for my baby boy and showed me the love of Christ in a beautiful way.

One day Diane said, "There's someplace I want to take you." I agreed and she took me to Hollywood Baptist Church in Dallas, Texas. That whole church surrounded me with love. They loved "the hell" out of me. One day I talked with the pastor and asked, "How can Jesus help me with all my drugs, drinking and men?" He answered, "Take your burdens to Jesus." I did, and His perfect love gave me perfect peace.

Lulu Roman
Singer/Hee Haw Show

September 2

Victory In Jesus

"...for I know whom I have believed, and am persuaded that he is able to keep that which I have committed unto him against that day."
II Timothy 1:12

Our lives are governed by divine destiny. God is in control at all times. When we're shaken or in trouble, we often feel forsaken, but we must realize God has a miracle sitting on a shelf engraved with our name, all ready to send.

The Scriptures say, "I know whom I have believed," not in what—but in whom—a person, the person of God. Our trust is not in a thing but in a living person.

We're to be persuaded, convinced that He is able to keep us. As long as you're persuaded, nothing can shake you. He is able to keep us until the judgment. "That day" refers to the judgment day, and His promise is to keep us until, "that day." Commit all that you have and all that you are over to God, for He promises to "keep."

Those who judge us and criticize us are not the final answer. God has the final answer for our lives and our lives are His responsibility if we've committed them to Him.

We're in a battle and it's the closing hours. We are promised in the Scriptures that we will be victorious through Jesus Christ. Through submission to the Holy Spirit we can help change the world. We must lay aside our denominational differences, be united by His love and together we will be conquerors. He is able, and He promised.

Jerry Barnard
Seminar Teacher

Living Before A Loving God

"...present your bodies a living sacrifice, holy, acceptable unto God....be ye transformed by the renewing of your mind, that ye may prove what is that good...." Romans 12:1-2

The very act of daily submitting ourselves to Jesus as Lord of our life is in itself the act of doing the will of God. Prayer in itself is an act of faith, and it's an act of faith when we submit ourselves and make Jesus Lord of our lives. It's one thing to accept Him as our Saviour, but it takes a lifetime of learning to daily make Him Lord of our lives. When we do make Jesus Lord of our lives, then we experience the real joy of living.

No matter how old we are, we come to places throughout our lives that are learning experiences. I've been a Christian thirty-three years, and recently I came to a new experience where I realized that there was still rebellion within my heart, something that I had been unaware of. The Lord is very gentle and loving towards us. He only gives us truth as we are able to move into that truth. I think that's so vital and so important in our lives, that we can never get away from it.

I John 4:10 says, "Herein is love, not that we loved God, but that he loved us, and sent his Son to be the propitiation for our sins." I believe that each of us is so loved by God, so much more than we realize, that we should believe love is the ultimate act of faith. And I also believe in the absolute love and honesty of God. So when the Lord says He loves me, He does, and I continually try to apply that to my life.

Sondra Barnard
Evangelist's Wife

September 4

God's In Charge Of Everything

"And we know that all things work together for good to them that love God, to them who are the called according to his purpose."
                                    Romans 8:28

    This scripture in Romans became my favorite when I was going to some Bible classes during Junior High and for some reason Romans became a favorite passage for me. I went to work in Las Vegas with Wayne Newton for about six months and there are not a lot of other brothers and sisters there, so I spent a lot of time in Denny's (restaurant) with my Bible, reading. Romans just seemed to really speak to me at that time as I was going through a lot of times with very little fellowship. There were not many people around that I related to. So I spent a lot of time in the Word then, and it really comforted me to know that even though I was there and I might have liked to have been someplace else, I felt like the Lord was using that, for my good and for His glory.
    I really feel like I have been called to His purpose and I've given my life to Him and no matter what happens on this earth, no matter how it may look from the earthly point of view, you know that it's the best thing for you. God's in charge of the total picture. That's a very comforting thing to me. And all of Romans 8 speaks of dying to self and living in the spiritual world instead of not being of the world. As long as you're being obedient to Him, and you continue to give your life to Him, He is going to take care of you and there's nothing that's going to happen to you that is not supposed to happen. That's how I interpret this passage.

Chris Christian
Gospel Music Artist

September 5

The Abundant Life

"...I am come that they might have life, and that they might have it more abundantly."
John 10:10

Mine was not a "sawdust trail" conversion nor a Damascus Road experience, but a gradual "living out" the new life I received when I was a child and accepted the gift of salvation. I grew up in a "hellfire and damnation" culture and felt that if something was "fun" it must be sinful. The discovery that Jesus came to make life more abundant, not more restrictive, was indeed good news to me. It made "salvation by grace" understandable after hearing so much legalistic, moralistic law from so many denominations. When I first understood the abundant life, I finally understood, "For by grace are you saved through faith; and that not of yourselves: it is the gift of God: Not of works, lest any man should boast" (Ephesians 2:8-9).

Understanding these scriptures made me more receptive to the "call" to go into the ministry. It has also been the underlying emphasis in my own ministry in the Episcopal Church. I feel that too many other people have had moralistic, legalistic religion laid on them and they need to hear *all* of the good news.

I accepted and received more "good news" when I was thrity-five and asked for the whole bundle at a conference. That's when I realized part of the abundant life included, "...he which baptizeth with the Holy Ghost" (John 1:33). I began to live "life in the Spirit" and living more fully as well as abundantly.

Rev. Chuck Murphy
Pastor

September 6

A Life That Is An Example

"...the Scriptures say that the world speaks evil of God because of you." Romans 2:24 (LB)

When God burned this verse into my heart, it was the first time I became fully aware of the fact that to the unsaved world, we are Jesus. Everything we do reflects, to them, what He is like. If we get mad and retaliate, that's their perception of what God does. If we don't keep our word with someone, neither, they figure, does God. If we gossip, so does God, and He's not to be trusted. When we identify ourselves as Christians, we had better walk and talk like the person from whose name we get that word, Christ. If we don't, then we are telling a lie, not only on us, but on God. And Revelations 21:8 tells us what will happen to all liars.

This scripture continually helps me keep my life in check. Everything I do, I try to think whether or not Christ would do it. Sometimes that makes it rough, but it has never failed to be beneficial.

Being a Christian is a special lifestyle. I'm grateful to be a part of God's wonderful family. His work in our lives is complete and supernatural. I was saved four years ago, and if God ever had a right to destroy someone for his sins, that was me. You name it, and I have experienced it. From dope, alcoholism, divorce, attempted suicide, riches to poverty, I've done it all. But thank God, the Lord Jesus never gave up on me. I turned the mess that was my life over to Him, and every good and beautiful thing that has happened in my life is a direct result of that commitment. God is merciful.

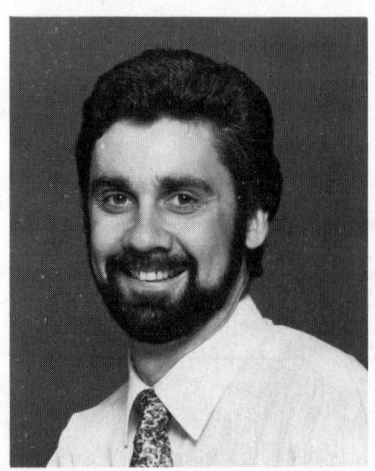

Rev. James H. Smith
PTL Youth Pastor

September 7

Acknowledge Him

"Trust in the Lord with all thine heart; and lean not unto thine own understanding. In all thy ways acknowledge him, and he shall direct thy paths." Proverbs 3:5-6

I've known the Lord since I was ten years old but have learned "to trust" Him in just the past year and a half. Learning "to trust," not rely on my own reasoning ability, has opened many doors for me to enjoy God's best. I've found trusting the Lord, leaning on Him, and allowing things to run smooth is far better than being on my own, wounded and upset.

In a pressured society that caters to selfish desires and ambitions, I am experiencing rest and provision as I trust in the Lord. The idea that you make your own opportunities prevails in the California "show biz scene." Without the Lord's instruction to "lean on Him," I would have given up acting and gone into another field. When I started honoring the Lord according to this verse, my life began to firm up. I found Christian friends, a good church and things started coming together.

Another verse that applies to the entertainment scene and to my life as a part of it is, "But seek ye first the kingdom of God, and his righteousness; and all these things shall be added to you" (Matthew 6:33). When everybody is seeking the perfect part, the rise to fame and the great opportunity, I've learned to seek righteousness and experience the peace, joy and abundance of God.

While many are seeking in the wrong way, the Lord has admonished me to seek Him and He will direct my paths.

Lisa Welchel
TV Actress

September 8

Confidence In The Shepherd

"The Lord is my shepherd; I shall not want...He restoreth my soul: he leadeth me in the paths of righteousness for his name's sake."
                                                Psalm 23:2-3

Because I know He is my Shepherd, I have everything I need. He gives me strength to do what most honors Him. He sends His angels to take care of us wherever we are.

In 1974, my husband and I were driving near New Florence, Pennsylvania and came very close to having a fatal accident. The car swerved to the side and knocked down a stretch of trees. I am sure the Lord had our guardian angels looking after us or we wouldn't be here today.

Further on, Psalm 23 promises, "You provide delicious food for me in the presence of my enemies. You have welcomed me as your guest; blessings overflow! Your goodness and unfailing kindness shall be with me all the days of my life and afterwards I will live with you forever in your home" Psalm 23:5-6 (LB).

We can stand on the Lord's promise that He will unfailingly show goodness and kindness toward us...just as a shepherd never harms his sheep.

Another scripture that assures us the Lord is ever watching over us is John 10:11, "I am the good shepherd: the good shepherd giveth his life for the sheep."

The Lord's promise to lead us in paths of righteousness has never failed.

Furnia L. Bakker
Jim's "Mom"

September 9

God's Love Protects

"He that dwelleth in the secret place of the Most High shall abide under the shadow of the Almighty."   Psalm 91:1

There is nothing more comforting or satisfying than knowing that you are loved and protected. Our Heavenly Father has so graciously provided divine protection and loving assurances through the promises of the entire ninety-first division of Psalms.

Every time I read these verses, I'm reminded of God's thorough provision for all those who trust completely in Him. I realize more fully that, indeed, the Lord is my refuge, my fortress, and my God. I don't have to ever be afraid of annoying circumstances, because He keeps me behind His shield—His perfect love and tender care.

Only eternity will reveal the countless dangers and snares of the enemy that have been thwarted by His divine intervention.

When I think of the strong Christian heritage of our family, too, I thank God for His faithfulness. More personally, I'm grateful to Him for sixty-eight years of *knowing* and walking in His love. Ever since I was saved at seven years of age, the Lord has fulfilled His promises to be with me at all times, provide for me, and direct my life.

I have complete faith in His promises and His protection. Years ago, I committed everything to Him, including my children. Today, I rejoice at God's faithfulness. My son, Jim, and the PTL organization are touching millions for Christ. I am fulfilled because His Word is true.

Raleigh Bakker
Jim's "Dad"

September 10

An Interceding Saviour

"...behold, Satan hath desired to have you, that he may sift you as wheat: But I have prayed ...that thy faith fail not: and when thou art converted, strengthen thy brethren." Luke 22:31-32

The one passage that has meant the most to me this year has been the place where our Saviour Jesus told Peter, "The devil is after you, and he will sift you as wheat, but I have prayed for you." That has been real special for me, in fact just this morning I had to get down on my knees and pray, "Lord, I have so many problems and troubles, just like everybody else, and, Lord, please pray for me."

That meant so much to me, to know that I could go to the Son of God, the Almighty, the Creator of the Universe. Yes, go to His Son and say, "Would you please pray for me just like you did for Peter, back when you told Peter, 'Now I'm going to pray for you and when you are strengthened, then you go and strengthen the brethren.'" So when I prayed this morning I said, "Lord, please just do this for me, just pray for me." And I believed that He did. I believe that He does it.

The Speers sing a song that's called, "He Is Ever Interceding," and that has blessed us this year because of sickness in the family. Brock and Faye's daughter has been real sick and we have relied on that scripture so very much. Knowing that He intercedes for us and He prays for us is very special to me. It's great that I can not only go to Him at any time, but also that He cares. That's the most important thing...that He loves me more than anything. He loves me, and He cares about me and He prays for me.

Kathy Watson
The Speers
Pianist/Vocalist

September 11

In Times Like These

"For if thou altogether holdest thy peace at this time, then shall...deliverance arise...from another place...who knoweth...thou art come to the kingdom for such a time as this." Esther 4:14

There are a number of challenges facing the church in these "last days." We have the charge to "go into all the world" preaching and teaching all about the love of God, the call to disciple new believers, making them "able ministers" and strong soldiers in the Army of the Lord, break down walls of doctrinal differences that separate believers, and care for the needy, oppressed, poor, and those confined. But perhaps our most sacred responsibility before God is to be totally available to Him at all times, to bless Him, to be blessed by Him, and to be a channel of His blessings to others.

Being at the right place at the right time will make the difference between effective results for good or chaos caused by indifference and apathy. The story of Esther is a beautiful example of God's sovereign care over His chosen people and an individual's selfless devotion to the welfare of her people at the risk of her own life. With little hesitation, Esther used her place in the kingdom to petition the king, expose the enemy of her people and retribution was made. Absolute obedience and trust in the Almighty God will reap manifold blessings. All God wants from us is our trust and availability. We, too, can be modern-day "Esthers" affecting our generation for God. In times like these, people of purpose, determination, and power with God are needed to be lifelines to Jesus. An old songwriter once wrote, "To serve this present age, my calling to fulfill." In times like these, we cannot afford the luxury of indifference, procrastination, or insensitivity.

Emily H. Walker
Writer

September 12

His Truth Endureth

"For the Lord is good; his mercy is everlasting; and his truth endureth to all generations."   Psalm 100:5

My home church gasped if you so much as mentioned the name of the Holy Spirit. When Paul was beheaded and all the apostles died, my church thought all spiritual healings and gifts died too. But God's Word proves itself, "Jesus Christ the same yesterday, and today, and for ever" (Hebrews 13:8).

One day as I read over Psalm 100 a light went on in my mind, for it said, "...his truth endureth to all generations." He's real! It makes no difference if God made the promise to Hagar and Ishmael, Moses and Isaac, and all the prophets great and small, it's good for my grandma and grandpa. We have an eight year old daughter and if Jesus tarries until she has children of her own, God's promises will be good for them, and even for their children. God's truth endures to all generations.

Once my mind got unblocked and I realized this truth was to all generations, I was able to enter into a relationship with the Holy Spirit and received the baptism. Don't be bound by thinking God's Word is bound—His truth is to all generations.

Just remember, "For the Lord is good; his mercy is everlasting; and his truth endureth to all generations." We can indeed live by the truth demonstrated in God's Word.

Terry White
Singer

September 13

My Keeper

"The Lord is thy keeper: the Lord is thy shade upon thy right hand."   Psalm 121:5

A few years back I was going through a hard time. I didn't see enough of my husband because I was asked to speak in one part of the country and he would be asked to speak in another part and our paths never quite crossed for much time together. I cried a lot and finally said to the Lord, "I don't know what I'll do if you don't help me." Shortly after I prayed that prayer, He showed me this verse that He'd be a keeper to me. He gave me a melody to go with it, and I went around the house singing this verse and believing it. As I sang the words of this Psalm, I would feel the Lord's strength welling up inside me and all the anger and resentment that the enemy was trying to put back in my life just left.

I had forgotten that our warfare is not fleshly but spiritual. I had to get a hold of God again and realize that no matter what we go through, whether it's a financial battle or a battle of the mind—if we will look up and praise God through the circumstances, He will lift the burden.

He *is* our keeper, all through the day, from the time we wake up in the morning until we lie down at night. He is continually thinking of us. Not only is He our keeper, but if we allow Him to be in every area of our life, He truly is a shade on the right hand and on the left. It's wonderful to rest in that assurance.

Wanda White
Singer

September 14

Sing Forth His Praises

"Make a joyful noise unto God, all ye lands: sing forth the honour of his name: make his praise glorious." Psalm 66:1-2

The Speer Family has been singing for God's glory for sixty years. Starting in 1920, through the 30's and now in the 1980's, we are still singing forth His praises. We see a trend of people wanting to come back to the old, solid foundations of the Bible and the old songs.

Mom and Dad were both music teachers who got saved in a singing situation. They both wanted to raise a family of singers—and they did. As soon as we were old enough to talk we were taught to sing.

Dad's call to sing was as definite a call as some men receive to preach. We sang at churches, revivals, and all day camp meetings with dinner on the grounds. "The King Is Coming" is our most anointed song; it has lasted the whole sixty years and the message of that song is as vital today as it was sixty years ago. The King *is* coming!

Dad wanted us to have a normal life during our school years and he taught music schools to support the family. During those depression days he was often paid in barter: eggs, chickens, milk, soybeans or potatoes. At that time we got twenty-five or thirty-five cents per person in concert.

As a family, we always try to uplift Jesus and the Word of God. Gospel music is God's Word set to music.

Brock Speer
Speer Family Singers

September 15

The Interceding Spirit

"...the Spirit also helpeth our infirmities:...we know not what we should pray...but the Spirit...- maketh intercession for us with groanings which cannot be uttered."   Romans 8:26

We have a daughter who is 28 years old and last April she was rushed to the hospital seriously ill. Our son called us and told us that the doctors might have to operate before we could get home. It was during this time Romans 8:26 came to my mind. Our daughter was in the hospital for five weeks, and for three of those weeks it was touch and go.

There was surgery to be performed and we were having a hard time coping with it. But I felt like the Lord gave us those three weeks to become prepared in our own minds for this surgery, because it was not like having just your appendix out, it was something that our daughter would have to live with for the rest of her life. Our daughter kept saying, "Mother, I feel like I'll have peace about it." So, peace came and the entire family accepted the surgery as what had to be done. It was either risk her life or undergo the surgery.

After our daughter was in the operating room for 3½ hours, the doctor came out smiling, and I didn't know what he was smiling about as this wasn't a smiling time. But he said that when they had gotten into surgery, it was discovered they could perform another type of surgery and do something that we didn't even know was possible. That was the reason, I believe, I had been thinking about Romans 8:26, as the Holy Spirit knew what to pray for, but I didn't. If I ever doubted that the Holy Spirit intercedes for us, that doubt is now gone.

Faye Speer
Speer Family Singers

September 16

Not Ashamed Of Christ

"For I am not ashamed of the gospel of Christ; for it is the power of God unto salvation to every one that believeth...." Romans 1:16

They call me "Big Daddy" because of the speed records I hold. One highlight of my career was being the first one to make 250 miles per hour in the quarter mile. I was able to make that record because of a part God told me to put on the car. We didn't think it would work, but I obeyed, and sure enough it worked.

In my life everything I've thought was a terrible disaster has turned out to be a blessing from the Lord. I had an accident and lost part of my right foot. I saw pictures of that car blowing to bits and I realized any part of that car could have hit a vital spot and killed me instantly. I knew then the Lord had protected me in a wonderful way. While in the hospital, I had a lot of time to think; the Lord spoke to me and told me a way to fix my car. People said I'd never race again, but because of that device I've won more races than before the accident. It's really true, "all things work together for good...." I painted a cross on my car and started honoring Christ in my profession. A few people said, "What are you trying to do? Want to get "Big Daddy In The Sky" on your side? I took some flak but what I'm saying is, "I'm not ashamed of Christ."

I was brought up to think God was at church on Sunday, but now I realize that God is with us every minute of every day. Making a part in my shop I'll say, "Lord, I need a little help here." How quickly He comes to my aid. The Lord does help in everyday trials.

Don Garlits
King of Drag Racers

September 17

Do It!

"...Be strong and of good courage, and do it...."   I Chronicles 28:20

All Christians have times when they feel they lack the strength or courage to continue. They desire to do the work of the Lord, but, possibly out of fear or exhaustion, many live self-centered, laborless lives. Their ministry is limited, touching only a few when they have the potential to reach hundreds or thousands. If we decide to "do it," God will give us the strength and courage to accomplish great things. The rest of I Chronicles 28:20 continues, "...fear not, nor be dismayed: for the Lord God, even my God, will be with thee; he will not fail thee, nor forsake thee, until thou hast finished all the work for the service of the house of the Lord."

As a young person, I decided I wasn't going to put limitations on how God would use me. He would be my guide and I would follow His leading. This verse has encouraged me to continue on even though my body is weak and my heart often fearful. We are told, "I can do all things through Christ which strengtheneth me" (Philippians 4:13).

My father is a minister, which means I pretty much grew up in the church. When I reached an age of understanding, I challenged what I had been taught and went through a period of questioning. Then I accepted these truths as my own because of what I'd been taught and from the example of my parents. The Christian life should be lived in the positive, "And whatsoever ye do, do it heartily, as to the Lord, and not unto men" (Colossians 3:23).

Doug Wead
Author

September 18

The Written Word

"All scripture is given by inspiration of God... for doctrine, for reproof, for correction, for instruction in righteousness."   II Timothy 3:16

"If you want to be a good writer, you must be a good reader." I've heard that principle emphasized in my journalism courses and at writers' conferences. Reading books, magazines, newspapers and other publications helps a writer improve punctuation of grammar and learn various characters or plots. What better reading material, for the Christian writer especially, than the inspired Word of God.

The Bible contains stories of romance and struggle in the lives of individuals and nations, poetry in the Psalms, and parables. Paul gave Timothy a list of reasons for reading the Holy Scriptures "...for doctrine, for reproof, for correction, for instruction in righteousness." I apply all of those reasons to my journalism career for God and spiritual relationship with Him. I want God, through my Bible reading and prayer, to inspire my creativity and ability as a writer. The words I place on paper should minister to you, the reader, or the words are worthless.

When I've written an article or devotional that's accepted for publication, God deserves the byline or credit. He provides the inspiration for the writer today to pen His Gospel message, similar to the way He inspired the authors of the Bible. God's written Word will inspire you as you read the words of Jesus, apostles like Paul, or prophets like Isaiah. For additional inspirational reading, select from the numerous Christian publications available.

Janet White
Free lance writer/Housewife

September 19

Love Without Limits

"By this shall all men know that ye are my disciples, if ye have love one to another."
John 13:35

I was fortunate to have been brought up in a Christian home. I attended church from infancy and cannot even recall at what point I accepted Christ, but I must have been very young. The Lord has always been a part of my life.

Having been born with a birth defect, I spent time in the hospital from time-to-time during my earlier years. The most significant being when I, as a teenager, had a leg amputated. One thing that impressed me during these periods was that so many of the kids there had problems much more serious than mine.

About twelve years ago, my health began to fail. I became very frustrated at not being able to support my family. As a result, self-pity took over, as my thoughts and concerns were turned increasingly toward myself and my own problems. It was like a merry-go-round but with no way to get off. Prolonged use of medication only worsened the situation.

When I honestly took a good look at the situation, I realized that I had allowed things to get out of hand, and only God could unwind the confused mess I had made. I turned everything over to Him and His precious love refreshed me. Then we came to PTL, and I found great satisfaction in meeting and loving countless numbers of God's people who visit PTL. I believe Christian love is the greatest therapy there is. If you need rehabilitating, try it.

Norman Bakker
PTL Partner Host/Jim's Brother

September 20

An Eternal Hope

"Looking for that blessed hope, and the appearing of the glory of our great God and Saviour Jesus Christ."   Titus 2:13 (NASV)

After my nephew had lost his life in September of 1973, I saw for the first time how fragile life was. One month later I received Jesus as my personal Saviour, for I knew if I had been in my nephew's place, I would not have been right with God.

Sometime after I had gotten saved, I awoke one morning with Titus 2:13 on my mind. I got out the dictionary to see what hope meant. I found that it was looking forward to a future event with great expectation, as we all use that word in a wishful way.

I saw that by giving man hope, God was helping him to stabilize his life. So instead of looking at the situation that surrounded me, I began to look to the day when Jesus will return and judge the world. Something like that really sets my soul free.

Professional counselors tell us that man has to have something to look forward to. We all have hope that someday we'll be able to pay off a bill, or be able to retire, or maybe obtain a certain goal that we have set for ourselves. These hopes are ones that we may or may not obtain.

But the one hope that *will* occur is the return of Jesus. Knowing that Christ is to return someday is like having a rope tied about your waist attached to the throne of God. For even if things get rough, and if it seems our feet can't touch bottom, we still have that eternal rope, Jesus Christ, to hold on to.

Ron Steele
*PTL's September
Employee of the Month*

September 21

Standing Alone

"...if thou wilt hearken unto me...."
Psalm 81:8

I was in a bad car wreck with my brother and two sisters when I was just a baby. Because of my injuries, the doctors put me on a strong drug. After my parents took me home, I began having epileptic seizures.

To complicate things, every time I'd fall I was afraid to cry for fear of having another seizure, so I'd hold my breath and wouldn't let it go. Several times my heart stopped beating and my father had to rush me to the hospital.

My daddy and momma prayed a lot about my getting better. One day the Lord told Daddy to take me off that drug and I wouldn't have any more problems. The doctors said I would die if I were taken off the three daily dosages. My mother agreed with the doctors and so did all my aunts and uncles and other relatives.

Daddy had to stand alone in his decision—that he had heard what the Lord wanted him to do. Understanding that Jesus was his head and he was the head of our family, he took me off the drug. I have never had any more problems.

I'm grateful my dad stood by what he knew God had said. It showed me that standing up for what you know is right may not make you very popular. But through our obedience and willingness to stand alone, God will work miracles.

Heath Prewitt
Student

September 22

Love, Love, Love

"A new commandment I give unto you, That ye love one another, as I have loved you, that ye also love one another." John 13:34

Love is the most overused word in our vocabulary. It is the most used, least understood, and least expressed. The difficult concept of love leads to a tremendous analogy. I studied for eleven years the constant command for us to love, and all of its ramifications. I began to sense that God was trying to tell us something that is hidden from our eyes, and that is the wonder that God has built into man—how to love as He loves.

The whole Bible tells us to love, not because it is psychologically sweet or sentimental, but because hidden behind our feelings is a secret—the beauty and sacredness of every human being.

Love is medicinal. When people feel loved and accepted, inhibitions are erased and people are freed from depression and anxiety. At one point, I was afraid to love, having been raised in a severe British home with a mother that was a bit overwhelming. I became terribly defensive, chauvinistic, and masculine. I am most grateful for God's love that soothed my rough edges and made me a new creature in Christ Jesus.

If you have been hurt or afraid to love, say it! Commit yourself. Some say love has got to be more than words. That's true, it may be more than words, but it cannot be less. Say it.

Leonard Evans
Author/Bible Teacher

September 23

A Future And A Hope

"So now, since we have been made right in God's sight by faith in his promises, we can have real peace with him because of what Jesus Christ...has done for us." Romans 5:1 (LB)

These verses convinced me that once we release our full trust and life to the Lord Jesus, whatever the plans He should have for us will materialize. The peace we experience will be there to let us know we are fully in His will. The next verse enlarges on this, "For because of our faith, he has brought us into this place of highest privilege where we now stand, and we confidently and joyfully look forward to actually becoming all that God has had in mind for us to be" (Romans 5:2). We can become more than we ever dreamed when we let His plans take place, rather than our own. These verses seemed to turn a light on in my spirit as I read them. They helped me know that I have a great lot to look forward to when I am resting in His plans for my life.

After I was saved at the age of eight years old, I began to have a real desire to sing for the Lord. The Lord began to open doors for me, one of the most important ones with the Blackwood Brothers. Because of the experience with that group, the Lord called me into a full-time ministry on my own. Watching the Lord's plans develop in my life has been one of the most exciting things that has ever happened to me. In Jeremiah 29:11, the Lord tells us, "For I know the plans I have for you, says the Lord. They are plans for good and not for evil, to give you a future and a hope" (Living Bible).

Big John Hall
Singer

September 24

God Loves The Weak, Too

"We then that are strong ought to bear the infirmities of the weak, and not to please ourselves."
Romans 15:1

Americans are almost obsessed with a desire to be strong, whether it be physically, emotionally, financially, or politically. Weakness is viewed as failure, as our strong competitive instincts abhor defeat. We don't relish being even number two! But Paul was realistic enough to admit that life is filled with contrasts and opposites: tall-short, bright-dull, success-failure—and strong-weak. And in the Body of Christ, though these are opposite poles, we must come to see them not as differences that divide us, but as tensions within the unity of Christ.

Too often the strong take advantage of the weak, or at best, simply ignore them. Even Christians may forget that while the Scriptures speak of some who are "strong in faith" (Romans 4:20), and others who are "weak in faith" (Romans 14:1), all are included in the "household of faith" (Galations 6:10). Paul says that the strong have a responsibility to help the weak. This is true whether the weakness is physical, financial, moral, or spiritual. Just as Christ's strength has been repeatedly made available to us in our moments of weakness, so our strengths must be shared with the other members of the Body of Christ, each of us supplying what is needed for a healthy operation of the whole (Ephesians 4:16).

E. Judson Cornwall
Teacher/Author
Conference Speaker

September 25

Get Insight

"...Let not the wise man glory in his wisdom,...But let him...glory...that he understandeth and knoweth me, that I am the Lord...."   Jeremiah 9:23-24

Many years ago I saw from these verses God's values as opposed to men's. I saw that God was concerned that we have the knowledge of WHO HE IS. For years I cried out to God in faith to reveal Himself to me. He showed me that to study His character from His Word was one of the surest ways to get the revelation.

From the knowledge of God's character came the understanding of His ways. As I walked in them, in strict obedience to the Holy Spirit, I experienced a totally new dimension, an intimacy of friendship with God for which I was created. That produced fulfillment.

I was forever ruined for the ordinary!!

As I have diligently pursued after the knowledge of God, in order to make Him know, He has entrusted me with a worldwide Bible teaching ministry based upon the results of that pursuit.

The Lord says in Proverbs 4:7 (RSV), "The beginning of wisdom is this: Get wisdom, and whatever you get, get insight." Proverbs 9:10 (RSV) reads, "The fear of the Lord is the beginning of wisdom, and the knowledge of the Holy One is insight."

So if you desire to see who God is, and have not really been able to learn who He is, you can learn about the Lord the way I did. By just studying God's Word, the Bible, you will see a finer portrait of the Lord than any man could ever paint of Him.

Mrs. Joy Dawson
International Bible Teacher

September 26

Praying Always

"Praying always with all prayer and supplication in the Spirit, and watching thereunto with all perseverance and supplication for all saints." **Ephesians 6:18**

Prayer is that medium of communication that joins our seeking hearts to the heart of God. If we only believe, the altar of prayer will alter any situation. Our needs and God's fullness become one when united in prayer.

In prayer, we often wrestle the forces of darkness, but persistence and total confidence toward God produce unfailing victory. Even Jesus, virgin born, spent whole nights in prayer. The result of prayer was manifested in His ministry through a mighty demonstration of miracles.

II Chronicles 19:3 shows a clear picture of what prayer is. God said to Jehoshaphat, "Nevertheless there are good things found in thee, in that thou...hast prepared thine heart to seek God." Divine approval was given, not because he sought the hand of God, but because he sought the heart of God. When people turn to God in prayer, He knows how to turn the tide of any "storm of life."

We all go through battles. They increase and strengthen our faith when we learn the power of consistent, trusting prayer. We must remember, too, that prayer really doesn't change things. Prayer changes people, and people change things.

Allow the uplifting and fulfilling experiences of prayer to transform you into what God wants you to be. Seek Him diligently with all your heart.

Rev. Paul Jones
Executive, International Foursquare Churches

September 27

Living Through God's Word

"This is my comfort in my affliction: for thy word hath quickened me." Psalm 119:50

Having been saved over 27 years ago, I came to Christ as a result of a very traumatic experience in my life which involved the fear and dread of death and knowing if I did die in my spiritual condition, I would not have made it to heaven.

Satan has fought me in so many areas of my life and ministry, until this verse which sums up the faithfulness of God to my life personally. He watches over His Word to perform it, and He has certainly been faithful to fulfill it to me regardless of the crisis that I was facing.

In the Bible, there are many commandments and facts that concern us as Christians in our daily lives. And we should remember these scriptures throughout our everyday confrontations. First, we must remember God's Word is eternal. "The grass withereth, the flower fadeth: but the word of our God shall stand for ever" says Isaiah 40:8. And Matthew 24:35 mentions, "Heaven and earth shall pass away, but my words shall not pass away."

Jesus said in Matthew 4:4 that, "...Man shall not live by bread alone, but by every word that proceedeth out of the mouth of God." And if we do not know the Word of God we are in error, according to what is said in Matthew 23:29. But if we follow God's recorded law, then we are promised eternal life in Proverbs 13:13, "...he that feareth the commandment shall be rewarded."

Walt Mills
Evangelist/Singer

September 28

Prayerful Persistence

"And, behold, a woman of Canaan came out of the same coasts, and cried unto him, saying, Have mercy on me, O Lord, thou son of David...."   Matthew 15:22

Our society is so paced that if it isn't "instant" we have little tolerance for it. Christians, too, have made this same mistake. We say, "Do it right now, Lord!" We get so charged up to see results that we forget God's timing and divine providence are always perfect and His infinite wisdom is to be unchallenged by human, finite reasoning and expectations.

The Lord has brought this verse to my attention in a meaningful way recently. The woman of Canaan persisted in her petitions to Christ. She cried and even tried reasoning with Jesus, but she kept up her pleas for her daughter's sake. The Lord used this passage to illustrate the need for persistent prayer.

Christ never criticized her because she was unrelenting. He didn't say she was lacking in faith. He, in fact, told her because she would not give up she had great faith. Persistent prayer is not a sign of weakness of faith...it is indicative of pure and true faith in God. In that, you know He lives...and He has the answer...and He will give an answer.

I have a real compassion for people who feel condemned when they pray and pray and get no answer. But we've got to remember what Jesus taught us in Luke 18:1. "And He spake a parable unto them to this end, that men ought always to pray, and not to faint," or give up. Be persistent, continue in prayer.

Loran Livingston
Pastor

September 29

Beware The Counterfeit

"Many will say to me...have we not in thy name...done many wonderful works...then will I profess unto them, I never knew you...."
Matthew 7:22-23

My fascination with magic and illusion started when I was given a Peter Rabbit magic kit when I was only seven. An illusionist is one who creates an artistic effect that is illusion but appears as reality.

I began to seriously ask myself why I was here and where I was going when I was twenty-five. My two best friends, who enjoyed fame, wealth, and success, committed suicide. Through this, I was challenged to investigate the miracles of Jesus to determine if they were illusion, mesmerization or sleight of hand. After thorough investigation, I could no longer question the authenticity of Jesus Christ. I accepted Christ as Saviour and was completely changed and overwhelmed. No one had ever explained to me the power of the Holy Spirit. I was amazed to find that God doesn't want us to work for Him but to let His Holy Spirit work through us.

There is much psychic phenomena today being deceitfully labeled as Christian. There are psychic surgeons who, through sleight of hand and use of animal entrails, make it appear they are doing miraculous incisions; they appear to remove growths with no tools. They falsely claim they are doing it in the name of Jesus and display an open Bible. In Matthew 7, it speaks of these kinds of deceivers. To distinguish the counterfeit from the real, study the real, the Scriptures tell us, "...try the spirits whether they are of God...Every spirit that confesseth Jesus Christ is come in the flesh is of God" (I John 4:1-2).

Andre Kole
Illusionist

September 30

The Virtuous Woman

"Who can find a virtuous woman? For her price is far above rubies. The heart of her husband doth safely trust in her, so that he shall have no need of spoil."   Proverbs 31:10-11

When thinking of a favorite passage, this is the one that is very significant, as it instantly comes to the top of my head. There are so many verses that relate to music, specifically about praising the Lord with cymbals and drums, but Proverbs 31 is a favorite that I've read recently that I felt really contributed to my spiritual relationship with the Lord.

These verses help me in my relationship with my wife and family. It's an excellent passage for a woman, but I need to read it myself to help me relate to my wife, where she is. My wife and I have small children. We are raising our family, so this passage speaks to me about the role of a woman in the family. It helps me to understand my wife as a woman and how I can relate to her better. To know what God's plan for her is, to know His design for her as a godly woman, helps reinforce me as a godly man.

In this chapter, it tells how the Christian woman supports her husband and works and helps him in all the things he does. You can apply this chapter to your wife or to your mother, either way, it applies to the Christian woman.

As I was reading Proverbs, trying to find some wisdom to pass on to my children, I ran across the thirty-first chapter. Because it definitely related to my wife, this passage's significance struck me right away and the thought really blessed me.

Ron Tuttle
Drummer
Benny Hester Band

October 1

God Is With Us

"Fear thou not; For I am with thee: be not dismayed; for I am thy God...all they that were incensed against thee...they that strive with thee shall perish." Isaiah 41:10-11

There are not many "sure things" in this world today, few indeed, except the reality of God through the Lord Jesus Christ. As a balm soothes over aches, so does the Lord bring peace and assurance in the midst of the perplexing, difficult times we encounter.

We need never fear external circumstances that affect the physical, mental tests or material need, because our God has promised restoration, total supply, and relationship with Himself.

Israel must have deeply appreciated God's faithfulness and mercy to them, when He called them back to Himself in these passages, promising forgiveness, restoration, protection and divine provision. They were indeed the chosen of God set apart for communion with Him. They, too, were given the responsibility to write and preserve the Scriptures.

With all the blessings we enjoy today, perhaps the most precious is that of being God's people, called by God, just like Israel, to bear His name, experience divine protection and provision and relationship.

Fear of any kind has no place in the victorious Christian's lifestyle. Assurance in His perfect love for us dismisses them all. Take comfort in the fact that He alone has overcome all of our temptations. Even the strongest adversary submits to His authority.

Lester Sumrall
TV Host

October 2

A Friend You Can Feel

"That if thou...confess with thy mouth the Lord Jesus, and...believe in thine heart that God hath raised him from the dead, thou shalt be saved." — Romans 10:9

I asked Jesus into my heart about five years ago when I was seven. We were going to a Bible study at Pat Boone's house. I noticed my mother had brought extra clothes and a towel and I asked her why. She told me she was going to be baptized. I asked the preacher if he'd baptize me, too. He said, "You must have a heart relationship with Jesus Christ." He showed me Romans 10:9 where it says you must confess with your mouth and believe in your heart. So I prayed and asked Jesus to save me and was baptized with my mother.

Whenever I've had hard times, like a test in school, I've prayed and He's helped me. He's a friend you can really feel.

One night I dreamed there was a huge fire in the field behind our house. I dreamed I stamped it out. I read my Bible every morning, and the next morning I read Isaiah 43:2, "When thou passest through the waters, I will be with thee;...through the fire, thou shalt not be burned; neither shall the flame kindle upon thee." To me, that meant no matter what happens, no matter what fires I go through, the Lord will help me. In another dream, I was a sheep straying, then it changed and I was the impatient shepherd angry with the sheep. Then the Lord showed me Isaiah 53:6, "All we like sheep have gone astray;...the Lord hath laid on him the iniquity of us all." He let me know that although we sometimes stray He never gets angry or impatient.

Bridget Mary Scott
Student

October 3

Be Strong And Do Exploits

"...the people that do know their God shall be strong, and do exploits."   Daniel 11:32b

Knowing God is the single most important factor in successful living. True success is found only when we acknowledge our human restrictions and recognize His unlimited resources that are available to us through Jesus Christ the Lord.

God's people must realize that all their progress will stem from an intimate, personal relationship with their Lord Jesus Christ, who beckons them into a close intimate friendship with Himself. Those that are in such sweet communion with their Creator will be strong in their Christian life and will accomplish exploits by the power of His Holy Spirit. In these last days, it is absolutely essential for God's people to have this kind of relationship, because, as a church, we are called to do the miraculous to reach a dying, bankrupt world. As God is restoring His church, it is imperative that we heed this scripture in our lives.

Over the years, I have realized the absolutely essential necessity of a deep, ever-growing relationship, the more I see His power evidenced in my life.

I have been saved for twelve years, after a lifetime of searching—religion, intellectualism, rock music, booze, etc.—I was brought to the end of myself and accepted Jesus Christ as my Creator and Saviour whose right to the destiny of my life has empowered me to do exploits in His name.

Larry Tomczak
Author

October 4

God's Answer To Burnout

"There remaineth therefore a rest to the people of God. For he that is entered into his rest, he also hath ceased from his own works, as God did from his." Hebrews 4:9-10

Rest! Who has time for it? That's what I used to say. Besides, I reasoned, how can anyone rest when the world needs to hear about the reality of a living, personal God. So I forged ahead with marathon mothering and spiritual activities designed to accomplish THE GREAT COMMISSION. It never occurred to me that God Himself took a rest from creation...or that there were times when Jesus took time apart for rest and renewal, in spite of the cries for "just one more miracle-just one more."

This scripture pulled together the elements of "balance" that God was trying to infuse in His creation. Each of us starts with a full pitcher, and unless we keep refilling it, we'll be giving forth from an empty pitcher, in other words burned out.

I've always been an energetic go-get-em person. My optimism had no room for realism until one day I had this little talk with myself, "Nyla, who do you think you are, God? You're running your spiritual race at such a pace that you have no time to read the road signs marked 'caution' or 'detour ahead.'" I needed to keep three things in mind: (1) Never say yes or no, until God and I have had a chance to talk about it, 24 hours at least; (2) By saying no, on occasion, I give God a chance to call someone He's been trying to get; and (3) Above all, never neglect personal, private prayer time!!!

Nyla Jane Witmore
Writer

Forsake, Take, And Follow

> *"And when he had called the people unto him with his disciples also, he said...Whosoever will come after me, let him deny himself... and follow me."*   Mark 8:34

Being raised in a famous Gospel family, I sang Gospel music after I graduated from college because "it was the thing to do" and not a 100 percent commitment to the Lord. For a few years, I sang with my brother Ron in the Blackwood Singers. We moved to Nashville and had a few hit records on the Heartwarming label. Soon, however, our eyes became fixed on the things of the world, and we left Heartwarming, signed with Capitol Records and started doing country music. The first record we did made the top 20 Hot! Country singles chart and the following week I went solo with Ron promoting me.

Thereafter, I began to travel and sing with Dolly Parton, Kenny Rogers, Barbara Mandrell, and many others, at fairs, theme parks, etc. My record company offered me a very lucrative deal, but I was under conviction. I told the Lord that I would cut a Gospel record to show Him that I was okay. I determined that if the company turned me down, I would search my life. I went to the record executives and they turned me down. Thus, listening to the Lord, I left Nashville for Memphis and Ron began to arrange evangelistic meetings for me.

God began to bless with many being saved in the meetings. I'm not making near the money that I had been, but I am so much happier. That's because the Lord wanted R.W. Blackwood to sing and preach the Gospel. I now, through the Lord's help, have several Christian songs on the national radio charts. And it's all because I denied myself and took up the cross and followed Him.

R.W. Blackwood
Evangelist

October 6

Move That Mountain

"...whosoever shall say unto this mountain, Be thou removed...and shall not doubt in his heart, but shall believe...he shall have whatsoever he saith."   Mark 11:23-24

For years, I've heard this verse recited as though it were a poem. People expected to be healed by just saying a scripture. It was only recently the Holy Spirit made its real meaning come alive in my heart. The phrase, "shall say unto this mountain," really means we should speak the words of faith boldly and with authority. Once we learned this principle, it became the basis for the healing ministry my wife and I have shared for many years.

I can recall in one of our meetings a young lady who came for prayer for healing. She had a broken neck and several other broken bones as the result of a serious auto accident. Her body was badly disarranged. Just as I started to pray for her, the Lord spoke to me "to take authority over her body." With this added encouragement, I commanded her body to be healed, and her disjointed body aligned. What an awesome spectacle!

We all can possess this dynamic power to overcome the most difficult problem (including healing the sick). Learn how you, too, can move that mountain of doubt, fear, and sickness. Be prayerful, cultivate a relationship with the Lord Jesus Christ, and be obedient to His instructions.

We believe that this final end time outpouring of the Holy Spirit will enable ordinary people like each of us to heal the multitudes and introduce the transforming Gospel of Jesus Christ.

Charles Hunter
Evangelist/Author

October 7

God's Prosperity

"Give, and it shall be given unto you; good measure, pressed down, and shaken together, and running over, shall men give into your bosom...."   Luke 6:38

Giving is so important. It's the first principle (fixed law of God) I learned. The greatest love message I ever received was, "I want 20 percent of everything you have." It was God's way of helping me understand His prosperity.

As God spoke, I listened and obeyed without question. Until then, I had not honored God in giving. The most I had ever given to the work of the Lord was a wadded up dollar bill. I'm glad I learned that when God gets your money He gets you. It's only then we realize His Lordship and divine provision. He provides abundantly and His prosperity is not limited to the financial. He also gives generously in every area of human need: emotionally, spiritually, and physically.

If you can't trust God with your money, how can you trust Him with your soul?

As people give, they see the fulfillment of Proverbs 13:22, "...the wealth of the sinner is laid up for the just." God is supernaturally supplying manna to His children in the midst of economic chaos and runaway inflation.

Remember the Lord's teachings on sowing and reaping as recorded in II Corinthians 9:6, whether we sow sparingly and grudgingly or generously we will reap (receive) the same.

One thing is for sure: You can't beat God giving!

Frances Hunter
Evangelist/Author

October 8

A New Beginning

"...forgetting those things which are behind, and reaching forth...."   Philippians 3:13

It's important we do not look back on our past sadness. We've all had things that hurt, and we grow through them—death, loneliness, heartbreak, failures, broken relationships. The growing comes as we "forgot those things which are behind" and do not dwell on them and let them hurt us over and over again afresh.

Once, when I was going through a trying time, I was at the end of a two mile walk in the mountains, when suddenly, a white cloud of butterflies flew up. The butterfly has always meant "new creation" to me. That cloud of butterflies represented to me several people and several new beginnings with God. I saw this one particular butterfly fluttering up and down, and as I watched, it landed on a rock.

Then it hit me, we may be fluttering up and down, but when we get on the rock which is Jesus, we are going to level out. He will control our lives. The butterfly is created to fly and can reach any height, so can we with Jesus. We are the determining factor of what the Lord can do in our lives.

This verse tells us to "forget those things which are behind." If we have a problem behind us, we must say, "God created in me the desire to forgive and forget the past." When we do this, He will recreate in us just what Psalm 51:10 says, "Create in me a clean heart, Oh God."

Lyn Robbins
Producer

October 9

Go!

"Go through, go through the gates; prepare ye the way of the people; cast up, cast up the highway; gather out the stones; lift up a standard for the people." Isaiah 62:10

The Lord God said to Moses, "Go!" Jesus in the great commission said "go" into all the world. So often as I travel, I meet Christians with great ideas, great words of faith and yet—they are living in defeat. They are waiting for "an open door." But the door was opened at Calvary for, at the Resurrection tomb, Jesus won the victory!

If you are faced with a "closed door," in the name of Jesus, tear it down! Burst through! Go! As I have carried the twelve foot cross around the world and through 59 countries, over and over I have had to just hear the Lord saying, "Go! Don't look at the human impossibility, but look at me! I am with you—go through the jungle—go down the Amazon—go through the Middle East—go into communistic Eastern Europe."

Go! For the Bible says, "How then shall they call on him in whom they have not believed? and how shall they believe in him of whom they have not heard? and how shall they hear without a preacher? And how shall they preach, except they be sent?..." (Romans 10:14-15).

Go! Rise up from fear, cast off defeat and go in the power of the Holy Spirit to preach Jesus for the glory of God. For remember. "...How beautiful are the feet of them that preach the gospel of peace, and bring glad tidings of good things!" (Romans 10:15).

Arthur Blessitt
Evangelist/Author

October 10

Moving Toward God

"Even so faith, if it hath not works, is dead, being alone."   James 2:17

My dad was a Pentecostal preacher, but in spite of my upbringing, I ran away from home and God at an early age. Never once in all my years of growing up did I make any commitment to the Lord. I was a wayward preacher's boy, I drank, caroused and cursed. I was a truck driver and led a hard life. But, my wife Mary prayed for me for twenty years, believing and hoping.

One night, in a motel room when I was forty years old, the Lord caught up with me. I was watching the PTL Club and Gloria Elliot sang, "Sweet, Sweet Spirit," and there was a sweet spirit, the sweet Spirit of the Lord ministered to me through Jim Bakker. Jim explained the Gospel and how, "...while we were yet sinners, Christ died for us" (Romans 5:8). Then he explained how Christ proved He is God's Son, "...by the resurrection from the dead" (Romans 1:4). Then Jim quoted from Acts 2:21, "...whosoever shall call on the name of the Lord shall be saved." After Jim shared these verses he said, "Anyone who doesn't know God, get up now and touch your television as a step of faith. God loves you, He really does!" As though a hand raised me up, I was off that bed and over to the TV. There is no salvation in touching the TV, but in James 2:17 we're told, "...faith, if it hath not works, is dead...." My getting up off that bed was an act of faith. I moved toward God. Now, I can look back and see God's hand on me. I am now in the ministry and pastoring a church.

Wayne Victory
Pastor/Evangelist

October 11

No Greater Commandment

"and thou shalt love the Lord thy God with all thy heart, and with all thy soul, and with all thy mind, and with all thy strength: this is the first commandment."   Mark 12:30

I was raised in the church most of my life. Sad to say, my religion was really without Christ. I believed things about God but it was not really a firsthand experience only a secondhand religion. I was continually confused between the way I *should* live as a Christian and how I actually acted. I kept looking for someone to pattern my life after, someone who was really living out the principles of the New Testament. I went through Bible school and then on into the ministry thinking that to live out the principles of Christ was impossible; our duty was just to preach them. Then one day I met a young man who practiced what he preached; his life was an example to me. My life was revolutionized!

Suddenly I realized the problem was me all the time. I was living a life that was selfish, one to continually please myself, and not loving the Lord with all my heart, soul, mind and strength.

Then, I, a minister of the Gospel, bowed my head and my heart and turned from my way of selfish living to one that was pleasing to Him. I began to realize how important it is for people to see real examples of Christianity, to see the Christian life lived out as well as spoken. The Lord showed me a verse that should apply to our Christian walk, "...I live; yet not I, but Christ liveth in me: and the life which I now live in the flesh I live by the faith of the Son of God, who loved me, and gave himself for me" (Galatians 2:20).

Anthony P. Salerno
Executive Director
Agape Force

October 12

Free At Last

"If the Son therefore shall make you free, ye shall be free indeed."   John 8:36

Making Gospel music the most exciting music on earth is the thrust of my ministry. I am tired of seeing young people "trip" out on secular music, a cheap counterfeit to the satisfying Gospel in song. The freedom to be creative and initiate this form of music is especially important to me.

I came to the United States from Bulgaria, totally disillusioned, not able to cope with life. I was so wounded I was convinced that you just go through life to end up a clump of earth. I thought surely there must be some answer to this predicament of life, but what?

I escaped through the Iron Curtain and, even though I was excited about freedom, it took me about a year to realize that even in the most free country in the world, I was still a prisoner in my mind. It was as though the Iron Curtain was still around me but, this time, I couldn't see it or tell where it was. Then one day a few men walking down the street came to me and loved me and told me about the Lord Jesus Christ. God has witnesses everywhere, sometimes in the most unusual places. For sure, He has a way, time and place to reveal Himself, bringing peace, joy and fulfillment.

When I met Christ face to face, for the first time in my life, I felt real freedom. No more bondage, limitations or mind games. He had completely set me free to know, love and serve Him. I will sing His praises continually for His mercy and graciousness to me.

Georgian Banov
Gospel Singer

October 13

I'm Available

"Also I heard the voice of the Lord, saying, Whom shall I send, and who will go for us? Then said I, Here am I; send me."

Isaiah 6:8

Even as Isaiah was called to a life of complete surrender to the perfect will of God, so Christ has called me to lay aside my every ambition, goal and desire and has called me into a life of complete dedication to be a "living" sacrifice, holy, acceptable unto God which is my reasonable service. The following poem, that the Lord gave me, expresses my feelings best:

I'M AVAILABLE

I'm available, dear Jesus, To be used by You each day,
Guide me precious Lord and lead me In whate're I do and say.
May my words and all my actions Be a witness loud and clear.
That you're living in me, Jesus, Every day throughout the year.
To the one who is so lonely, May I be a friend indeed;
To those with heavy burdens, Help me meet their every need.
Lord, I do not ask for fortune And I do not ask for fame,
Lord, my only prayer is, "Use me," In your precious, Holy name.
Now I don't have much to offer, but I give to you my all,
'Cause I've heard your tender voice; I've answered to the call.
And I know that I don't need to have some great ability,
For all you ever asked is that I be available to Thee.
Then by your Holy Spirit I will be what I should be,
And I'll hear You say,
"Well done, My Child,"
When Your precious face I see!

Linda Grubic
PTL Staff

October 14

He's Established My Goings

"I waited patiently for the Lord; and he inclined unto me, and heard my cry. He brought me up also out of a horrible pit...."
                                                           Psalm 40:1-2

I have been saved for ten years. I enjoyed a lifetime in show business and received the world's rewards of fame, money and social position. Then, I lost it all. I sank to the bottom of a pit. Praise God, as He promised, "He brought me up out of a horrible pit, out of the miry clay...and established my goings." God proved Himself true to His Word in my life and gave me love, forgiveness and renewal.

I want to spend the rest of my life telling the world that there *is* an answer to life. The one and only answer is in the surrender of one's life to Jesus Christ.

The Word tells us that not only does Christ rescue us, but He gives us a joy. "But let all those who take refuge and put their trust in you rejoice; let them ever sing and shout for joy, because you make a covering over them and defend them; let those also, who love your name, be joyful in you and be in high spirits" (Psalm 5:11).

These verses are significant in my life because they are proof that His Word is alive and powerful and relates perfectly to where I am today. The "horrible pit" expressed exactly what my life was before I knew Him. He truly, "...set my feet on a rock..." (verse 2, Psalm 40) and now He is using me in this present day to glorify His name.

Jack Searle
Singer

October 15

No Excuses

"Seek ye the Lord while he may be found, call ye upon him while he is near: Let the wicked forsake his way, and the unrighteous man his thoughts...."   Isaiah 55:6-7

One of the biggest hindrances to people coming to the Lord is the hardened state that develops when people become bitter, resentful and angry at God for disappointments, tragedies and loses in life. They enter depression and slump into self-pity, blaming God for negative circumstances. However, I am convinced that we make this mistake, that of blaming God and becoming bitter, because we really don't know Him. If we truly knew Him, we would be assured of His love and care. Knowing God is the single most important decision anyone will ever make in this life.

We must *know Him!* The only way to get to know Him is through praise. Praise Him in the morning, praise Him in the evening. Whenever we realize how much we have to praise Him for, get to know Him personally, and praise Him continually, He will deny us nothing.

It is also important for us to praise Him in all situations. We have no excuses to hate God or to fail to give Him due respect, love and service. I learned this lesson when my son literally died in a go-cart accident. He was going full speed when he collided with a parked truck. After being told that the doctors could not do him any good, I slipped away from his room to the lobby to collect my thoughts. Once there, every negative thought crowded my mind as the enemy tried to distort my vision of God and His love. Through it all, I was saved, my son touched, and no bitterness took root. We have no excuse.

Chris D. Schlabach
Evangelist

October 16

A Gift From God

"And whoso shall receive one such little child in my name receiveth me."
Matthew 18:5

This verse is very significant in my life due to the fact that I was an abused child. From earliest childhood, I was beaten and misused. A child is a gift from God, one meant to be loved and protected. In God's eyes, the way we treat our children is the way we are treating Him.

Children are important to God and He will not let those who mistreat them go unpunished. In Matthew 18:6 (Living Bible) Jesus declares, "But if any of you causes one of these little ones who trusts in me to lose his faith, it would be better for you to have a rock tied to your neck and be thrown into the sea."

I feel so deeply about the misuse of children I founded the Hank Snow Foundation For The Prevention Of Child Abuse And Neglect, Inc. in 1977. I want to do all I can to prevent children going through a childhood like mine.

When the disciples inquired of Jesus who would be greatest, He called a small child to Himself and answered, "...unless you turn to God from your sins and become as little children, you will never get into the Kingdom of Heaven. Therefore anyone who humbles himself as this little child is the greatest in the Kingdom of Heaven. And any of you who welcomes a little child like this because you are mine is welcoming me and caring for me" (Matthew 18:3-5, Living Bible).

Clarence E. (Hank) Snow
Entertainer

October 17

Sent By The Lord Of Peace

"Then said Jesus to them again, Peace be unto you: as my Father hath sent me, even so send I you."   John 20:21

So many, many Christians never know how they have been sent, although they recognize that the Lord has commissioned them to go. This scripture is of double importance to me in that, on two occasions in my life, it was shown to me as a "directive" in a time of need. It perhaps, more than any other scripture, has been a foundation in the whole of my ministry keeping me from the doubts and frustrations in the call of God.

As a result of this statement by Jesus, I have found peace through the years in my calling and have been able to follow it in the New Testament to find exactly how Jesus was called and sent, thereby knowing what I am sent to do. If one wishes to know how one is sent, then one must first know how Jesus was sent.

Most important of all He, with this scripture, defeated the lies of Satan in regards to my call. In 1955, I had finally surrendered to the call of God in my life to preach the Gospel, and had sold a thriving business and my equipment. The devil attacked me and questioned the call of God in my life. In desperation, feeling defeated, I turned to the Lord and asked for His help. I opened the Bible and let it fall, and as it fell open, my eyes were glued to John 20:21. I closed the Bible and have never doubted the call on my life since that day.

George T. Stallings
Pastor

October 18

The Joy Of Anticipation

"And when these things begin to come to pass, then look up, and lift up your heads; for your redemption draweth nigh." Luke 21:28

In the very middle of Christ's message on the second coming, He stops and talks to us concerning our attitude toward things that happen in the world. It is not necessarily the happenings in this world that affect us, rather, it is our "reaction," our disposition, temperament, and personal management under stress, that determines our emotional and spiritual well-being.

The Lord continues as He describes the numerous problems arising out of the world's conditons. He describes, very clearly severe oppression caused by great fear and distress of nations with perplexity. In other words, the world reaches an "impasse." The Greek word for this situation is "Aporia" which means "no way across."

Even under these circumstances, we have a formula for victorious living. We are exhorted in this verse to "Look up! Lift up your heads" or "be elated with joyous anticipation" because "Our redemption draweth nigh." Release is on the way!

When you and I react to adversity by looking up with glorious hope, not only are we lifted in our own spirits, but we become a "Cultivator of encouragement," and evoke a good atmosphere around us.

So, friend, look up. Anticipate the wonderful things to come. "For He (the Lord) that will come, shall come."

Kenneth R. Schmidt
Author/Teacher

October 19

Renewed Like The Eagle

"Bless the Lord, O my soul: and all that is within me, bless his holy name. Bless the Lord, O my soul...thy youth is renewed like the eagles."
Psalm 103:1-5

In this passage of Scripture, we are admonished not to forget *all the benefits* from the Lord, such as forgiveness of all our sins, healing from all our diseases. I have experienced many healings but have had three miracles from the Lord during my lifetime.

The first one was when I was totally paralyzed and could not even lift any part of my body, I had lost all control of my organs. Doctors had given me up, but one night God, in His omnipotent power, reached down and healed me. The second miracle occurred when the Lord healed me of a severe asthmatic condition.

My latest miracle was 4½ years ago, when my doctor told me X-rays had revealed a tumor as large as a grapefruit in my pancreas and spleen area. The doctors gave me no hope of living and were positive I was full of cancer. I went into the hospital and three specialists stood by to see the extent of the cancer and assist in the surgery. To their amazement, they removed the tumor along with half my spleen and half my pancreas and found no sign of cancer. Those three specialists later told me that I was a miracle and they had expected me to die on the operating table.

That is why this Psalm is so special to me, especially where He tells us, "...who forgiveth all thine iniquities; who healeth all thy diseases...." Praise His name, I know He does!

Rose Schmidt
Evangelist

October 20

Power For Today

"But ye shall receive power, after that the Holy Ghost is come upon you: and ye shall be witnesses unto me..."   Acts 1:8

Power. Everyone wants it, few can handle it. But, for the children of God, we have all the forces of heaven at our disposal for effective witnessing, and so that Jesus Christ the Lord will be revealed in the hearts of mankind. Mighty demonstrations of His authority and power are being witnessed by millions around the world as God's instruments are preaching the Gospel of Jesus Christ with more boldness than ever before, with the evidence of the presence of the Holy Spirit who brings healing and deliverance.

On a recent Haitian crusade, record breaking numbers of people were in attendance, as many as 70,000 on the final evening. Multitudes came to the Lord, and many were healed. One night going to my car, a little nine year old boy grabbed my leg and held tightly. A fellow pastor interpreted the Creole that the child was speaking; he had been born blind, but when I had prayed a mass prayer during the service, he was healed. Praise the Lord! There were many other testimonies of God's miracle working power, and I know He has allowed this kind of demonstration of His love to draw men to Himself. This same power is available to every believer. It is gained by faith. God honors faith. Where there is a demonstration of the power of God, men, women, boys and girls are freed to enjoy the love of Jesus. The only hindrance is the proliferation of negative preaching and teaching. Don't allow it. Accept this power, the Holy Spirit for yourself, today.

R.W. Shambaugh
Evangelist

_____ October 21

God's Protection

"For he shall give his angels charge over thee, to keep thee in all thy ways." Psalm 91:11

People ask me sometimes, "Aren't you afraid before you attempt to drive your motorcycle through a wall of fire and jump over a row of automobiles?" I'll have to be honest with you, the message about Jesus I share before and after the jump concerns me more.

As a motorcycling stunt man who formerly worked two years on the road with Evel Knievel, I know a dangerous jump attracts a crowd. But I also know God wants me to motorcycle for Him. When people come to see the stunt, I explain the symbolic meaning behind each part of the jump.

The ramp I accelerate on approaching the jump symbolizes how each of us is launched into this life. A wall of fire at the end of the ramp signifies the gates of hell which await the person that doesn't know Jesus as Saviour at life's end.

The cars I jump over represent the mountains and valleys of life. But I keep my eyes fixed on the other side where my motorcycle will touch the ground again. Once the jump is completed, I ask the people in the audience to make a commitment for Christ.

I know my Heavenly Father will get me safely through the wall of fire and over the line of cars because He has a job for me to do on the other side. God will provide His divine protection for you in whatever work He calls you to perform.

Gene Sullivan
Motorcyclist/Evangelist

October 22

His Grace Is Sufficient

"The Lord is not slack concerning his promise...but is long-suffering to us-ward, not willing that any should perish, but that all should come to repentance." II Peter 3:9

A trip that was to be our vacation, and my introduction to wilderness camping, and my initiation into my newly acquired ready-made family, turned into a disaster that only God could resolve. But God is big enough, merciful enough, and desirous of us enough, to love us and move in our behalf, even when we are not walking in right relationship with Him, yet. He, indeed, rescued my family and set us on the road to intimacy and involvement with Himself. If you've ever wondered how much God loves you, in your weaknesses, let me reassure you, His love is infinitely more perfect than what we could ever imagine.

Forty miles out in the wilderness on a tiny island, my family and I began camping. As a storm arose three days later, my husband and I were struck by lightning, destroying eighty percent of our nerve endings, blowing my husband's ear drums, charring our bodies, and leaving little hope for our survival. But prayer works. My father who had raised us alone, my brother and me, was a Christian who believed God for our salvation for many years, and I'm convinced that it was his prayers and God's timing that brought our miraculous healing.

That day I experienced what it feels like to die without God. Eternal separation from God is indeed hell. We received His love and were joined with Him. Don't wait for tragedy; live for Him now!

Wilma Stanchfield
Author/Speaker

October 23

Overcoming The Enemy

"No weapon that is formed against thee shall prosper...This is the heritage of the servants of the Lord, and their righteousness is of me, saith the Lord." Isaiah 54:17

When I was eight years old, God called me into the ministry. I thought at the time I was to be a Missionary Nun because I was Catholic. I found out later that God had other things in store.

I was filled with the Holy Spirit in 1971. But three years later, my marriage ended tragically in divorce. I was left with two small sons to raise alone. In 1975, though, God through His love and compassion sent to me my future husband, Parker Snow. We were eventually married in a big wedding, with my two sons giving me away.

After being married for two years and having a miracle baby, I was struck down by a rare and incurable disease. I became paralyzed and lost my hair, fingernails, eyebrows, and eyelashes. The specialists said I wouldn't live, but God said differently. In I Peter 2:24, the Word says, "By whose stripes ye were healed." Through Parker's and my faith in Jesus and His Word, and by standing through all the evil reports, within eighteen months God had totally healed me.

Isaiah 54:17 was given to me in 1974 by a minister. He told me I would stand on it the rest of my life, and so far he has been right. Through every storm, persecution, valley, trial, and tribulation, this scripture has given me the strength to continue. I have now stood on this verse through a divorce, an incurable blood disease, having a miracle baby, fear, and raising three sons. Through it all, God's Word is true and it has made us victorious in every situation.

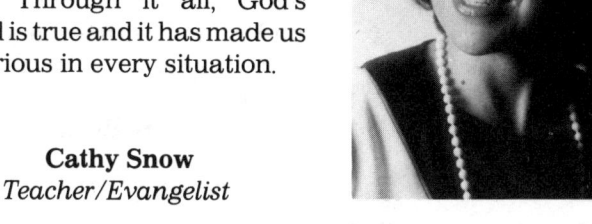

Cathy Snow
Teacher/Evangelist

October 24

Broken, Melted, And Molded

"Being confident of this very thing, that he which hath begun a good work in you will perform it until the day of Jesus Christ."
Philippians 1:6

One day, together, my wife Sherry and I asked God to work in us, to break us, melt us and mold us. That's just what God did and we went through extreme times while He "performed His good work."

He broke down the areas of rebellion in my life. I had always resented authority of any kind, although I didn't openly flaunt it. I was like the little boy whose teacher told him to sit down and he did, but said, "I'm sitting down on the outside, but on the inside I'm still standing up." I had the idea I could do everything "my" way and the Lord kept putting me in situations to break that rebellion toward authority and me to trust in Him.

Then He began the melting process. I had so many barriers of fear and mistrust toward other people. These barriers were walls that kept me from relating to other people. I had to be melted so I could relate both to others and to Christ.

As the molding process began to take place, God began shaping me into a vessel that was able not only to receive love, but to give love.

Our marriage relationship changed as these areas of my life were broken, melted and molded. God did "perform His good work." As my wife trusted in me, I became built-up to the point where I was able to fulfill my role as head of the household.

God has molded me into a vessel, so that I could reach out and share with others. And what He has done for me, He'll do for you!

Terry Rostek
Associate Pastor
Church On The Way

October 25

The New Life

"Therefore if any man be in Christ, he is a new creature: old things are passed away; behold, all things are become new."
II Corinthians 5:17

In March of '62, I experienced becoming a "new creature in Christ." I needed to become a new creature, because the "old creature" was a rebel to life. I gave vent to an uncontrollable temper, I was unable to accept responsibility in my marriage and I sought release from all this through alcohol.

A burdened, praying friend invited my wife and me to church where Christ's wonderful plan broke our hearts with love. "But God commendeth his love toward us, in that, while we were yet sinners, Christ died for us" (Romans 5:8). We surrendered our lives fully as the light of the Holy Spirit flooded our souls.

Certainly II Corinthians 5:17 was true when it said, "Therefore if any man be in Christ, he is a new creature: old things are passed away; behold, all things are become new."

And, as His 'new creature,' God sent me to Bible College and trusted me to pastor a church. Since then God has also allowed me to go on preaching missions to the Philippines, Korea, India and Japan.

The change I experienced in my life is because of becoming a "new creature" in Jesus. God doesn't try to direct us in a slightly different direction. He makes a whole new person with new desires and new goals. A Christian is somebody he wasn't before, not a changed life...but a new life!

Pat Shaughnessy
Pastor

October 26

Rejection

"He is despised and rejected of men; a man of sorrows, and acquainted with grief...he was despised, and we esteemed him not."
Isaiah 53:3

Rejection is the most devastating problem people confront. Christ suffered rejection and He can support and comfort us when we suffer rejection. Isaiah 53:3 tells us, He was not only rejected, but despised. In Hebrews 4:15, we are reminded, "...we have not a high priest which cannot be touched with the feeling of our infirmities; but was in all points tempted like as we...." I have counseled people seared by rejection. It is the most brutal weapon we can use against anyone when we, by word or deed, say to someone, "You're in the way, things would be better without you and the sooner you get out of the way the better."

Many children suffer great rejection from parents, peers and teachers. Some are scarred for life from these terrible rejections. In school, if a teacher rejects a child because they're not the same color or same creed, they are contributing to the delinquency of a minor when that child rebels against society.

How can we handle rejection? Analyze your rejection. Many times we're rejected not as a person but the things about us. We may have bad breath or bad attitudes. It may be that we should clean up a bit, whether it's our person or our personality. We also have the right to reject rejection. Just say to yourself, "I don't accept this rejection." Remember, too, Jesus Christ is "...the stone which the builders rejected..." (Matthew 21:42) proving rejection by men isn't always important.

John Stallings
Singer

October 27

God's Phone Line

"Call unto me, and I will answer thee, and show thee great and mighty things, which thou knowest not." Jeremiah 33:3

The Holy Spirit is always faithful, and God is our only hope. This verse in Jeremiah 33:3, "Call unto me, and I will answer..." is almost like a telephone connection we can have with God. He invites us to call and promises He will answer.

There are many instances in our lives as a family where God has answered as definitely as though we did have a phone connection. In 1973, when America was going through a great crisis, we prayed and asked God to give us a song that would bless America. He gave my husband the words and music to the song, "Learning to Lean," and it has proved to be a blessing to thousands.

Another answer from the "direct line" was when we had a burden for the over twelve million people a year who go through the gates of Disney World in Orlando, Florida. That gate is only fifteen minutes from our home. We called to the Lord with our burden and He answered, "You can't build a church with traveling people, but you can evangelize them." We opened our home to people and it's packed out every meeting. God is richly blessing us and others through this outreach.

The Lord invites us to call on Him. He even promises wisdom. "If any of you lack wisdom, let him ask of God, that giveth to all men liberally, and upbraideth not; and it shall be given him" (James 1:5).

Faith Stallings
Singer

October 28

Be A Seed Planter!

"But ye shall receive power, after that the Holy Ghost is come upon you: and ye shall be witnesses unto me...unto the uttermost part of the earth."   Acts 1:8

The heartbeat, pulse and cry of the Holy Ghost is that He came to seek. Then He gave us equipment, the power of the Holy Spirit, so we could help Him in this seeking.

In Luke 14:23, Jesus said, "And the lord said unto the servant, Go out into the highways and hedges, and compel them to come in, that my house may be filled." The word "compel" is much stronger than talk, ask or invite, it means to force.

The Holy Spirit's burden and vision for the Kingdom of God is for the people in the church to get out of the church and become soul-winners for the Lord Jesus Christ.

God wants us to plant seed in good ground for a good harvest. Matthew 13:8 relates, "But other fell into good ground, and brought forth fruit, some a hundredfold, some sixtyfold, and some thirtyfold." When we plant the "seed," we will realize the harvest, sometimes thirtyfold, sometimes sixtyfold and sometimes a hundredfold.

I was only five and a half years old when the Lord gave me a vision of hell. I saw a round globe and people were climbing up and falling off into a lake of fire. This vision gave me an overwhelming desire to reach people with the Gospel of Christ.

Rev. Vinal A. Thomas
Pastor

October 29

We Have A Future And A Hope

"For I know the plans I have for you, says the Lord. They are plans for good and not for evil, to give you a future and a hope."
Jeremiah 29:11 (LB)

It was during my freshman year at Oral Roberts University that I noticed this scripture on a plaque. At the same time, the Lord was speaking to me about a singing career. To me, this scripture was a special message, just for me. When, in my sophomore year, I was faced with leaving school because of lack of funds, the Lord confirmed His interest in my developing a singing career by allowing me to become a part of the World Action Singers, and thereby receiving a full scholarship. How completely our God plans for us!

The Lord is truly Alpha and Omega, and I'm assured He knows "the end from the beginning." Everyone and everything that touches me is in harmony with His design for my life. I've witnessed many miracles these past ten years after having begun to walk under His direction. One special miracle that still blesses me today was the salvation of my cousin, who was saved while she listened to one of my albums. Others have written to me about the presence of the Lord that is communicated as He fulfills His purposes through the gifts He's given me. Others testify to wonderful healings, miraculous and divine deliverance of all types of afflictions. To God be the glory.

I am more fulfilled and challenged than I could have ever imagined. The Lord is quite thorough in His preparation and plan for each of us. We do, indeed, have a future and a hope.

Stephanie Booshada
Singer

October 30

Communicating Comedy

"A merry heart doeth good like a medicine...." Proverbs 17:22

Comedy is a way of propagating a message. My partner Dave and I have done musical plays and comedy together since we were very young. About five years ago, the Lord changed our lives and we changed our message. We want to communicate that we don't have to wait until we're crossing the bridge to figure out how to get across, but that Christ has already taken care of the bridge before we get there.

Many comedians are communicating humanism—that's where they're "coming from"—that there's no right or wrong. Often movies and performers make fun of the Gospel in some way. Our comedians of today are like the old-time jesters in the king's court, they reflect the thinking of the day. The pain of some performers is so intense it comes through. Their lives are very difficult, constantly traveling, often on uppers and downers to keep going, not treated well. Christ said, "...out of the abundance of the heart the mouth speaketh" (Matthew 12:34). When they speak, the pain of their hearts comes out.

We were warned people would misunderstand our comedy, think it blasphemous. We're not poking fun at God but finding our humor in man's response to a loving God. God said, "A merry heart doeth good like a medicine..." (Proverbs 17:22). Being a Christian is fun! We want to communicate that.

Dan Ruple
Isaac Air Freight

October 31

Motivation Miracles

"for as he (a man) thinketh in his heart, so is he...." Proverbs 23:7

Miracles, unusual occurrences of God's presence, are still happening today. Because of God's motivation, a miracle happened to me, changing my life from failure to success.

As a teenager, my mother planted this seed, "real strength is in the Lord." But I paid her no attention. I was in control of my future. Many years passed and I established my own business. I ran it my way. Finally the business was about to go under. Financial experts told me "you haven't a prayer." I was crushed as I left that meeting. Driving home I began sobbing and pulled off the road. Prayer was *all* I had left. That day I asked the Lord to help me. In return, I promised to uplift Him and share His glory in every way I could. God's faithfulness became evident as I started to put Him first, sought Him diligently in prayer, trusted others, and worked to the best of my ability. Soon my business was stable and finally successful, even beyond my expectations.

I have come to believe that motivation is the difference between success and failure. It is the blend of acknowledging God first and committing yourself to accomplishing a task. When you believe in God, have confidence that you can succeed, commit yourself to accomplishing (working for success not waiting for it), take good care of yourself, do not indulge in self-pity, enlarge your talents and complete each task with excellence, you, too, can realize miracles in your life.

George Shinn
Author

November 1

Press Toward The Mark

"I press toward the mark for the prize of the high calling of God in Christ Jesus."
Philippians 3:14

We must never stop being aggressive in sharpening and using our talents for Christ. Even in the face of very difficult circumstances we must reach for the eternal prize that God has set before us and not let the problems of the present or past prevent us from securing our calling. Like the apostle Paul, I've never felt I've arrived but that God has a lot more out there for me. "Brethren, I count not myself to have apprehended: but this one thing I do, forgetting those things which are behind, and reaching forth unto those things which are before, I press toward the mark..." (Philippians 3:13-14). We must keep our eyes upon Christ, "...the author and finisher of our faith..." (Hebrews 12:2). When circumstances say, "give up," Christ says, "press toward the mark...."

Before I was born, the doctor said I'd be stillborn. My godly, Greek grandmother rebuked Satan, in the name of Jesus, to release his grip on her daughter and dedicated this unborn child to God. The Scriptures tell us, "I was cast upon thee from the womb; thou art my God from my mother's belly" (Psalm 22:10). God honored my grandmother's prayers and I am now a living testimony of His grace. I determined to turn over any of my talents to Him. I've learned you never stop striving "for the prize," you give your very best and continue to PRESS!

Dino Kartsonakis
Gospel Pianist

November 2

The Wisdom Of God

"But the wisdom...from above is first pure, then peaceable...full of mercy and good fruits ...without hypocrisy."   James 3:17

As a Christian film producer, I see many circumstances much like the false-fronted buildings on a set. They appear important and of substance, yet can easily be moved and changed. The real dialogues of the maturing Christian require the quality of wisdom as described by James in this passage. It is God who has built for us the stage of this world so we can imitate Christ with attitudes and relationships that glorify Him.

My personal challenge is to emphasize, demonstrate, and communicate all the principles and divine order emphasized in the Bible, in word, action, and deed. Since numerous verses declare, "wisdom to be the principal thing," James 3:17 reveals the kind of wisdom we are exhorted to know as Christians.

The wisdom of God is first, pure, or uncontaminated with dross or evil. Our infinite, sovereign God is omniscience, His knowledge is without limits or restrictions and true to His nature, His wisdom is pure, holy, and infallible.

The wisdom of God brings peace, wholeness, mercy. For who else could know the thoughts of we humans, look beyond our faults and minister to our needs?

The wisdom of God is stable and consistent. When we are "rooted and grounded in Christ Jesus," our lives reflect relationship and direction, far beyond human interpretation.

Kenneth Bliss
Film Producer

November 3

Give Excessively

"...He which soweth sparingly shall reap also sparingly;...he which soweth bountifully shall reap also bountifully." II Corinthians 9:6

This scripture describes God's desire for us to prosper and be liberal givers, inasmuch as we are created in His image. God has always been a giver: everything from creation to salvation through Jesus Christ.

In Acts 11:27, Agabus prophesied of a drought to come over Bible lands. Paul and Barnabas authorized "The Great Relief Offering," which is described in chapters 8 and 9 of II Corinthians. The Gentile churches sent offerings to Jerusalem during this time of need. Paul is explaining that if you will give beyond your own local needs, God will bless you so abundantly that you will be able to abound (give) to *every good work*. Then, Paul further encouraged them by saying, "Every man according as he purposeth in his heart, so let him give; not grudgingly, or of necessity: for God loveth a cheerful giver. And God is able to make all grace abound toward you; that ye, always having all sufficiency in all things, may abound to every good work" (II Corinthians 9:7-8).

Then, Jesus explained the ministering of seed back to the sower to perpetuate and multiply the blessing cycle, "...He hath dispersed abroad; he hath given to the poor: his righteousness remaineth for ever. Now he that ministereth seed to the sower both minister bread for your food, and multiply your seed sown, and increase the fruits of your righteousness" (II Corinthians 9:9-10). Paul did not expect one to be led, *but for every man to purpose in his own heart* and give accordingly.

David D. Copple
Stewardship Ministries

November 4

What Is Faith?

"So God's blessings are given to us by faith, as a free gift...and this promise is from God Himself." Romans 4:16-17 (LB)

God "speaks of future events... As though they were already past." This is His definition of what faith really is.

It is the confident assurance that something we want is going to happen—Hebrews 11:1. Many have confused faith with hope. Hope always refers to a future tense. Faith is now, in the present. It is the certainty that what we hope for is waiting for us, even though we cannot see it up ahead. If you really want to walk the life of faith, begin to think of "...future events with as much certainty as though they were already past." Believe it's already accomplished "even though we cannot see it up ahead." These are the two keys for anyone who really wants to walk the life of faith. You don't have what you're asking for except by faith... faith in the now.

In 1975, the communists took over Portugal. I was arrested and lost my sense of direction, because I looked at the circumstances, not at God. For forty-five days I lived in the opposite of faith...fear. One day God came to me and renewed me again, reminding me that He is, "Jesus Christ the same yesterday, and today, and for ever" (Hebrews 13:8). I caught faith to believe our work could continue. Shortly, the communists were overthrown, we renewed the building of our Bible college and the country is on its way to stability. All because of a "now" faith.

Sam Johnson
Missionary/Evangelist

November 5

He Who Loves Much

"Therefore I tell you, her sins, which are many, are forgiven, for she loved much, but he who is forgiven little, loves little." Luke 7:47 (RS)

I'm proof that God loves good guys too. I grew up in church, did everything expected of me and always thought God was impressed.

I thought I was better off and looked down on sinners. If we're not looking honestly at our own lives, it's easy to fall into self-righteousness and judgments.

At the age of twenty-one, God gave me a hard look at John Fischer. Externally I might not be involved in more things of life than others, but on the inside I was a very selfish person.

Thankfully, I saw myself as a sinner, because finally I was able to understand the cross, salvation, and forgiveness. I needed it myself.

Everyone has to encounter their own personal sense of need for forgiveness. The Lord said, "Blessed are the poor in spirit....," they're blessed because they see their need.

Now my daily walk with the Lord is contingent upon my honesty with myself and my need. As I do that, I constantly receive more and more of His sufficiency in my life.

As a result of His grace, it unlocks my love for Him in response.

We all have much to be forgiven and much love to return to the Lord in response.

John Fischer
Singer

November 6

He's Inside!

"...greater is he that is in you, than he that is in the world."   John 4:4

"Greater is he that is in you, than he that is in the world," became very real to me while I was deep in prayer several years ago. I suddenly realized that the God I worship and serve is not just a million miles away somewhere in heaven, but He is HERE, actually dwelling inside me.

My prayers didn't need to "get any higher than the ceiling," they really didn't need to get above my nose. It was real! He's inside me! The Great One is living within me! Since that day, I have become much more "God inside" minded.

In II Corinthians 6:16, we are reminded that this indwelling demands holiness on our part, "And what agreement hath the temple of God with idols? for ye are the temple of the living God; as God hath said, I will dwell in them, and walk in them; and I will be their God, and they shall be my people."

He is there to help, protect, guide, strengthen, heal, teach, and empower us to serve Him in a greater, holier, lovelier way.

His promise to strengthen us is found in Ephesians 3:16, "That he would grant you, according to the riches of his glory, to be strengthened with might by his Spirit in the inner man." What a promise! All the riches of His glory are at our disposal.

Kenneth Copeland
Evangelist/Teacher

November 7

Praise Ye The Lord

"Praise ye the Lord..." Psalm 150

The 150th Psalm tells us to "Praise ye the Lord. Praise God in his sanctuary: praise him in the firmament of his power. Praise him for his mighty acts: praise him according to his excellent greatness. Praise him with the sound of the trumpet: praise him with psaltery and harp. Praise him with the timbrel and dance: praise him with stringed instruments and organs. Praise him upon the loud cymbals: praise him upon the high-sounding cymbals. Let every thing that hath breath praise the Lord. Praise ye the Lord."

I like this chapter because God gave me a talent with which to play. Just being able to give a little of my life back to the Lord by playing with The Travelers makes me feel great. That's what I want to do with my life, just play for the Lord, whether it be with The Travelers or anybody else.

Every time I play, I think of Psalm 150 because we used to have trouble going into churches because of our contemporary music. Before we began reading this chapter, our music would discourage many people. But now, when we show people Psalm 150, everything seems to fall in place and we're more readily accepted. That's why this passage means so much to me.

Wesley Foy
Musician

November 8

No Condemnation

"There is therefore now no condemnation to them which are in Christ Jesus, who walk not after the flesh, but after the Spirit." Romans 8:1

I now realize that my life has been turned around from what it once was, and I never have to worry about being condemned by God for my past.

His plan of salvation is free of condemnation since I made the choice to follow Him, and walk after His Spirit and not things of the flesh.

He promised that if I mortify the deeds of the body through His power, I will live. But, He warns if I walk after the flesh, I will die.

Romans 8:1 became my favorite verse when I realized that flesh and things of the flesh will someday pass away, but His Spirit can never die. Praise the Lord!

I accepted Jesus as my Saviour when I was fourteen years old. For most of my life I have been active in the church, teaching, singing and serving wherever I was asked.

Five years ago, I realized that I had been seeking applause and recognition of men and was walking after things of the flesh. It was then that I started seeking God's Spirit, and found a whole new meaning to serving God, and walking after His Spirit.

Romans 8:13 reminds us of this, "For if ye live after the flesh, ye shall die; but if ye through the Spirit do mortify the deeds of the body, ye shall live."

Bob Johnson
PTL Retail Manager

November 9

Called To His Purpose

"And we know that all things work together for good to them that love God, to them who are the called according to his purpose."
Romans 8:28

My parents divorced when I was just a little girl five years old. I was absolutely devastated and felt such terrible rejection. The doors of my grandma and grampa's house opened to my eight-year-old brother and me. Even though I was too young to comprehend God's plan and know "...all things work together for good...," looking back, I know without a shadow of doubt that the Lord had His hand on my life and has indeed worked things out "for my good."

Through rain, sleet, snow, and heat, my grandparents walked with us the five miles each way to church every single Sunday. We saw their consistent example lived every day of their lives. We learned about Jesus, that He loved us and cared what happened in our lives. Even when there were disappointments, times when our parents didn't show up for special events, embarrassment around other children because of divorced parents, not being able to write down my real parents names on forms filled out at school, still, the Lord was working things out for my good.

Grandma was the only one working those lean years, money was tight, but somehow she found the money to give me piano lessons. That started my musical career. I met my husband through music. We later became involved in a full-time ministry with the Speer Family. This led to a full-time ministry at PTL as Staff Soloist and Associate Producer. I'm thankful that all things *do* work together for our good.

Jeanne Johnson
Soloist
PTL Associate Producer

November 10

A Heart To Respond

"...The harvest truly is great, but the laborers are few: pray ye therefore the Lord of the harvest...send forth laborers into his harvest."
Luke 10:2

Early one February morning in 1951, I was awakened to find my husband about three feet off the ground with excitement that God had given him an idea for a student movement which would be worldwide, and that we were going to sell our businesses, move to the UCLA campus, and begin to live by faith. I was bewildered. I didn't know anyone who lived by faith. After all, we had set goals for our lives. This idea was not particularly appealing to me. I had many apprehensions, the vision was too great. But after a few months, the Lord confirmed Bill's vision, and I earnestly prayed for wisdom and a heart to respond. Soon it was our vision together.

Too often when God wants to use us as vessels, we challenge the ability of God to perform His Word in us. Or perhaps, we are too comfortable where we are in God and are not willing to be living sacrifices for the kingdom's sake. We need to take a good look at our commitment to Jesus and sometimes ask for a heart to respond.

Through the years God has continued to work in our hearts. We have seen growth and changes, but the concept remains the same—evangelism through discipleship, training, and placement. We have seen millions liberated to serve effectively as the Holy Spirit has revealed Jesus through our ministries, and other faithful witnesses. It is time, right now, to live consistent Christian lives. For some, this maturity will begin the minute you ask Christ for a willing heart.

Vonnette Bright
Minister's Wife/Teacher

November 11

Face The Son

"Thou wilt keep him in perfect peace, whose mind is stayed on thee: because he trusteth in thee."   Isaiah 26:3

The Bible greatly emphasizes the proper use of the mind, because our behavior is determined by our thoughts. The devil is the author of all distress, despair, and discouragement. If we entertain his disparaging thoughts, then we will live in constant defeat, never knowing the peace of God. But, if we fix our minds, not on the problem, but on a bountiful, gracious Lord, His peace crowds out the unrest. If I'm sitting close to a fire and get too warm, what is the remedy? Should I move closer to the fire? Of course not! I move away from it. In the same way, if I'm overcome with fear, anxiety, and despair, what should I do? Should I dwell more on the thing that's causing my distress? No! I must center my attention not on the problem, but on the Lord who is the answer.

When I was a little boy I used to try to jump over my shadow, but I couldn't do it. I even tried to outrun my shadow, but I couldn't do that either. My shadow was always in front of me. Then, I made the startling discovery that when I faced the sun, my shadow was always behind me. This experience illustrates the truth of Isaiah 26:3. If I dwell on distressing things, they are always before me, and I walk in the darkness of their shadow. But when I turn to Jesus, the sun of my soul, all those dark things are behind me, and I walk in the light of His blessed presence. The Lord emphasizes this thought again in saying, "Be careful (anxious) for nothing; but...let your requests be made known to God" (Philippians 4:6).

Jerry Horner
*Professor,
Oral Roberts University*

November 12

He'll Finish What He Starts

"Being confident of this very thing, that he which hath begun a good work in you will perform it until the day of Jesus Christ."
Philippians 1:6

Availability, trust, obedience are the ingredients for any successful Christian endeavor.

I had never realized how important it is for us, as Christians, to recognize the tremendous investments God has in all of us and how He can use that investment to demonstrate His love and grace to the world. Just after graduating from high school, I began looking for a job. I was unsure of what I had to offer and lacked confidence in projecting myself. I had, of course, prayed and prayed but didn't sense positive direction. It was a little disturbing. I was asked to send an audition tape to the PTL Singers. I was very apprehensive. Did I really have a chance? Surely there were much better singers, more experienced and qualified people than I. But I was soon to realize that the small talent God has given could become something of blessing and honor and praise to the Lord when He's given the right to develop and use it. When I was hired, I couldn't believe it. God is entirely gracious and a wonderful teacher. It was this experience that made this scripture a reality to me.

Since I started singing with the PTL Singers, God has amazingly increased my ability, and continually gives the confidence that He is able to do exceeding, abundantly above what we ask or expect.

Jackie Gouche
PTL Singer

November 13

With Healing In His Wings

"But unto you that fear my name shall the Sun of righteousness arise with healing in his wings; and ye shall go forth, and grow up as calves of the stall."   Malachi 4:2

When my husband Dave and I were engaged, I became pregnant and eventually had an abortion. This permissive, irresponsible act opened us up to more satanic influences and involvement. Our lives were completely contradictory. After we were married, I spontaneously miscarried, and for thirteen months we tried to have another child. It was at this time, too, I began having symptoms later diagnosed as systemic lupus. Later when our son Blake was born, I finally asseverated acute lupus. It was living death, with warts, infections, hair loss, not to mention the emotional deterioration, high blood pressure, headaches and arthritic complaints. All seemed hopeless.

Dave, however, had known for five years the hell I was to live. When the symptoms first appeared, he, being a medical doctor, had done a "work-up" and knew the prognosis. Thank God we met the Healer and came face to face with His magnificent power to save and heal. But our salvation was not manifested until we had come to the place where all was stripped away; pride, vanity, indifference, apathy, and selfishness. This was the anguish I was to bear and Dave to endure as well.

After exhausting all available crutches, medicines, psychiatric counseling, vitamins, etc., I reached out to God in my own primitive way, and He heard me. My hunger for God and the miraculous recovery I experienced touched Dave and moved him to the point of salvation and joy in Jesus. God is real, He heals, He saved, there is none like Him.

Kathleen Kovacs
Speech Therapist

November 14

Knowing God's Perfect Peace

"Thou wilt keep him in perfect peace, whose mind is stayed on thee: because he trusteth in thee."   Isaiah 26:3

Peace is the "missing factor" in lives today. We surround ourselves with things and people. But peace is conspicuously absent so much of the time.

Jesus told the disciples just hours away from the cross, "My peace I give to you!" Not just peace during the good times, but peace even in the midst of crises and heartache.

Peace is not automatic with salvation; it is a developed characteristic accomplished in our lives by the Holy Spirit. It comes as the believer leaves the spiritual cradle and becomes involved in spiritual walking with the Master.

This type of walk means being reconciled to His plan for your life. "Reconcile" means restoring harmony and communion. When we are reconciled to God, our minds and thoughts are brought into harmony with God's mind and thoughts. Then we experience His peace.

It is sometimes observed of married couples that the longer they are married, the more like each other they become. This is true spiritually: the more we are married to Christ by salvation, living under His guidance and walking in the light of the Word, the more we become like Him.

If you are missing peace in your life, take time now to focus your thoughts on Jesus Christ. Practice keeping your thoughts on Him both in good times and the bad. As you do, His perfect peace will abide in you.

Dan Betzer
*Speaker/Revivaltime &
Every Day With Jesus*

November 15

His Spirit In You!

"Know ye not that ye are the temple of God and that the Spirit of God dwelleth in you?"
I Corinthians 3:16

I asked Jesus to be my Saviour when I was seven years old, but I never made Him Lord of my life. I grew up in church and thought, "I'm a Christian so I can't have any fun in life." When I went to college I broke loose. I still thought I'd go to Heaven some day.

Then, after I'd married and reached all the goals of my life, I realized that didn't bring happiness or joy. I had good movie and TV roles, but something was missing. Also, I gradually realized I was not going to live forever.

I went on a church retreat. I saw that everything I'd lived for was for self-interest, always pushing for my own interests. Later, I went to this church where people were speaking in tongues. I doubted it was genuine. About the fourth time there, I prayed, "Lord, if it's from you—show me. I'm an actor and I'm not going to put on a show for anybody. I want to know beyond a shadow of a doubt if it's from You." HE showed me—that night I spoke in tongues and I've been talking "funny" ever since. More important, I have given the Lord the Lordship over my life that He desires.

When you accept Christ, you have a spiritual being inside you. It was like I'd been in a dark room and someone turned on the light. I'd been stumbling in the dark all my life and the Holy Spirit's coming to indwell flooded my life with light. Reach out and receive it! It's yours!

Jim Hampton
Actor

November 16

Commitment To Excellence

"Therefore my beloved brethren, be firm, (steadfast) immovable, always abounding in the work of the Lord...that your labor is not futile."   I Corinthians 15:58 (NAS)

In Christ, we are being emotionally compelled to be the most outstanding in thought, word, deed and action. Whatever we're involved in, we've got to be God's best because God is appearing to others through us. We are His ambassadors. As we continually excel and allow God to make us outstanding, it becomes a part of our practical, everyday relationships.

I once heard a wise preacher say, "I'd rather see a sermon than hear one." When we excel for the Lord, we're doing just that. We are demonstrating that we're willing to do and be "more than enough" for Christ's sake, thereby showing the world the reality of Christ in our lives.

We should not only share a message but be one. What we believe about Jesus we should express in every part of our lives, our words, our deeds and manner of life. Our emotions should say "yes" to God and be in harmony with the Word of God. Our mind, will and emotions must be one.

Our call is to excellence and not only excellence but "always being superior." That means *always* giving your very best for Him. As we are firm, steadfast, immovable and always abounding, then we can claim God's promise that our labor in the Lord is never wasted or to no purpose.

Rev. Evelyn Carter Spencer
Author/Teacher

November 17

Enter Ye In

"Enter ye in at the strait gate: for wide is the gate, and broad is the way, that leadeth to destruction, and many there be which go in thereat."   Matthew 7:13

The Foursquare Church was founded by my mother Amy Semple. She probably blazed a trail for women in the work of the Lord more than any other woman. However, she was a real mother in every way. She cared for our needs and prayed for us when we were sick and we were healed. My mother moved in God's Spirit, and as she moved, countless thousands were healed in her ministry. When she was taken from us, the Lord gave us the assurance that He'd keep the work going. We learned at that time a ministry wasn't built on a person, but on Jesus Christ our Lord.

When the call of the Lord first came to my mother, she tried to escape it. She was brought to death's door and God said to her, "If you'll serve Me, I'll give you the strength of ten women," and He did. The message she always preached was, "Jesus Christ the same yesterday, and today, and for ever" (Hebrews 13:8). One day she was preaching that Jesus heals the sick and a little boy with his arm in a cast came forward and said, "You preached Jesus heals the sick, can He heal me?" My mother prayed for him and he took his cast off and his arm was completely healed. From then on, healings took place in her meetings by the tens of thousands. One time Mother prayed for the sick eight solid hours. The Lord put a special anointing on her life. But, it was because she was willing to obey and "...seek...first the kingdom of God" (Matthew 6:33).

Dr. Rolf McPherson
President, Foursquare Gospel Church

November 18

Forbid Them Not

"...Jesus said, Suffer little children, and forbid them not, to come unto me: for of such is the kingdom of heaven." Matthew 19:14

Our desire is to reach kids with the Gospel. Too many are not sensitive to what Jesus had to say about children. When speaking with His disciples in a dispute over who should be greatest, He called a child to Him and said, "Whosoever shall receive one of such children in my name, receiveth me..." (Mark 9:37).

Our organization, "Supergang," was born out of a desire to reach these children for Christ. We realized early in our ministry that much of the teaching material was written over twenty years ago. Kids are in tune, they need an aggressive approach. We wrote our own material to move at the kids' pace. We had a tremendous response. We've started "The Supergang Club" that kids can join, they get a button, we offer albums and comic books. Kids need an alternative to stand up to peer pressure, a club for Christian kids.

We deal with the issues kids deal with every day—grumpy people, unfairness and hurt feelings. We help them respond in a Christ-like manner.

There is a big void in child evangelism in many churches. There are seldom meetings just for children and almost never evangelistic meetings directed specifically toward them. It would be good for us all to remember that when children were shoved aside in Jesus' presence, He said, "...Suffer the little children to come unto me, and forbid them not: for of such is the kingdom of heaven God" (Mark 10:15).

Tom Brooks
Director Supergang

In Service For Him

"And I will restore to you the years that the locust (and canker worm) hath eaten...."
Joel 2:25

Last year I retired from my job as president of a furniture company in Thomasville, N.C. After 36 years with the company, the Lord moved me out of the business world to use my talents for Him. I had worked as a furniture designer and gained experience as an interior decorator.

When I was nine years old, I accepted Christ as my Saviour. And in 1973, I found a deeper walk with the Lord when I received the baptism of the Holy Spirit. Resigning my job with the furniture company opened an exciting new way to work for God.

By giving my decorating skills for His service, I've helped several major ministries in the United States with their interior construction. For instance, I helped design the offices of the administration building at Oral Roberts University in Tulsa, Oklahoma. God also lead me in aiding Pat Robertson and Ken Copeland in their building programs.

All those 36 years in the secular field prepared me so the Lord could use me in a special way in decorating His structures. It reminds me of the verse in Joel where He promises to make up the years of the cankerowrm. One year of full-time service for God will restore five or ten years that seemed spent on my own ambitions.

Remember, it will never be too late for you to accept Christ, be filled with His Spirit, or begin doing what He wants you to do.

Katharine Lambeth
Laywoman

November 20

Studying For God's Approval

"Study to show thyself approved unto God, a workman that needeth not to be ashamed, rightly dividing the word of truth."

II Timothy 2:15

I have always been greatly moved by ministers that could explain the Scriptures in simplicity. I have done a fair amount of studying on some of the other religions and cults in the world, so that when other people, who are not involved in Christianity, ask me what it is that governs our lives, I am able to explain it from a Biblical standpoint as the Holy Spirit gives me utterance, and not just from my own understanding.

Wanting to learn the Word of God more, so I can explain it better, is what motivates me. A member of one cult talked to me and left me with so many unanswered questions. That brought me to the realization that Jesus is either who He said He was, or He is the biggest liar of our time. That conversation caused me to study the Scriptures even more.

II Timothy 2:15 says, "Study to show thyself approved unto god, a workman that needeth not to be ashamed, rightly dividing the word of truth." When we do study what the Lord has presented in His Word to us, then we can learn everything that we need to know about Him and realize that Jesus indeed was the Son of God.

Studying and becoming wiser should be a goal of all Christians, as I Samuel 2:3 tells us that "...the Lord is a God of knowledge...." And Proverbs 1:7 emphasizes just where our knowledge comes from and just how important it is, "The fear of the Lord is the beginning of knowledge: but fools despise wisdom and instruction.

Therlow Foy
Musician

November 21

Following Christ

"...I count all things but loss for the excellency of the knowledge of Christ Jesus my Lord: for whom I have suffered the loss of all things...that I may win Christ." Philippians 3:8

Through the years, many people have approached me and said, "Tom, you sure are lucky, getting fame in Hollywood and all of that."

While I can truthfully say that I am grateful to God for the opportunity to use the ability He has given me before so many people, nothing else is compared to the deep inner peace and joy of knowing Jesus Christ as Lord and Saviour.

The worldly fame, popularity and good pay are all fleeting satisfaction. Plus, they are not really ours to begin with, but merely gifts from God.

But the love of God is something that lasts. No one, nothing can take it away. And no matter who you are, or what you are, it is available to you.

Not all of us can have the same gifts or talents, that is what makes the Body of Christ so interesting. And I enjoy the fellowship one to another so very much. It has nothing to do with who is a construction worker or a singer, it doesn't matter.

What matters is that we follow Christ. That is what is really satisfying!

Tom Netherton
Singer

November 22

The Sweet Shepherd

"The Lord is my shepherd; I shall not want. He maketh me to lie down in green pastures...He restoreth my soul...I will dwell in the house of the Lord for ever."   Psalm 23

    This is so important to me because it gave me a peace when I was lying on the labor room table being prepared for an emergency Caesarean section. Satan was trying to destroy two of God's children through toxemia. I had already lost one baby at eight months of pregnancy and here I was again at 7½ months with severe toxemia. Our baby and my life were in the shadow of death. I prayed and asked God for His peace, and when He brought Psalm 23:4 to mind, I knew He was there with me.

    There was a calmness and as I went under for surgery, I knew my God was guarding and guiding all the way. I can't explain the peace that passeth *all* understanding, but He was preparing a table for me even in the presence of my worst enemy. The Lord's blessings and His unfailing love brought forth our son Joshua to definitely carry out Joshua's message in the Old Testament, "As for me and my house, we will serve the Lord."

    The Lord has been my shepherd from the time I was young, for at the age of nine I accepted Jesus as my personal Saviour. But not until I was in college did I really understand about my salvation and the Holy Spirit. That's when I realized I had to make the commitment for myself, and not for my parents. Since then I have realized every day with my Lord is definitely sweeter than the day before, as the Lord is truly my shepherd.

Diane Bogart
PTL Voices

November 23

Honesty With God

"...to give unto them beauty for ashes, the oil of joy for mourning, the garment of praise for the spirit of heaviness...." Isaiah 61:3

When I was fifteen years old, my father died and I refused to understand why he couldn't have lived. I grew angry and bitter toward God for not preventing his death. For the rest of my childhood and into my adult years, that anger was buried deep inside me...buried so deep I didn't even acknowledge its presence.

For years I served God in the image I wanted of Him, instead of my conforming to His likeness. That hidden anger and rebellion against God caused me to make mistakes during those years of my life.

One day, someone pointed out to me the anger in my heart. My first reaction was, "Not me, how could I be angry." Then I asked the Lord to examine my heart showing me the secret places of it. That's exactly what He did. Maybe I knew all along the resentment was there but couldn't be honest with God.

Many times when we're talking to God, it's hard to verbalize the burdens and problems that clutter our hearts. A lesson I learned from overcoming anger concerns God and His Word. God knows the very thought and intent of our hearts. And as Isaiah said, He wants to give beauty for ashes, joy for mourning, and praise for heaviness of heart. Be honest with God about your secret shortcomings and hidden hurts. He wants to heal your heart.

Hazel McAlister
Author

November 24

Get Ready!

> *"...in the last days, saith God, I will pour out of my Spirit upon all flesh...your sons and your daughters shall prophesy...young men shall see visions...."* Acts 2:17

Our daughter Kelly was diagnosed with an incurable kidney disease. In search of a miracle we found Jesus as Baptizer in the Spirit, Healer and Deliverer. At that time God gave me a vision of my life's work. I saw women coming together unto Him, worshiping and honoring His name as they were healed spirit, soul and body. I have been privileged to see God pouring out His Spirit upon His handmaidens without measure.

In John's Gospel we are told: "Say not ye, There are yet four months, and then cometh harvest? behold, I say unto you, Lift up your eyes, and look on the fields; for they are white already to harvest" (John 4:35). We are a people chosen to live in the fullness of time when this scripture is coming to pass. Doubly blessed, we are the ones God's Spirit is being poured out upon. Our generation is commissioned to deliver the end-time message, "Get Ready!" We are to "get ready" for the greatest revival this world has ever known. We are to "get ready" for supernatural outpourings of His power and glory.

Matthew 24:14 says, "And this gospel of the kingdom shall be preached in all the world for a witness unto all nations; and then shall the end come." We are the ones laboring in His fields that are white unto harvest. We are the ones to minister His healing and wholeness to a world of broken, hurting and rejected people and see God glorified.

Helen Cregger
*Aglow President
South Carolina*

November 25

Divine Guidance

"Trust in the Lord with all thine heart; and lean not unto thine own understanding. In all thy ways acknowledge him, and he shall direct thy paths."   Proverbs 3:5-6

Proverbs 3:6 was the scripture motto hung on the wall when we were first married. Being a petty officer in the Coast Guard in the early 1930's with a low salary, this scripture buoyed us up and helped us to lean on the Lord and seek His guidance in all things. It was like a beacon to us in our decision making, for by acknowledging Him and asking His guidance, we acknowledged our own weakness and He gave us the promise of His unfailing care. Acknowledging Him in our lives and conversation is also a major step in soul-winning, and what a blessing to see God honor His Word.

I was first saved at the age of ten in a revival meeting, and baptized in Lake Stevens, Washington. I'll never forget how the Holy Spirit tugged at my heart during the altar call singing of "Just As I Am." Later, during a term in the Navy in submarine service, my testimony wavered a bit, but the Lord answered an anxious mother's prayers for her oldest son, and kept me from deep sin or bad habits, and provided a Christian buddy as more reinforcement.

Coming out of the Navy unscathed by the scars of sin, I was welcomed home to find my folks had experienced the truth of the full Gospel, and I was soon baptized in the Holy Spirit. God has allowed a few bumps along the way, but He has never failed us in our daily walk, in raising the family, and finally in our business experience as head of the fastest growing and second largest cutlery company in the USA.

Al Buck
Author

November 26

Where Eagles Soar

"Ye have seen what I did unto the Egyptians, and how I bare you on eagles' wings, and brought you unto myself." Exodus 19:4

During my research trips to the Sinai while I was writing "Where Eagles Soar," I had a chance to study the habits of these beautiful birds. Riding the thermals, they often soar completely over the occasional thunderstorms that devastate the lower regions. That is what God did for the children of Israel. He not only delivered them from the slavery of Egypt, but lifted them from the things designed by Satan to destroy, and brought them to Himself.

As I have looked at my own life, caught in the snare of self-satisfaction and later in the terrible prison of legalistic religion, I have seen God's grace manifested in a magnificent way. Every day we face new and menacing thunderheads. All around me there is devastation and destruction, but God still lifts His children on eagles' wings...brings them unto Himself.

It is from the heights we begin to see as God sees. The eagle can spot a rabbit from 20,000 feet, so keen is his eyesight. At the same time he can see for sixty miles as he floats above the earth. So it is as we soar with eagles...seeing the tiny things, but more importantly, knowing what is over the horizon as well.

God used the lowly dove to convey His blessing and to speak of peace. He said He loved the little sparrows and knows whenever one falls from the sky. He used ravens to feed the prophet, quail to feed the multitudes, a rooster to remind Peter of his fault. But it was the eagle he used to lift our sights above the ordinary to a God who is over all the earth.

Jamie Buckingham
Author/Pastor

November 27

The Establisher Of Our Thoughts

"Commit thy works unto the Lord, and thy thoughts shall be established." Proverbs 16:3

During August of 1978, I was reading daily the chapter in Proverbs that corresponded with the date of the month. On the 16th of August, I read, "Commit thy works unto the Lord, and thy thoughts shall be established" in Proverbs 16:3. As my wife and I shared and discussed this scripture, the phone rang and I was offered my present position at PTL.

Hebrews 4:12 speaks more on how our thoughts are established: "For the word of God is quick, and powerful, and sharper than any two-edged sword, piercing even to the dividing asunder of soul and spirit, and of the joints and marrow, and is a *discerner of the thoughts* and intents of the heart."

This verse tells us, God's Word discerns our thoughts and even the intentions of our hearts. When our lives are truly committed to the Lord, when we read His Word and let it work in our lives, then our walk, thoughts, and even the intentions of our hearts will line up and be in accordance with God's perfect will.

It was during my senior year in college, that my wife (then my fiancee) and her parents came to know Christ in a personal way. Their peace was so tangible, that I "caught it." Since then, I have enjoyed the supernatural "...peace of God, which passeth all understanding..." (Philippians 4:7) and the joy of letting the Lord control every aspect of my life.

John A. Franklin
PTL Vice President
Finances

November 28

A Promise For Every Occasion

"Thy way is in the sea, and thy path in the great waters, and thy footsteps are not known."
Psalm 77:19

I have learned God has a promise for every occasion. During World War II in 1943, my wife and I and our two children were on a troop ship traveling from India to America. We were sixty-nine days traveling in submarine infested waters. The whole trip had to be made in blackout conditions and the ship zigzagged every three minutes to avoid torpedoes. At one point we picked up survivors from a nearby sunken ship.

Circumstances indicated it would be nearly impossible for us to get through without an attack. To add to our anxiety, the captain announced a raider had been sighted and extra precautions must be enforced. I was concerned, our children were so small they would need our help if they were to survive an attack. I walked the deck praying for the safety of all aboard, when suddenly, for no apparent reason, a rainbow appeared on the horizon. This gave me great peace and the assurance from Genesis 9:13, "I do set my rainbow in the cloud...as a token (sign) of a covenant between me and the earth." Flooded with peace, I returned to my cabin, opened my Bible and these words jumped out at me, "Thy way is in the sea, and thy path in the great waters and thy footsteps are not known" (Psalm 77:19). This assured me our way was not known to the enemy. I knew without a shadow of doubt this promise was for our ship. The peace that passes understanding was mine until we safely harbored in New York.

Dr. Alfred Cawston
Missionary Statesman

November 29

You Are An Individual

"As you have therefore received Christ...walk ye in him. Rooted and built up in him, and stablished in the faith."
Colossians 2:6

There are many things we do today that take joint effort, for example, team sports, and then there are situations that occur that only you, individually, can take care of, like choosing just the right shade for that special outfit, bearing grief, or experiencing God. Especially today, when women's rights are an issue, every Christian woman should know who she is, who her God is and be settled in Him. This scripture is especially meaningful to all who want to do more than maintain, those who want to grow and develop.

Christian women come in all shapes and sizes. It is so easy to say that today's Christian woman must be this way, or act like this, believe like that, or react like this, but what we must realize is that we are unique. Only God knows what He wants for us. Helping every woman discover what God has for her, aware of her individuality and worth in the kingdom of God is what our ministry is all about. It is vital. Sometimes we forget that we are not to be carbon copies of each other, instead, we are to be conformed to the image of our Lord Jesus Christ. He, alone, sets the standards as dictated by the Holy Scriptures.

So many attitudes, traditions, and trends are changing, quickly. For this reason, every woman of every Christian period should know what is expected of them and where their contributions can best benefit the whole. Trends are trends, you are an individual. God will lead you to respond.

Dale Hanson Bourke
Editor Today's Christian Woman

November 30

Christ In Me

"I am crucified with Christ...and the life which I now live in the flesh I live by the faith of the Son of God, who loved me, and gave himself for me." Galatians 2:20

Living this life as Christ would has been foremost on my mind lately. I've asked myself, when situations arise, "How would Christ react under these circumstances?" Then I've asked, "How would He minister to the hurts of those who have been bruised, ignored, or forgotten?" In each instance, I've determined to be the best possible example of Christ, giving myself totally to those who need His love.

When people come to hear me sing, I want them to hear a message that uplifts Christ, and when they leave, I want them to remember Christ and not me. For we are told in Colossians 3:3, "For ye are dead, and your life is hid with Christ in God." So when it comes to making impressions, striving and pushing to get ahead, we all should remember that "we are dead," and let Christ live His life through us.

The more I realize the depth of Christ's love and sacrifice for me, the more I rejoice in my salvation. I know my limitations more clearly, and I depend on my Heavenly Father more. How sufficient He is. Count yourselves "dead" to the striving of the flesh. Step out and live by faith in the Son of God and know that it is only His wonderful presence in our lives that produces victory and fruitful ministry to others.

Karen Kelley
Singer

December 1

Pressing On The Upward Way

"I press toward the mark for the prize of the high calling of God in Christ Jesus."
Philippians 3:14

As Christians, we should set a goal and when we reach that goal, set a further goal. As you continue pressing on with the Lord, He will continue to give you new victories. I am sixty-two and still singing and on the go, not even thinking of retiring. I'd rather wear out for the Lord than rust out for the devil. We must continually keep reaching out, I call it the "pace of faith." Many retire and in six months half of them are dead because they don't have any remaining goals. Keep active, keep setting goals for the Lord; spiritual goals.

Every race is run for a prize. II Timothy 4:7-8 gives us a brief glimpse of the prize awaiting us in His presence: "I have fought a good fight, I have finished my course, I have kept the faith: Henceforth there is laid up for me a crown of righteousness, which the Lord, the righteous judge, shall give me at that day: and not me only, but unto all them also that love his appearing." Believe it, it's a reality, that some day we will appear before our Lord and receive our crowns. What glory if we can appear before Him and *know* we have been faithful in "pressing toward the mark for the prize..." We're told in I Corinthians 9:24, "...they which run in a race run all, but one receiveth the prize? So run, that ye may obtain." To obtain, to win, you must set goals. So set your goals high...then run to win!

James Blackwood
"Mr. Gospel Music"

December 2

A Loving And Saving God

"For God so loved the world that he gave his one and only Son, that whoever believes in him shall not perish but have eternal life."
John 3:16 (NIV)

God didn't just tell us that He loved us, He showed us He did by giving His very own Son. Now that's what gets me. I really can't understand God's love, but I know it's real because of what He *did*.

Love, as far as God is concerned, is something you do. That compels me to live my life in a way that says, "I love you, Lord." Like God, I want to show my love and not just tell about it.

When I was young, I had this verse memorized in both Spanish and English, without really understanding it. But God's Word is alive and, as I grew older, it became real in my heart.

I John 3:16 goes even one step further in explaining the love that God and Jesus have for us. Once again God's love and Word became even more real through this verse. It says, "This is how we know what love is: Jesus Christ laid down his life for us. And we ought to lay down our lives for our brothers (NIV).

We can only begin to understand what the love of God is all about when we accept God's Son, Jesus, as our personal Saviour. I was nine years old when my mother (evangelist Aimee Cortese) was preaching in a small church in Puerto Rico. At the end of her sermon, I knew I had to decide on my own to live for Jesus. You see, I thought I was a Christian because Mommy and Daddy were. That night I found out I was a Christian because I made the choice.

Damaris Carbaugh
Singer

December 3

Faith To Accomplish The Impossible

"But without faith it is impossible to please him: for he that cometh to God must believe that he is, and that he is a rewarder of them that diligently seek him." Hebrews 11:6

During a crisis in my life this scripture became very real to me. It was a matter of calling upon God with an honest and sincere heart. The Holy Spirit revealed this truth to me, and day after day, I would wait in the presence of God standing upon the thought that if I come to Him and believe that He is a rewarder of those who diligently seek Him, I could expect Him to reward me.

Late at night, I would wait before God when things seemed totally hopeless, but I stood upon the truth of God's Word. The Holy Spirit began to illuminate the truth of who God really is. He is bigger than all my problems; He is concerned with everything that touches me; He is ready and well able to solve my crisis situations. As these truths were opened to me, my faith began to rise. These two facts surfaced in my relationship with Him; first, He is my Heavenly Father and provider; second, if I sincerely and consistently sought Him in prayer and deed, He would reward me. For two years I stood on this scripture, and it brought me through one of the greatest crises in my life.

God performed miraculous things in my life during this period of time, just when I needed Him the most. He moved me from a minister who knew God could do things, to a minister who knew God could do "all" things. Equally as important, He revealed His eminence and power, all things are, indeed, possible to those who believe that God is.

Rev. Marvin E. Gorman
Pastor

December 4

Soul Food

"Therefore I say unto you, What things soever ye desire, when ye pray, believe that ye receive them, and ye shall have them."
Mark 11:24

I accepted a pastor's invitation to church when I was eight years old. In his sermon, he told me Jesus loved me, hell was very hot and heaven was very sweet. I determined I wanted to go to heaven and prayed, "Jesus, thank you for dying on the cross for me and for your coming alive again. I give my life over totally to you." I received assurance I was saved and shortly after my whole family came to the Lord. My grandmother had been praying that my brothers John, Coman and myself would minister for the Lord. That prayer has been answered as our ministry to the Lord has taken us around the world.

A short while ago, my faith was challenged when I had a serious problem with my voice. A thoughtful friend, Rev. Tilton, sent me some tapes entitled, "Soul Food Scriptures." These scriptures built up my faith and indeed became my soul food in that trying time.

The above verses encouraged me along with Mark 11:23, "...whosoever shall say unto this mountain, Be thou removed, and be thou cast into the sea; and shall not doubt in his heart, but shall believe that those things...shall come to pass; he shall have whatsoever he saith."

The Word of God healed me and my voice became more vibrant than ever before in my twenty-six years in the ministry.

Roger McDuff
Evangelistic Singer

December 5

Renewed Mind

"If you abide in me and my words abide in you, ye shall ask what you will, and it shall be done unto you." John 15:7

To me, abiding in Him and His Word abiding in us, sums up the Christian life Jesus wants us to live. First of all, we have to abide in Him to experience His joy, peace and power. The alternative is not to abide in Him, and then we experience frustration, restlessness, and dissatisfaction. The choice is ours.

"If my words abide in you..." promises over and over that if we meditate on and obey God's Word, all of it, He will bless us and our families and our nation; give prosperity, success and answer our deepest prayers. This allows Him to use us to His purposes while we walk on this earth. What greater joy than this?

"You shall ask what you will, and I will do it." Jesus said those unbelievable words and then He asked us to believe them. I do! "Abiding in Jesus," is living close, snug in His arms, hearing His heartbeat and knowing His will. When we slip out of fellowship, He lets us know by the ache and loneliness we feel, that we are no longer abiding. However, we are always welcome to come back into His inner circle of love.

Reading His words keeps our earthly mind transformed by His mind. "And be not conformed to this world: but be ye transformed by the renewing of your mind, that ye may prove what is that good, and acceptable, and perfect, will of God" (Romans 12:2). This keeps us on track and with His perspective in view.

Marabel Morgan
Author

December 6

His Mercy Endures Forever

"Oh, give thanks unto the Lord; for he is good: for his mercy endureth for ever."
                                        Psalm 136:1

    I've often wondered what our world would be like if the mercy of God were withdrawn. If there were no pardon and forgiveness, or if, indeed, God dealt with us justly after all our sins. We would have no hope and certainly no redemption. Because mercy means you receive pardon when you justly deserve judgment, it gives added credence to God's pure and perfect love for us. I'm most grateful, too, that His mercies are renewed every morning.

    Whenever I mess up and miss the mark, which happens entirely too often in my life, I can go to Psalm 136 and be assured that my Father's mercy endures forever. I can count on His mercy and forgiveness. But, even though the Lord is merciful, we must never use His pardon as a license to sin. Many are like me. I didn't need a license to sin before I was saved, and I don't need one now for sure. As I read the entire Psalms, I'm reminded over and over, I can be restored to right relationship with our Saviour. This entire division lists all the mighty works of God and reminds the reader that God ever gives us the flexibility of growth, even with the mistakes that come with developing ourselves in God.

    Bishop Fulton J. Sheen once said, "The closer I got to God, the holier God looked and the filthier I became." God is holiness absolute, and in order for us to have a relationship that's personal, we must be able to gratefully acknowledge His mercy.

Carl Bunch
Singer

December 7

A Promise Of Strength

"I can do all things through Christ which strengtheneth me."   Philippians 4:13

Having found the Lord in 1944, I have been saved for nearly 40 years. I was in the service of my country and was restless, searching, always searching for something to calm the tempest that raged within. I turned to strong drink but found out that it didn't satisfy. One night I stumbled up the street of an Army town, attracted by the sound of singing. I stood there trying to figure out what these people were doing. Then I heard it! "If you are weary and heavy laden, there is rest for you." At the strong urging of these Christians, I followed them down to the church and was powerfully saved. I thank God that men were interested in the souls of people like me.

As an Indian boy, I had found myself surrounded by white people, resulting in my being intimidated to the point that I regarded myself as somewhat of a second class person. This continued until I was almost grown. What a glorious revelation it was when I discovered that God had been standing by me all those many years, waiting for me to declare Him Lord and Master of my life. God is color blind and still desires to make us conquerors.

In times of diversity in my Christian life, when the winds of the enemy threaten to blow me off course, I begin to implement the promise given to us in Philippians 4:13. God has been abundantly kind to me ever since that day I found Him when I was a young man in the Army.

John McPherson
Missionary/Evangelist

December 8

You Gotta Serve Somebody

...if we believe not, yet he abideth faithful: he cannot deny himself."   II Timothy 2:13

After enjoying the blessings of easy success, one day my world fell in. One night a young boy came to the door at 2 a.m. and told me my 14-year-old Jennie had been in an auto accident. She went through the windshield and her skull was shattered, it was a terrible fright.

Jennie was five hours in the emergency room and seven hours in the operating room. The whole twelve hours the words from Bob Dylan's album kept playing through my mind. I hadn't paid that much attention to the words before, I'd just stuck the tape in while I ran errands around town. But now, in this extreme emergency, the words buried in my subconscious came back to minister to me. The words asked, "When You Gonna Wake Up?" and repeated, "You Gotta Serve Somebody." I knew I'd gone my own way and hadn't paid any attention to the living God in a long time.

Now I prayed, "Save my daughter, oh please, save my daughter."

My life flashed before me; I saw a very sloppy way of life, far from God. I became convicted of my lifestyle, the pot, the booze, the fast life. Right there, I made a decision to commit my life to God. Hours later, the doctor said he'd pieced the splinters together and hoped Jennie would be all right. Ten days later, she was out of the hospital.

I'm so glad God is faithful, even when we haven't been.

Maria Muldaur
Gospel Recording Artist

December 9

A Pathway For Our Desires

"Trust in the Lord with all thine heart; and lean not unto thine own understanding. In all thy ways acknowledge him, and he shall direct thy paths." Proverbs 3:5-6

Sometimes we find it hard to see God's will in our lives. But I believe, from my own experience, that if we are daily walking with God and trusting that we are in His will, then as we look back over the circumstances of our lives, we can see how He leads us to be just where He wants us to be.

We can run around for years planning out perfect little lives for ourselves, but if God is not the center of that life, then it can never be the perfect life for us, for without God, we can never be truly happy.

When I was in college, I studied to be an opera singer. It was during those years that I became a Christian through the witness of a campus Christian group. I had attended church for 13 years, doing all the right things—attending Sunday School, singing in the choir, being active in youth groups, etc., but in all those years I had never heard about the possibility of having a personal relationship with God. But through that group I came to accept the Lord.

After I became a Christian, I had a real desire to sing Christian music. When Lawrence Welk asked me to join his show, I didn't see how it could possibly be God's will for me because it had nothing to do with either opera or Gospel music. But I trusted in Him and now, as I look back, I can see His leading in it all because I am now doing what I desired to do in the beginning—to sing Christian music.

Kathie Sullivan
Singer

December 10

Father Does Know Best

"Holy Father, keep through thine own name those whom thou hast given me, that they may be one, as we are."   John 17:11b

God watches out for all of us, and if we walk in a daily commitment with Him, He will never let us go astray. He will mold you, strengthen you, and keep you "accepted in the beloved." You, too, will be able to fellowship with other saints of God in the beauty of Christian love.

I have personally felt the weight of the enemy's deception and destruction. A product of a broken home at age seven, I never felt secure or truly loved. Even though I was sent to church, I never had real life role models to pattern my behavior or approach to God. The only reality I had was what I accepted as reality from the scripts on the television series, Father Knows Best, and my co-star, Robert Young. So at sixteen, because I had been typeset as Kathy, petite, dimpled youngster on the series, I was rejected by the industry that had become my life. I dropped out of school and married a boy I had known only for a month. During that marriage, I lost eight babies, became addicted, dropped out of church, and ended up in jails and mental institutions.

In the subculture that is the drug scene, no one really cares, everyone is disillusioned. I became suicidal, I even overdosed three or four times, before a man in jail introduced me to the love of God. Now I know security and true love. I have a Heavenly Father who cares about everything that touches me, and you.

Lauren Chapin
Actress

December 11

The Importance Of Your Faith

"That the communication of thy faith may become effectual by the acknowledging of every good thing which is in you in Christ Jesus."
                                           Philemon 6

Positive affirmations are vitally important in the development of the life of faith. The Bible says faith works. It is a heart and mouth experience. With our hearts we trust in God's grace. With our mouths we confess victory through His promises. Fear is an obstacle easily overcome by using this heart/mouth formula.

In 1976, a growth the doctors found was diagnosed as cancer, and I was scheduled for surgery. Fear gripped my entire being and I questioned God repeatedly, shattered and overcome with self-pity. Thank God for my wife who brought me face to face with what it was doing to me. Together we claimed God's promise of deliverance and boldly expelled the spirit of fear. Immediately I was set free, and seventy-two hours before surgery, the growth fell off. Praise the Lord!

I'm convinced whatever your need, if you speak these affirmations, you'll be whole:
Fear has no part in my heart.
There is no room for gloom.
I rejoice in Christ, my choice.
What I confess, I possess.
God giveth me wealth and health.
I'm sold on being bold.

Don Gossett
Minister/Author

December 12

The Never Ending Battle

"Being confident of this very thing, that he which hath begun a good work in you will perform it until the day of Jesus Christ."
Philippians 1:6

To the detriment of a victorious Christian life, many people push themselves for perfection, becoming exhausted emotionally and rendering themselves helpless and nearly hopeless. All because they fail to recognize that our efforts alone, without God's supernatural strength, is self-defeating.

This past year I have looked at myself and what God is doing with me in a different way. I used to have the feeling that the Christian life was a never ending battle, and I would never measure up. When I discovered it was not what I did, but what God has already done, it was a wonderful revelation.

This simple statement, "He which hath begun a good work...will perform it," gave me the strength to live freely in Christ. Not free wantonly, but by taking the emphasis of my doing, and putting the emphasis on what God has and is doing in me, I have fresh, comforting assurance that the Lord is in control of everything that touches me.

God has given me the assurance that He started the work, and He'll finish the work. I can be confident, too, that someday the work will be completed. It took the "monkey" off my back freeing me to relax and do my very best with no strain. Now, if I fail, it doesn't shatter me. It's God's project, and I've been promised He will perform it.

Jon Mohr
Singer

December 13

Seek Him Daily

"Being confident of this very thing, that he which hath begun a good work in you will perform it until the day of Jesus Christ."
Philippians 1:6

Above all else, knowing God intimately and seeking Him is the most important relationship we will ever cultivate. Neither His gifts nor material gain should precede our desire to "know" Him. I'm learning to never take the things of God lightly but to be totally committed to Christ and a body of Christians in a church. He's teaching me lately not to be lax but to get with it and become serious about the things of God.

In order to grow, we must be willing to look at our weaknesses and allow God to show us how to live in victory. Harmony with God and others cannot exist with bitterness and resentment in our hearts. I've come to realize that when I'm feeling bitter towards anyone, I'm only hurting myself. Quite often the other person isn't aware of my feelings. In the beautiful garden of spiritual attributes, we must continually weed out bitterness, as a careful gardener would, to insure a productive harvest or continued growth.

Bitterness can cause others to fall and be wounded in their spiritual lives. We're admonished in Hebrews 12:15, "Looking diligently lest any man fail of the grace of God; lest any root of bitterness springing up trouble you, and thereby many be defiled."

Sometimes we need to look back over the past year and see if we have grown in the "inner one." It's a good feeling to know you react differently to things as Christ "performs a good work in you."

Luanne Mohr
Singer

December 14

He Giveth And Giveth

"Give, and it shall be given unto you; good measure, pressed down...and running over...For with the same measure that ye mete...it shall be measured to you again." Luke 6:38

Love is the key to all that is God! I learned this shortly after I was born again. I thought I had nothing to give God until He showed me that seeds are stuff of which great trees are made. I gave, I tithed, I ministered to others and the more I gave, the more God returned. After a while I started to think that God was like a computer—push a button and He responds.

He soon showed me the error of my thinking. As He began to work on my motives, He showed me that love is the essential key, that faith works by love.

The essential nature of God is to give, but He gives because He loves. I know that as He is, so am I in the world. "God so loved...that He gave" (John 3:16).

Because of God's grace we have a music ministry. This would have been unthinkable a few years ago. I was lying in a hospital bed and my doctors told me that, as a result of an accident, my right vocal chord was severed. They told me I would be unable to sing or even talk normally again. Praise God, He saw my need, looked beyond my fault and restored my voice miraculously by His grace. That's God!

His is the love that gives! He gives, and gives and continues to give. I have experienced healing miracles, and deliverance from near disaster while flying. He has expended our Joe Bias Ministries to an overseas ministry with Swedish young people. He continually gives of His love.

Joe Bias
Singer/Joe Bias Ministries

December 15

The Good Success

"...the law shall not depart out of thy mouth; but thou shall meditate...day and night...observe to do...all that is written there in...then thou shalt have good success."   Joshua 1:8

Success, apart from God, is not true success. Very young, I set goals for myself; one was to become bank president. As I succeeded in realizing all my goals, they didn't bring happiness. Financially, I'd achieved all my goals and many I hadn't dreamed of. But it was only after the age of forty, when I accepted Christ as Saviour and took Him as my partner, that I knew real success.

I came to know Christ in a deeper way while praying for a friend. He was in the hospital awaiting surgery for painful kidney stones. The Lord prompted me to lay hands on him and pray according to James 5:14-15, "Is any sick among you? let him call for the elders of the church; and let them pray over him, anointing him with oil in the name of the Lord. And the prayer of faith shall save the sick, and the Lord shall raise him up...." I'd never done this before, as I prayed and asked Jesus to touch him, I believe He did exactly that. My friend's countenance changed visibly before my eyes, it was as though a charge of electricity passed through him.

Later in the parking lot, God said to me, "I want you to touch people for Me." That experience revolutionized my life. The next day, my friend called me from home. He no longer required surgery, the kidney stones were gone.

After experiencing the world's empty success, I learned of God's true success as recorded in Joshua 1:8, the success from God.

Doug Mobley
Evangelist

December 16

Details

"Search me, O God, and know my heart: try me, and know my thoughts: and see if there be any wicked way in me, and lead me in the way everlasting." Psalm 139:23-24

A lot of people talk about being "detail people." In the secular marketplace, it is a valuable asset to any employee. But more than we could ever dream of being, our Heavenly Father is a detail person. He knows every little thought, every action, every word, everything that we do.

Unless you are trying hard to live according to the Word of God, the verse above is not one you would recite often in your prayers. Yet regardless, God does search our hearts, and we as His children need to be ever mindful of that, and live knowing that.

Every day in my work, I try not to forget this, in every decision, every job, every meeting...whatever, I want to do the best I can do before God.

Always looking back, I ask myself "Did I do the best I can?" "Did I do it right?" "Was it pleasing to God?" And through searching myself, I can better prepare myself to be searched and tried by God.

Let the Holy Spirit minister to you in this area today. I know, by my own experience, that it will make it easier in your walk with Him tomorrow.

Richard Ball
PTL Vice President
Marketing

December 17

Availability Over Ability

"But Jesus beheld them, and said unto them, With men this is impossible; but with God all things are possible." Matthew 19:26

God didn't have a whole lot of raw material to work with when I was born. I was premature, weighing less than three pounds, affected by a borderline case of cerebral palsy. Though the Lord saw fit to preserve the lives of my twin sister and me, for a long time, I didn't see how I could be of any use to Him.

Not being able to walk right, being small and slight, with eyes that didn't work so well, what purpose could God have for my life? All I could think of was the many things I couldn't do.

But when I became a teenager, the Lord "beheld me," as He said the words above to me. He said, "Yes, with you, it's impossible, but I don't look on the outward appearance. I'm not concerned with your physical body. I'm not worried about what you think you can't do. I don't need your ability, because all of the possibility is in My hands. All I need is for you to become available for My use, and I can do wonders through you."

I said, "Yes, Lord! With me, it's impossible to even walk right, but You will walk through me. With me it's impossible to save anyone, but You're going to use me to lead many to You. With me, it's impossible to heal the sick, but with You, I can lay hands on them, and they'll get well. I can't love of myself, but You can love others through me!"

No matter what you might think your handicaps or limitations are today, Jesus is looking past them right now, straight to your heart. He wants to know if you're willing to let Him be everything it's possible for Him to be through you! Pray right now, "Use me, Lord! Take me and spend me for others today.

Ron Hollings
PTL Staff

December 18

Beautiful Promises

"Whereby are given unto us exceeding great and precious promises: that by these ye might be partakers of the divine nature...."   II Peter 1:4

Whenever our God does something, He does it very well! There is no such thing as half a blessing from God. He either does something or He doesn't do it, whichever brings Him the greater glory, and will be the most beneficial to His kingdom. But this fact remains, He is well able!

I am a living witness that God honors His Word and is capable, willing and delights in blessing His people. The Bible is full of promises that attest to this. God is for us. We can receive all that we need by knowing and claiming His promises to us, His children. The Word of God is His Will. If we would only take the time to read His Will, becoming acquainted with the provisions, we would realize how very rich we are...rich in the fact that all the forces of heaven are working circumstances for our good and rich in the fact that our loving Heavenly Father has provided bountifully for spiritual, emotional, physical, intellectual, and social fulfillment in the lives of all who love and trust Him.

When everything looked hopeless for me, God intervened, and as His Word said, set me on a course of health and salvation. You see, I was a leukemia victim. I grew so ill that I was given up to die. Even the talent to sing was nearly cut off. Doctors said that I would never sing again. But what the doctors didn't know was, I had learned whose I was, and His Word lived in me. God honored His Word. Today I am whole.

Jerry McGrath
Singer

My Soul Followeth

"My soul followeth hard after thee: thy right hand upholdeth me."   Psalm 63:8

I was saved at the age of nine and gifted with music at the age of eleven. Although I played and sang for my local church most of my childhood and adult life, it wasn't until recently that I went into full-time ministering for the Lord. Full-time service has been one of the most rewarding experiences of my life. Now I can say I really know what it means to live by faith and what a joy it is to see God at work in our lives.

I often sing the Scriptures and every time I sing Psalm 63 I am especially strengthened by the words. It is true, "Because thy loving-kindness is better than life, my lips shall praise thee" (Psalm 63:3). One day, when I was traveling, I read the words of this psalm and this promise from verse 5 became so real, "My soul shall be satisfied as with marrow and fatness; and my mouth shall praise thee with joyful lips." My desire is to praise the Lord with joyful lips. I knew, in my spirit, what David meant when he wrote the words of this psalm. In verse 7, it continues, "Because thou hast been my help, therefore in the shadow of thy wings will I rejoice." "In the shadow of thy wings," and the phrase, "hard after thee," mean in a very close, personal and tender relationship. This psalm speaks over and over of the praise of the lips and mouth and giving God the glory.

Morris Chapman
Singer/Evangelist

December 20

Peace In The Midst Of Fear

"When thou passest through the waters, I will be with thee...rivers...shall not overflow thee...neither shall the flame kindle upon thee."
Isaiah 43:2

The resurrection power is so invincible, we can be certain the Lord never forsakes, even in the midst of obstacles we consider impossible. Often we become afraid when we can't handle things. If we trust, He'll do anything, just for us.

Because of our stand for Jesus, my husband and I have been firebombed, shot at, threatened and jeered, but the Lord has always delivered us. It is a real temptation to give in to fear during these testing times, but it is important to realize that one of Satan's greatest tools is fear.

We are living in the "end times" spoken of in the Bible: "Men's hearts failing them for fear, and for looking after those things which are coming on the earth" (Luke 21:26). But we have a promise from God that He will be with us, through fire, through water, through all things. We know, that we know, that we know. That's certainty.

Shadrach, Meshach and Abednego had to go through the fire, but their clothes didn't even smell of fire. With God's abundant protection, they passed through unscathed. You, too, can walk in peace during these fearful times if you meditate on the promises of God. If we get our eyes and ears on God's Word, fears are reversed and we receive His peace. We can't have His peace unless we meditate on His Word. "Faith cometh by hearing, and hearing by the Word of God."

Pat Moehring
Heritage School
Music Director

December 21

Trust, Delight, Commit

"Delight thyself also in the Lord; and he shall give thee the desires of thine heart. Commit thy way unto the Lord; trust also in him; and he shall bring it to pass." Psalm 37:4-5

Not long ago, I sang at a prison for about 100 inmates. I was a little scared beforehand, but the sweet special love of the Holy Spirit came down on us, and it touched me very deeply.

I began to pray earnestly that the Lord would enable me to get into prison ministry more often. I knew of Chuck Colson's prison outreach, and I really wanted to work with him. My faith wasn't very great, but I committed this wish to the Lord and then just sort of forgot about it.

Well, soon thereafter at a convention where I was singing, Chuck Colson was the featured speaker. I put aside my shyness after the final banquet and caught up with him just before he left the building. "Mr Colson," I burst out, "I want to sing in prison—can I help you?" He kindly invited me to join him in an upcoming visit, and I've been working with him regularly ever since in prisons all over the country.

It's such a temptation, if you have a ministry that you think the Lord wants you to do, to get anxious and strive and try to open doors for yourself, but I've found out that you don't have to do that. Just seek the Lord, and hand it over to Him and let it go-- almost forget it. God will open the door because He definitely wants us to serve Him. He needs every one of us He can get! And He loves surprises, so why try to figure everything out for yourself?

Honeytree
Singer

December 22

Darkest, Darkest Mission Field

"...the dayspring from on high hath visited us, to give light to them that sit in darkness...."
Luke 1:78-79

    If it were not for my own blindness, I would never have had a burden for the huge mission field of the sightless. I see God's plan that the "all things" of Romans 8:28 have made me aware of the problem of the blind. And what a vast mission field this is! There are forty-two million sightless in this darkest of dark mission fields.

    Once in a large crowd, I felt a tug at my coat sleeve. When I asked what he wanted, someone told me he was blind, deaf and mute. I gave him my hand and with a laborious system of communication, he spelled out, "I wish I was dead. You don't know how lonely I am. I live in a totally dark and isolated world. I wish I was dead." I in turn told him about my friend and Saviour Jesus, "...a friend that sticketh closer than a brother" (Proverbs 18:24). Before we parted, he was happy and rejoicing in Jesus. It was like the Lord spoke to me then and said, "This is why you're blind."

    I began a ministry of radio and sending out Braille tracts. Our broadcast, *That They Might See,* originates from Chicago and is carried worldwide. After the program had been aired two weeks, we had our first convert. I spoke and said, 'Don't take your life, there's hope in Jesus." A very excited seventeen year old called and said she'd gone to her room to take sleeping pills and cut her wrists. She turned on her radio to cover her suicide when the program led her to Christ. She is now happily married, full of joy and rejoicing. Praise Him!

Dr. Ralph Montemas
President, Gospel Association/Blind

December 23

Get Wisdom And Understanding

"Wisdom is the principal thing; therefore get wisdom: and with all thy getting get understanding." Proverbs 4:7

I believe this verse is not just a simple invitation, I also feel it is a divine commandment! God tells us here that wisdom is the most important thing we can have, and that we should acquire all the wisdom and understanding we can get. Having established the importance of wisdom, I feel God is telling us that we should be concerned, not with what wisdom is, but rather who wisdom is according to Scripture.

By revealing this verse to me, the Holy Spirit has shown me what to ask for, so that I may be constantly filled with the Spirit. Several verses that may help us are: I Corinthians 1:30, "But of him are ye in Jesus Christ, who of God is made unto us wisdom..."; I Corinthians 2:7, "But we speak the wisdom of God in a mystery, even the hidden wisdom, which God ordained before the world..."; and Proverbs 8:5, "O ye simple, understand wisdom...."

I am constantly saved. Salvation is the ever present love of Jesus Christ in my life and even when I don't keep the faith, Jesus says that He does.

When I was 15, I asked the Lord into my heart at the altar of a small church in San Diego where I lived. But it wasn't until recently that I have realized the Spirit of God and the ministry He offers in the gifts of the Spirit.

Jack Bradford
Singer/PTL Voices

December 24

Finer Than Gold

"Blessed is the man that endureth temptation: for when he is tried, he shall receive the crown of life, which the Lord hath promised to them that love him." James 1:12

If there's anything I have, any love to give, it is all because of God. He is everything to me. A relationship like this didn't come easily, I suppose that's what makes it so meaningful.

I spent thirty-five years in darkness. The whole entertainment scene: broadway shows, concert stages around the world, films, parties, drugs, airplanes, motorcycles, sports cars, the whole gamut, including the fantasy of the playboy lifestyle became a reality for me. But it was a totally empty, death-oriented trip. Once you have been to the mountaintop, there are few more highs to experience, so there is only the way back down. Coming down, sometimes, can be quite drastic. I lost sixteen friends to drug overdoses. All were talented, well-known show business personalities. What a waste. But that is the lie of deception Satan uses to persuade us to turn away from God. But it is only a lie!

I believed the lie myself, and right at the bottom of my life, I reached out to the Lord. Isn't it tragic that some of us wait until they have bottomed out to look up? But God is always there, and once we call out to Him, He hears, answers, and restores. Once cleansed, we are as pure, before God, as newborn babes because the blood of Jesus erases every trace of the nature to sin. Then as we continue to walk in Him, even through fiery trials, our witness shines finer than gold.

Barry McGuire
Singer

December 25

Good Tidings Of Great Joy

"...Fear not: for, behold, I bring you good tidings of great joy, which shall be to all people....born this day in the city of David a Saviour...Christ the Lord."   Luke 2:10-11

What a thrill it must have been for the shepherds of Bethlehem to have been singled out by the angel of the Lord and be invited to take part in the first Christmas ever celebrated by the world. Some 2000 years later, we can all still celebrate this special event.

Of all the accounts in the Four Gospels, the passage in Luke has always been my favorite as it vividly described the events leading up to and the actual birth of our Saviour, Jesus Christ. Christmas actually became alive to me as I would sit down and read the first two chapters of Luke and view how the real story of this special holiday unfolded.

Growing up, what a joy it was to see the bright lights and tinsel that would adorn our small midwestern town around the Christmas season. As one strolled the city streets, usually Christmas shopping, the winter chill would pierce the physical being.

But no matter how cold it ever was on the outside, one's inner being was warmed by just knowing that the holiday celebration was in recognition of God being born in the flesh. It was a feeling that could never be put in the proper words, knowing the Son of God had come to redeem us.

Then as gifts would be exchanged Christmas morning, one could not help but think of a gift that was given to mankind on Christmas Day centuries ago. A Saviour, which is Christ the Lord.

Ron Kopczick
Writer

December 26

Our Bodies, His Treasure

"The life is more than meat, and the body is more than raiment."   Luke 12:23

If we are to take the Gospel message to the world, good health, strong bodies, sharp mental and reasoning capabilities are a must. These, along with a vibrant, dedicated faith in the Lord Jesus Christ, will reap amazing results for the Kingdom of God.

We must learn to be consistent in good health practices. Good health is not an option if we are to be effective in ministry.

Years ago I was teaching in a medical school in Kansas City and practicing medicine part-time. One night in a nearby rooming house, a forty-two year old man died of a heart attack. It really upset me. Shortly after that we were taking out the gallbladder of a twenty-four year old woman, filled with gallstones. I was concerned. Why doesn't every forty-two year old man die of a heart attack or every twenty-four year old woman have gallstones? Finally I had an idea that there must be a chain of health. If there is a chain of health, much of it is genetic or runs in families, and perhaps the weakest link in this chain of health is nutrition. So I coined the word, "Nutrigenetics," and I wrote a book with the same name, describing hypoglycemia.

There are many influences that can harm our bodies. Sugar is one of them. Not to restrict our dependence on this health robber is an indication that we don't value good health. These bodies are God's treasures to fill with His Spirit and dwell in. Can we do any less than protect this precious instrument? I say no.

Dr. Richard Brennan
Author

December 27

The God-Connection

"These things have I spoken unto you, that my joy might remain in you, and that your joy might be full." — John 15:11

Man craves *greatness*. We possess an obsession to expand, grow and improve. We were born for the "High Place." We instinctively gravitate toward *increase*: spiritually, mentally and financially.

The "seed of need" was planted by the Creator. God made Himself a *necessity* for human happiness. Like the missing puzzle piece, the life-picture doesn't make sense until He is included. We were built for *connection*. The ear demands sounds, the eye demands sights, the mind wants negotiation, the heart seeks companionship.

The *God*-connection-it is the bridge from failure to success.

Popularity is not success. Popularity is people liking you. Happiness is *you* liking *you*.

What is success? Happiness is success. Happiness is "feeling good about yourself." It is not necessarily fame, money, or position. It is knowledge and awareness of your worth in the eyes of God.

You are here on purpose, designed and equipped for a particular function. You must discern and develop the God-given abilities He invested at your birth. It is only when those gifts are being used properly that you will feel and know the value God sees in you.

Two forces are needed for total happiness: 1) The Person of Jesus Christ, and 2) The Principles of Jesus Christ. One is the Son of God, the other is the system of God.

Joy was set in motion on this planet at Calvary.

Mike Murdock
Singer

December 28

The Faithful Saviour

"Satan hath desired to have you...But I have prayed for thee, that thy faith fail not: and when thou art converted, strengthen thy brethren."
Luke 22:31-32

It is such a comfort to remember that in spite of our failures and weaknesses, He is always faithful to us. Jesus is interceding for us so that our faith may not fail. I became a Christian when I was a junior at college. At the time of graduation, I thought of becoming a pastor, but I had neither the passion nor strong sense of calling. So I chose to work as a businessman.

In the third year of my business career, I moved to the McDonald's Corporation, which was just starting to introduce its hamburger business to the Japanese. I began to be promoted very rapidly. The more success I attained, the more enthusiastically I became involved in my job.

Within me, however, I found something unhealthy was developing. I was seeking the glory of this world. My wife, observing the change which had taken place in me, once remarked, "You are indeed dead; dead with hamburgers." How precisely she painted my spiritual state!

One night, in March of 1975, God began to talk to my heart. I was in bed with a high fever when the Holy Spirit said to me, "Kenichi, you are laboring to build up your own kingdom, not mine." I was struck with fear for a moment, but I took the Bible and began to read the Gospel of Luke to calm myself. Jesus impressed me with His love so vividly through the verse above, that I had no doubt that my sins of disobedience were forgiven and that He chose me to become a full-time minister.

Kenichi Nakagawa
Japanese PTL Host

December 29

The Harvest Is White

"Be sober, be vigilant; because your adversary the devil, as a roaring lion, walketh about, seeking whom he may devour."

I Peter 5:8

I believe America is in trouble and needs a spiritual rebirth. But, praise God, we are seeing "grass roots" people come alive for Jesus.

We are warned in Scripture to, "...watch out for attacks from Satan, your great enemy. He prowls around like a hungry, roaring lion, looking for some victim to tear apart...remember that other Christians are going through these sufferings too" (I Peter 5:8-Living Bible).

People are sensing the urgency of these last days. Recently, during revival services at Melodyland Church in California, over six thousand walked the aisles for salvation. I saw an alcoholic delivered from bondage as he came and declared, "I've got to have help." Three days later, his wife called, sobbing with joy, because it was the first time in twenty-two years he'd been sober.

Debbie, a seventeen year old who planned to take her life one night, came to the meeting instead. God delivered her and set her free, replacing joy for her deep despondency. Over 260, hardcore, hard-acid and heroin junkies have been completely delivered from lifelong addiction.

I can never thank God enough for what He's doing. We declare the uncompromising Word of God, and His Holy Spirit convicts and converts. Praise God!

Dwight Thompson
President
World Outreach Ministries

December 30

Touched By Our Weaknesses

"For we have not a high priest which cannot be touched with the feeling of our infirmities; but was in all points tempted like as we...."
Hebrews 4:15

Older people often forget they were ever teenagers. An effective parent has to remember how they feel. We're more prone to force kids to do "what we want" than we are to understand what it felt like to go through those problems. We are not "touched with the feeling of their infirmities."

On the first day of junior high, kids get an opposite perspective; up to that point they've been comfortable in the home, they've taken instructions and reproof. But as they hit adolescence they realize, "Hey, I'm able to make some decisions on my own. I need to separate from Mom and Dad." If you're going to separate, you take an opposite approach. Teenagers go through a period of negativism; it's their way of saying, "I'm becoming my own person. I'm not just the Smith boy or the Jones girl." Parents get angry, and that causes more rebellion in the teenager. It's a vicious cycle of escalating stubbornness, and you don't out-stubborn a teenager.

They need help and not condemnation; you need to accept your teenager as he is. They are more open to the potential negative results of peer pressure if there is no communication in the home.

Become sensitive to the hurts, struggles and feelings going on inside this new developing person. Christ, our High Priest, was touched with our feelings and hurts. Help your young person to know they're created in God's image, then they learn to feel positive about themselves and can stand up to peer pressure.

Bruce Narramore
Psychologist

December 31

Trusting For The Right Direction

"Trust in the Lord with all thine heart; and lean not unto thine own understanding. In all thy ways acknowledge him, and he shall direct thy paths." Proverbs 3:5-6

I learned early in my Christian life that the only way to real victory and accomplishment as a believer was to trust the Lord Jesus Christ to keep me and to guide me moment-by-moment in the same way and by using the same faith I used when I received Him as Saviour and Lord.

This, I take it, is the real meaning of Colossians 2:6, "As ye have therefore received Christ Jesus the Lord, so walk ye in him." In the same way that one receives Christ Jesus as Lord, one also trusts Him for every step along the way. The Proverbs passage assures me that if I really *want* the will of God and ask for it, He will see to it that is what I get—a precious truth, indeed!

In the course of making many decisions in life, one has the choice between relying merely upon a judgment made upon the best organized facts one can gather, or on the other hand, making that decision through the guidance of the Holy Spirit based on the facts that one can gather. I learned the hard way that the best and most lasting decisions are made through absolute commitment to God's Holy Spirit, based upon His infallible Word, the Bible.

Today, as President of The King's College, I rely upon the presence and guidance of God's Holy Spirit for decisions that are made day by day. I find the best procedure is to gather all the facts, pray over them, and then trust God to guide in His perfect will.

Robert A. Cook
President
The King's College